'THIS IS JUST THIS.
IT ISN'T REAL.
IT'S MONEY'

'THIS IS JUST THIS.
IT ISN'T REAL.
IT'S MONEY'

THE OBERON ANTHOLOGY OF CONTEMPORARY IRISH PLAYS

EDITED AND INTRODUCED BY THOMAS CONWAY

HEROIN by Grace Dyas

Trade by Mark O'Halloran

The Art of Swimming by Lynda Radley

Pineapple by Phillip McMahon

I ♥ Alice ♥ I by Amy Conroy

The Big Deal edited by Una McKevitt

Oedipus Loves You by Simon Doyle & Gavin Quinn

The Year of Magical Wanking by Neil Watkins

OBERON BOOKS
LONDON

WWW.OBERONBOOKS.COM

First published in this collection in 2012 by Oberon Books Ltd
521 Caledonian Road, London N7 9RH
Tel: +44 (0) 20 7607 3637 / Fax: +44 (0) 20 7607 3629
e-mail: info@oberonbooks.com
www.oberonbooks.com

PB ISBN: 978-1-84943-391-4
E ISBN: 978-1-84943-672-4

Cover image by Gary Coyle

Printed and bound by Marston Book Services, Didcot.

Visit www.oberonbooks.com to read more about all our books
and to buy them. You will also find features, author interviews and
news of any author events, and you can sign up for e-newsletters
so that you're always first to hear about our new releases.

Contents

Introduction

Something of the enterprise of playwriting itself is being re-imagined in these plays. These playwrights ride in no slipstream of the identifiably Irish play or even the play *per se*. An inhabiting of the theatre comes before the construction of the dramatic world, an interrogation of the medium before the *bon mot*, a self-conscious use of language before garrulousness. To trade by what playwrights, Irish or otherwise, are known *by* or *for* is subordinated to a commitment to become in the theatre.

Unsurprisingly, then, working through the volume is a commitment to cosmopolitanism before any foregrounding of so-called Irishness. As world-citizens these playwrights address audiences. For all that, we can say with confidence that each of them is concerned with what is unfinished business in Ireland. It becomes astonishing, in this light, to reflect just how often these plays revolve around the question of sexual identity.

In *The Year of Magical Wanking* Neil Watkins takes us through twelve months of a gay sexual odyssey. Along the way the audience look into and, it might be said, look past excesses, not alone in the content but in the story-telling – inflated accounts, parodies, multiple personae, levels of artifice, rhyming couplets, an abundance of styles – to seeing the story-maker in his particularity. Frailty as the common ground of our humanity proves to be more binding here than sexuality is (needlessly but nonetheless) divisive, and the lightness we experience on arriving at the destination he has chosen for us, is in every way keyed to the person whom we meet.

The Big Deal looks to work in the opposite direction for a similar destination of grace, finding a register and a performance language that is seemingly without style. It relays testimony from two Irish citizens who underwent sex reassignments (outside of Ireland) at a time when they found themselves in marriages to individuals of that self-same gender to which they would reassign. Actual diaries and correspondence between the principles form the material for this play where Una McKevitt's authorial touch is, strictly speaking, exercised through the editing and the theatricalizing of the 'found' material. Performing this material means in practice playing for high stakes. Audience members, to connect with these stories, risk destabilizing cherished ideas and it is far from a passive activity to attend this play.

Oedipus Loves You places Oedipus on the psychoanalyst's couch in the twenty-first century, together with his family, and what registers as plague is less of an external nature than it is owed to the paralysis of their sexual lives. Their desires are catered for, it is the twenty-first century after all, but are not sated: they still demand placation. Here, their options coalesce around self-harm or reputational damage. And so, it is less a sense of heady abandon than enervating abandonment that runs through the play. And it is this sense of abandonment that begets its attitude – an ironical submissiveness before the abandonment by everyone and everything in the universe, an embrace of abandonment in a grunge pose.

I ♥ Alice ♥ I engages with a present-day struggle in Ireland more directly than any other play in the collection: the struggle for full marriage rights for same-sex couples. Which is to say, it discountenances 'civil partnership', recently placed on the Irish statute books, as anything like sufficient. Even so, parodying the verbatim play as it does, its subversion goes further than a genre, further even than challenging the attitudes against same-sex marriages. Its subversion goes all the way to upsetting the status of what is real and what is performance in a composition keyed to the precise *effect* of those who perform within it: the writer-director-actor, Amy Conroy, and actor, Clare Barrett. Here, we should know, nothing is as it seems.

Trade brings us to where, to my knowledge, no verbatim account has ever taken us, where the imagination alone goes – the moments before a young man trades his body for sex with an older man. The older man speaks of his troubles, comes to recognize the precipice on which he balances, experiences his future as do-or-die. But for once a dramatization of Irish male identity holds off from exonerating him of the charge of exploitation. Rather, for all his bravado and reticence before the important questions, it is the vulnerability of the young man that hits us hardest.

Two sisters hold the centre of *Pineapple.* One is a young mother looking askance over the book of her sexual history, prompted by the attentions of a new lover who promises to be different. The other is a teenager at the point of writing out, as in a first draft, the pattern of her own sexuality. Weighing reality against opportunity, likelihood against desire, in a context of begrudging state support, the play finds a metonymical equivalence between their stories and those outside the theatre. (Axis Arts Centre, Ballymun, where the play premièred, sits in the shadow of the Ballymun Tower Blocks.[1]) Teeming, eye-popping social drama and at the same time, just a handful of the stories available from the infinite number in Ballymun, it is at once riveting and generous, attention-grabbing and stepping out of the way.

The Art of Swimming tells the story, as the play itself lets us know, of 'Mercedes Gleitze: the first British woman to swim the English Channel. This I did in 1927 aged twenty-six and it took fifteen hours and fifteen minutes.' From this is woven a metaphor for the construction of self-hood outside class and gender boundaries, with materials that appeal as concrete achievements, from drives that can never fully be known. In this performance we are aware of watching two people become more themselves, Mercedes Gleitze, as her story unfolds, and Lynda Radley the writer-performer, as she tells it. In each case, however, we are aware that this *growing* is an effect of the theatre. Whatever about its passing itself off as a lecture on the art of swimming, it is a fathomless example of the art of theatrical storytelling.

HEROIN might be said to buck the trend by identifying its unfinished business in the realm of social policy. But the stories of addiction here are neither accusatory of the individual nor the usual parade of 'junkies' pointing to state neglect. Rather, the play brings us into ethical contact with the individual story and leaves open what ensues. And for all that the play rehearses a history of Irish delusion, it questions the uses to which we put history. It collapses time into that ethical encounter in the present. It asks us to see the addict now, in her present fullness of being. It asks us to stop, look, listen, make eye contact, engage, recognize, before

---

1. Social housing in north Dublin, close to Dublin airport, that has been the by-word for social trap in Ireland throughout its forty-five-year history – its demolition, begun in 2005, is ongoing.

moving on. Whatever has or hasn't worked in the past, whatever models of representation we were wont to have the addict fall into, we start again and we start by seeing again.

In these plays you will recognize a conscious exercise of what I choose to call theatre's 'materiality'. The audience is, somehow, to complete the plays. The concrete experience of theatrical circumstance itself is to be available to our attention. Here is a conscious embrace of theatricality as a principle of composition.

Let us explore this further in relation to each of the plays.

Trade by performing during its première run in the bedroom of an actual guesthouse on Dublin's north-side, explodes the realism to which it cleaves exaggeratedly, to leave us in the spoor of its theatricality.

The Big Deal at no point asks us to connect the performer to the text, rather from 'stand-ins' we get our bearings in the text, from proxies we locate ourselves vis-à-vis these stories of metamorphosis.

HEROIN builds for us a framework, an environment, a relationship with the actors, but leaves it entirely up to us to erect on them what illusions we will.

The Art of Swimming is at once a journeying and a remaining in our theatre seats, an exhilarating remembering and a bittersweet re-calibration to the present.

The Year of Magical Wanking builds artifice on artifice, all the more to see the person just there.

Oedipus Loves You is all the time getting to the 'what's just there' – a flaming barbecue, a paddling pool, a live grunge band, the director issuing notes from a cubicle onstage – all the while it invokes Thebes.

I ♥ Alice ♥ I invites us in to meet, as it were, 'Granny' – two 'authentic' middle-aged women as lovers – and when we ask, 'why the nervousness', replies 'all the better to see you with, my dear', or 'why the wigs', replies 'all the better to hear you with, my dear', or 'why the…', whereupon we realize how malevolent and 'wolfish' are *our* own presumptions.

Pineapple is firstly a drama, but secondly a monument – a tribute to those residents of the Ballymun Tower Blocks who are relocating, redesigning their homes and re-making their communities and identities even now as we watch *or read* the drama.

The terms by which identity itself comes into play, the opening of the field of play, the raising into collective experience the exercise of that play: an urgency in the playwriting would appear to lie precisely here.

'I only met Patrick once. I was passing by Cathy's office and she said call in. I said, "okay, but I won't be me, I'll be Sean," and she said, "call in anyway, I'll be Patrick."' (*The Big Deal*)

The exercise of playfulness of identity and the question of the reading of that playfulness would seem to be the wheel to which these playwrights put their shoulders.

'Leave on your smalls just. Your boxers. Let me look at you. I don't want a show or anything.' (*Trade*)

It is not enough, so these playwrights would seem to say, that 'we' get on with 'our' play. Rather the range of terms recognized as 'play' is to be re-negotiated by everyone, vouchsafed by everyone, to be a part of our collective witness, our collective possibilities, to be an experience *imaginable* by everyone.

'Both Alices move back. Alice Slattery prompts Alice Kinsella subtly. They check the "map" on the wall. They give each other a reassuring glance.' (*I ♥ Alice ♥ I*)

You are entitled to think that we are coming here to the question of 'visibility', of making visible what has hitherto been concealed. But you might also be prevailed upon to recognize – which is to touch on theatre's province and majesty – what is a reconnecting with the power of the invisible.

'If it helps you to have a more fulfilling theatrical experience you can imagine that I *did* decide to spend the exorbitant amount of money they were asking for in the second-hand clothing shop where I found an authentic period swimming costume – you know, one of the ones that comes down to here (*indicating thighs*) and looks like something a wrestler might wear. It was navy blue and made out of cotton jersey.' (*The Art of Swimming*)

You'd also be forgiven for thinking these Irish playwrights hadn't heard.

'But your needs, young one. Your needs! Let that be your number one concern from here on in.' (*Pineapple*)

Perhaps they've chosen not to hear, perhaps they were determined to tune in elsewhere.

'On alcohol, on ketomene, on coke.

On poppers, on my own, on with the porn.

On headshop herbal smoke, I am reborn.

On x-tube I'm used and abused by ghosts.'

(*The Year of Magical Wanking*)

Perhaps no such choosing had even been involved. Perhaps they kept out of step because it had nothing to do with them, or because it had no story in which they could see themselves.

'"Please don't panic," she said, "but I saw you two in Tesco. I saw your kiss and it was beautiful."' (*I ♥ Alice ♥ I*)

Sure, in the real world economic pressure is being brought to bear on them just as much as on anyone else.

'This is just this. It isn't real. It's money.' (*Trade*)

Sure, they are as alive as everyone else to the changed realities.

'Keep it up now

Keep it up

Keep it the fuck up

Keep it up now

Go for it

I dare you

See what happens' (*HEROIN*)

But the sense of urgency would appear to be directed elsewhere.

'In the open sea you have no idea what's coming next. You must make your peace with currents and tides. You must learn how to track them. You have to swim straight but you cannot waste too much energy on looking up so you learn blind how to navigate a straight liquid line. You must learn how to swim in the dark.' (*The Art of Swimming*)

It would appear to be directed to a re-negotiation both *in* and *of* the theatre that is, if anything, coming to a head.

'I don't know. It's kind of reassuring. Like being half-asleep and knowing that you don't have to wake up. I think it suits us here this plague.' (*Oedipus Loves You*)

Other fronts have ceded sovereignty here. These playwrights give no quarter. They engage the theatre, and engage us in the theatre, on their own terms. We can insist on reading from the historical moment into these plays. Or we can take them at their word. It is for us as readers, just as we have as theatre-goers – frequently scandalized, enthralled, shamed, appalled, unburdened, tickled pink – to decide.

Acknowledgements

I wish to acknowledge the contribution of photographer and performance artist, Gary Coyle, who generously provided the cover image, 'Forty Foot' (2005).

To the writers, editors and the wider personnel behind each of the plays, my heartfelt thanks for your generosity, patience, attention to detail and commitment to the anthology through each of its phases.

To Andrew Walby and the team at Oberon books, equally heartfelt thanks for the vision, support, commitment, unstinting labours, good humour and spirit of adventure that you brought to this, the most collaborative of publications.

Thomas Conway
September 10, 2012

Selected texts by Grace Dyas from
HEROIN
BY THEATREclub

HEROIN was authored by Grace Dyas in collaboration with Barry O'Connor, Lauren Larkin, Gerard Kelly, Rachael Keogh, Graham Ryall and The Men's Group at Rialto Community Drug Team.

The performance text is a combination of improvisation from the actors, written testimony from interviewees in Rialto and Dolphin's Barn, Dublin 8, Rachel Keogh's autobiography *Dying to Survive* (Gill & Macmillan, 2007) and authored texts by Grace Dyas. The interviews and the texts authored by Grace Dyas are the sole texts detailed here.

HEROIN was performed by Barry O'Connor, Lauren Larkin and Ryan O'Conor (first production, performances 1 – 3), Conor Madden (work-in-progress and first production, performances 4 – 9), Ger Kelly (work-in-progress, second through fifth productions), Dylan Brophy (aged 12) and Ross Kenny (aged 11).

Stage Designer	Doireann Coady
Lighting Designer	Eoin Winning
Costume Designer	Emma Fraser
Producer	Sarah Murphy
Sound Designer	Frank Sweeney
Researcher and Producer	Shane Byrne
Assistant Director	Dylan Haskins
Assistant Designer	Emma Fraser
Assistant Lighting Designer	Eoghan Carrick
Production Manager	Helen Collins
Stage Manager	Emma Fraser
Assitant Stage Manager	Niamh Denyer
Sound Operator	Gavin Hennessy
Stage Manager	Gemma Collins
Production Assistant	Shirley Somers

Dublin Fringe Festival, 8–17 September 2010, Smock Alley Theatre

axis, Ballymun, 24–26 March 2011

Dublin Theatre Festival (as part of ReViewed), 4–9 October 2011, Smock Alley Theatre

Noorderzon Performing Arts Festival, Groningen, The Netherlands 16-19 August 2012

Draíocht, Blanchardstown, 10 & 11 October 2012

Winner of Spirit of the Fringe Award 2010.

Author's Note

The following is a selection of the written texts in the play *HEROIN* that was made collaboratively in 2010. The action of the play proper in our version of *HEROIN* moves from the 1960s to the present day while a living space is constructed on stage live. Because the performance is largely unscripted, that is, it follows a rigid rules structure that the actors improvise within – or what happens is set but how it happens is not – I have elected not to include stage directions. Because the performers do not play 'characters' but rather 'personae' or 'versions of themselves', I have omitted character names. I would invite anyone wishing to stage this piece to use these texts, along with their own rigorous research process, to create their own narrative using these texts as a framework. I would advise that anyone wishing to stage it should also read Rachel Keogh's book *Dying to Survive* and seek her permission if they wish to include it. Ultimately, for a million metaphysical paradoxical reasons, it would be impossible for anyone to stage the version of *HEROIN* that I 'wrote'. However, I invite you to use these texts to make your own. I would also refer readers to an essay that I wrote for *Irish Theatre Magazine*, as it provides the necessary context for how this work was produced collaboratively, which I think will be of interest to the reader... The essay can be found at: http://www.irishtheatremagazine. ie/Features/Current/This-is-about-everything-that-ever-happened

SECTION ONE. THE NINETEEN SIXTIES SECTION. THAT IS WHAT THIS SECTION IS CALLED, OKAY?

– This is a story about heroin.

– We're moving now
We're moving

Hope comes
Hope goes

Swings and roundabouts

Post boxes are being painted from red to green

We're building boxes on boxes to cut the landscape
We're seeing progress loom over our heads
We're living in mansions

We've got our own doors
We've got our bathrooms
We have mansions
With balconies too high to see our children

Sean Lemass is helping us play catch up
We're moving now
We're going

Foley St. has fallen down
We're up and out
We're on
We're gone

We're getting televisions to watch troubles
We're cleaning out our lungs

We're coming home to roll spliffs

We're getting paid
We're contributing something
We're staying here

We're coughing and dying of consumption

We're turned on

We're rejecting our parents
We're not concerned with material goods

We're making our children lambs of god
We're cleansing their souls with leather straps
We're sending our daughters to breathe in steam

We're drinking too much
We're leaving them at it

SECTION TWO. THE NINETEEN SEVENTIES. THE SECTION
THAT DETAILS THE EVENTS OF THE NINETEEN SEVENTIES.

– This is a story about Joey.

– Joey started drinking at eleven and smoking hash at
fourteen. He came from a big family. They were the first in
their block to get a television.

He thinks his dad might have stolen it, but he's not sure.
He says he did poorly in school due to behavioural
problems and poor concentration. His mother called a
priest to the house when he was caught stealing to pay for
drink and clothes. For a short time he served as an altar
boy.

When he was caught stealing again, he was sent away.

When he came home, he started taking painkillers;
palphine, diphenol. He took heroin first in 1978, when it
was beginning to creep in. He vomited for hours after his
first smoke. People he hung around with offered him some,
a well-known Dublin criminal family –

– Who?

– He would have tried anything at the time. He didn't even
know what it was, and didn't get much out of it either, at
first. He started injecting almost immediately. He knew he
had a problem before he went to prison again.

– This is a story about me
My da drinks
My ma smokes
I don't get on with them
Stay outside
My ma is a saint
My da is a cunt though
I'm never there
Close your eyes
Lean forward
Every muscle in your body
Can you feel it?

My ma has a new fella
Don't like him much
Can you feel that?
My da is a cunt
He's a fucking cunt
Can you feel that?
And I'll never be like him
Haven't seen me ma in weeks
My da props up the bar
Lean forward
Close your eyes
My ma is gone out with her friends
They did their best but we hadn't a hope
My da lost his job
When all the factories closed down
Started drinking
Me ma is grand really
They really did do their best but we hadn't really a hope
My ma is dead
She died this morning
She's gone
And she's never coming back
He's just always fucking nagging me
And I just
It gets very
Ah for fuck's sake
See you
See you
You can smile all you want
That's all I'm saying
Fucking stand-up comedian
That's all I'm saying

Fuck him
Fuck him from a fucking height
That's fucking hilarious

Easy
Easy

Stay fucking easy
Alright
Okay
Alright
You're gonna pay for that
Alright deadly
Cheers
Yeah grand

Are you actually serious?

I'm gonna bite your face off
I'll rip your fucking head off

Go for it
You prick
Do you think I won't?

I'll rip your fucking head off

Keep it up now
Keep it up
Keep it the fuck up
Keep it up now
Go for it
I dare you
See what happens

– We're changing now

We're getting corrupt
We can't remember who we're voting for

We're hearing about streets worth killing for
Somewhere we've never been

Poppies are growing
Millions of red poppies
Leaders are changing
Moving and starting to sell in a place we've never heard of

An oil crisis ripples and sends us somewhere else

We're changing to the decimal
We're swapping our skirts for trousers
We're leaving or staying to do nothing

Our factories are closing down
We're signing on
We're up and out

Our mansions are falling down
Our lifts are broken
Our children are playing with broken glass

We're being ignored
We're second-class citizens
We're having more children to get bigger rooms
Streets worth killing for cloud the agenda
So they tell us it's not happening

Hope falls
Swings and roundabouts

There's a war on
That means we can't rob banks
There's a crisis that means
We can't get jobs

We forget what we can do
We have nothing
We feel like less

Some of us take it
Some of us don't
Some of us can't
Some of us won't

Our mothers are crushing benzo's against their teeth
Our fathers are drinking Guinness and talking about the
British

We're living in ruins of mansions
We've got nowhere to go and nothing to do
We're stealing pills from our mothers to calm our nerves

We're climbing over our neighbours on the stairs

We're fine though
Because none of this is happening

They're telling us it's not happening

SECTION THREE. OR SOMETHING. THE EIGHTIES. THIS IS WHAT HAPPENS IN THE EIGHTIES.

– She's after having a baby now
A little girl
I think it's with her ma

I got pulled out of the bed by the ankle
Pushed out to the landing
Punched in the stomach
Fell down the stairs

When we got broken into we didn't get a new window for
a few weeks
And we got a letter yeah
A letter off the corpo
Saying that we were being fined
For breaking our tenancy agreement
Can you believe that?

I met a fella, I suppose that was how I got into it
More often than not,
It's always a fella

This place is not on a map
It's not on a map of Dublin

I can't get anything on tick now and that's a fucking
problem
No labour till Wednesday
What the fuck
What the fuck

I guarantee you
No I guarantee it
If this was happening in Rathgar
They'd do something about it pretty quick

Walked up with a knife
Give me your bag love
Ran away
Scored

Every day the sickness gets worse
You start off being careful
But eventually you don't care
It's just like
You need that ya know
You need that
And if you can't get it you'll do fucking anything

I knocked at the door and a young wan answered
Told her that her da left something for me upstairs
Walked upstairs and looked around
Came back at the weekend
Took it all

During the 1980s anyone from the south inner city who
had a video player got it robbed
It was tragic

Started going over once a week and bringing the boxes
back on cargo ships
It was fucking easy
It felt like they weren't even trying to stop us

Nobody touches you when you have the virus
And you know you feel very alone

I came back from the disco and kneeled down at the statue
of the Virgin Mary
It started lashing raining
And I prayed till the morning

Little fuckers
Little fucking fucks
If it isn't nailed down they have it away
Fuckers

You go in with a shopping bag
Take the whole arm of jumpers
Into the bag
You walk out
Once you don't look like you're on drugs nobody notices

We call the police but nobody comes
Taxis won't pull in under the arch
My mother cried when I said I was moving in here

My da bought me a bottle of brown phi and locked me in
my room for weeks

Nobody talks to you when you're sick
They know you're sick
You can't even buy milk in shops
You only talk to other people who take drugs
And you make friends with people who take drugs
And that's just it

Open your handbag and offer out the Valium
Sure we're all brothers and sisters in Holy God's family

I went to my doctor and he told me all he could do was tell
me to stay off the gear
He said I should go to my priest

Hands go around your waist and it makes you breathe in
Get your fucking hands off me
Close your eyes
Maggots and mould and rot
Feel the sick coming up and falling out my mouth
He never fucking stops

Smack in the jaw
Taste blood
Slam the door behind me

Put your hands over your ears and say lalalalala

Smack in the jaw
Taste blood
Slam the door behind me

– They even took our new curtains and my mother made
them for us as a wedding present

Come on to the pub son
I'll buy you a few pints

Stay off that fucking dirty stuff

Hands go around your waist and it makes you breathe in
Get your fucking hands off me
Close your eyes
Maggots and mould and rot
Feel the sick coming up and falling out my mouth
He never fucking stops

– I remember just thinking
How can I live here?

I came up the stairs and I just saw runners
His brand new Nike runners hanging there
In the air
I went and got me ma

We take their names at the entrance to the blocks. If
they've no business here we ask them to move on.

We know each other. They're our own. They're one of us.
And they're laughing at the drug watch.

Are we doing the right thing here? We think we are. But
are we doing the right thing here, really?

Can we talk about this here? Is it okay, to talk about this
here, like this?

He wants help and he can't get it
And God knows when he'll ask again
I do leave the place crying

Things have got worse
They're only going to get worse
They're not getting any better

This could have been a good place
It could have been brilliant here
A great place to rear a family
And now
And now

– We're unstable
Walls are falling
We're reshuffling and stopping and starting
We're under pressure
We're making words for things we didn't have words for
before
We're making rules about something new

People are refusing to eat
For streets we've never walked on

We're in debt
We're spending nothing
Our mansions are turning into ghettoes

It's too hot in our towers
We're serving time until we're moved on
We're wheeling our prams for hours
We've started to lie about where we're from

We're colder than we've ever been
We're seeing faces change
We're having our windows broken
We're watching our tellies being stolen

We're spreading new diseases
We're waking up to spacemen
We're holding up the shop van

We're robbing chemists
We're swallowing cough syrup
We're being found in forests

We're dancing in our casuals
We're walking home at sunrise
And hiding our eyes

We're finding veins
We're scoring
We're borrowing
We're dyin' sick
We're freezing cold when we wake up

We puncture our skin to make ourselves warm

Swings and roundabouts

We're coming together to say no to drugs
We're shooting to kill
We're taking names
We're organizing
We're meeting and talking
We're marching on houses

We're beating not treating
We're moving their furniture out one by one
We're talking to gun bearers
We're kicking each other to death
Our names are in the newspapers

We're moving the quiet ones out to the suburbs
We're keeping the bad with the bad

We're praying to Holy God to remove heroin from us
We're looking at the sweat on Jesus's brow
We're doing 'The Stations of the Cross'

We're not being encouraged by getting free needles
We're not interfering in God's Holy Plan with
contraception
We're spreading diseases we know nothing about

We're stealing to pay for our habits
We're shooting to recover our debts
We're suffocating in our boxes
We're drinking whiskey for our regrets

It's okay though
None of this is really happening
They tell us it's not happening

SECTION FOUR, YEAH? THE NINETIES. THINGS HAVE BEEN
GETTING WORSE FOR A VERY LONG TIME.

– The footpaths are painted green, white and orange.
The streetlamps are beginning to flicker.
You can feel the sun on your back.

There's one less family at mass.

Corrugated iron windows. The grass has been burnt.
Destruction. Don't say too much. You don't have to.

The space is as big as eleven acres, or as small as one.
Looming over you. You're standing across the road. It feels
like the city has just stopped moving. It hasn't. But that's
how it feels. You can hear humming. A red car passes you.
You don't see many of those nowadays.

Looking at all the windows makes your eyes squint.
There's all these holes in the walls and you wonder about
them.

If you look past the railings that cage the whole thing in,
you can see the dirty syringes in the muck where the grass
used to grow. Or maybe you just saw that on television.

You walk inside and you can feel the weight of people
inside. If you look up, it feels like everything might fall
down.

There's a Guard *[policeman]* standing here 24 hours a day.

He has to stand here all day.

And there's a van at every block.

There are no other parts of the city now and this is a war
zone.

– A war zone is better than a famine though.

– Yeah.

This is where everyone feels like they're serving time, and
the whole country comes to buy drugs.

And you can even buy a gun here, now that the troubles are over.

But you're afraid to actually own anything, in case it gets robbed.

Where were you when Ireland lost in Italia '90?

– That was the first time I saw me da cry.

– This is the part where everything gets terrifying.
Where all the colours are dark and nothing makes sense. Everybody is acting on impulse, or autopilot. This is the bit where we all stood up and ran. We left empty flats behind us and people moved in and started banging up.

This is the bit where the hero dies of AIDS, and the heroine gets raped.

Where the baby was born with an addiction, where the mattress was set on fire.

This is when her ribs were broken. Ireland lost in Italia '90.

This was the moment when we got rich. And you might say, if you weren't there, that this was when we split. Before we were all together, and some of us were poorer or less well off than others. But now this is the part where we've all succeeded, and everybody else has fucked it up for themselves.

This is the moment before the end of the war. The bit where the most people die. The bit where the most irrational choices are made. The camera pans out and all the casualties are lying in the street.

This is when we'll feel like we can't take it anymore. Where we'll declare that we want to die. Where we'll decide that the situation is inevitable, and that change is impossible.

Things have just been getting worse for a very long time.

We might come together for the very first time. We might organize effectively for change. We might use our fists. But when it comes to tell the story, we won't be able to remember.

This is when we'll knock it all down. Because we're at our rock bottom. And now we need to fight.

This is what it feels like when pressure builds. When the emersion is left on for too long. When the pot boils over and something has to happen. This is the bit where the guy who was saying 'What are you looking at?,' actually beat up the guy who was looking at him.

– We're moving now
We're going

We're putting ourselves on the agenda

God is saying they can't grow poppies anymore

They're flying over Columbia with poisons

We're purring
We're swimming
We're going for gold

We're spending money
We're teaching children
We're wearing tracksuits and getting our rings engraved

We're coming together and doing things we saw in films
We're getting guns and nicknames
We just don't give a fuck

We're killing Veronica Guerin
We're paying off our mortgages
We're getting jobs in Industrial Estates
We're hearing the secrets from industrial schools

We're moving

We're kicking Josie Dwyer
We're packing out our prisons

We're taking down our net curtains
We're going on holidays to Spain

We're buying a new car
We're complaining about insurance
We're building
We're moving
We're blaring rap songs out our windows

We're hopeful
Swings and roundabouts

We're watching Saturday morning television
We're wearing multi-coloured caps
We're playing with our Pogs
We're robbing cars and driving in the park
We're walking into the bushes

We're in an epidemic
We're jumping off a tower block
We're collapsing our veins
We're injecting into our feet
We're living in stairwells

We're taking ecstacy with our Evian
We're getting our pictures in the papers

We're easing the sickness with methadone
We're going to clinics twice a week
We're breaking our balls to help people
We're raising a profile
We're understanding the situation
We're on committees
We're strategizing
We're forward thinking

We're building help in our communities
We're making our marches bigger

We're hearing that Brenda's got a baby

We're containing it off the beaten track

We're hiding from tourists
We're left to our own devices
We're killing each other

I'm sorry
We can't say it's not happening anymore

SECTION FIVE. THE TWO THOUSANDS. YOU ARE NEVER GONNA UNDERSTAND.

– I'm not doing this tomorrow night.

– And you know, you feel very alone

– She can read that book all she likes but she's never gonna understand

– I'm sorry
I am sorry
I don't think I can do this anymore

I'm lost
I'm falling apart
I'm losing
Sorry

I'm sorry but
I don't think I can do this anymore

I'm sorry
I am really fucking sorry
I just want it all to end

I don't think I can stay quiet anymore
I don't know what to say
I'm sorry
I am
It's all my fault
Nobody forced me to do anything
It is all my fault
And I'm sorry

I'm sick
I'm really feeling sick now

I've lost it all

And I need help
I don't want to do this anymore
I don't want to do this anymore
I don't want any of this anymore

Okay?
None of it
Nothing

I'm lost

I would like to be able to join in
I would like to calm down

Look at me
Please
Can you just look at me?

I feel like I never had anything to lose

I can't do this anymore
I can't even wake up
I'm finished
I don't even know this
I can't even notice

Can you please tell me what to do?
Can you please tell me what the fuck I'm supposed to do?
I don't know how this works

I wish I could see a video of my life
I wish someone had recorded it
I wish there was a record
I wish I was caught on CCTV

Help me
Please
Can someone just help me?
Please

Can you just look at me?
Can you just look at me?
Please?
I think that might help

Look at me
Look at me
Look at me

I'm sick
I'm really fucking dying sick now
Please

– I'm in my dress just waiting to sing, look lovely, etc.
This is what happened
We took drugs
We took any drugs we could get our hands on
Because we were scared of being normal
Of having to live with our heads
Because horrible things happened to us
Or because nothing ever happened to us
Because our fathers drank and battered us
Because our mothers never washed our uniforms
Because we had no socks
Because we couldn't tell the time
Because we couldn't tie our laces
And we felt nothing
And we didn't know how
And we ran

And I was there and I saw it

This is what happened
I was there and I saw it
And I wrote my name on a wall

This is what happened
We took drugs
Because we wanted to take drugs
We wanted to feel different

This is what happened
I stole handbags and wallets
And I smashed windows with bricks
This is what happened
I took cocaine
And crack cocaine
And I mixed my methadone with heroin
And I lied to the relieving officer
And I ran

This is what happened, my uncle took me into a room and
told me to undress
This is what happened, I slept under a bridge
This is what happened, my teacher humiliated me in front
of the class
This is what happened, my brother was better than me
My daughter kept crying
I didn't know what the fuck else to do
I couldn't fill in the form

I couldn't give directions
I spread the poison
And nobody mentioned it

This is what happened
We were told we were nothing
We had nothing

This is what happened
Our address came with a stigma
We never did well in school
Our parents were bad parents
I was there and I saw it
And I wrote my name on a wall
I was there

This is about everything that ever happened

Because we needed to talk about this
Because we couldn't
Because we needed to be on the dark side of life
Because we believed in God
Because we left the empire
Because we saw our fathers peddle death to people we
didn't know
Because we never saw anything
Because we were bored
This is what happened
I was there and I saw it
I was there
I was there

Because we had no sense of pride in ourselves
Because our parents shouted over our heads while they
cleaned our faces
Because we injected cigarettes
Because we mainlined McDonald's
Because we rubbed vodka into our pores
Because we were disqualified in Italia '90
Because Tony Gregory had the balance of power
Because we needed something to feel well

Because we ran

This is about everything that ever happened

One day you will wake up and you won't want this
anymore
You will see everything laid out in front of you
For the first time
You will really see what's on offer
And you won't want it

It's the minute when the choice is there
It only lasts a minute though

One day you're caught or you have no veins to inject into
And you claim that this is a crisis, a desperate problem that
you need help in overcoming
A photograph of thirteen people, everyone of them dead
but you
And now you have to look at it and stop running

We learn to find hope in small things
In the mundanity of everyday life

We are afraid of reliving our past, that looking back might
finish us off altogether
Nobody is forcing us to
Nobody can

We're getting something to take the sickness away

We learnt to find hope in the small things

We're sleeping in one of thirty detox beds

We are afraid of reliving our past
But we've collapsed all our veins
We can't take one more turn on
So they gave us something to take the sickness away

We can't bury what had happened under a ton of drugs
We can't face thinking about what happened
We're taking something so we won't get sick
But we're not getting better

We're drug free, and we've never looked back

We're starting to live in the world again
We're trying to be adults, but we never learnt how to be
children

We've stopped stealing, we're legal, above board
And almost as sick as ever

Sick, but different

We're telling our story

We're sweating and our teeth are rotting
They gave us something so we wouldn't get sick
But we are not getting better

We were bored
And the temptation was too strong
We couldn't move forward
We couldn't face it
So we ran again

We smoke heroin at the weekends

We are confronting it all head on
We feel all the pain and the guilt
We surrendered
We are were powerless
And we are still sick

We have switched to smoking crack

Our teeth are rotting and we can't even smile
We can't go on holidays without their permission
But we are were living
We are here
Still
Just
Just here

We are here
We are standing here

In the moment that is the aftermath and the beginning
But we don't know what yet

– We're sticking around for longer
We're fighting a war on terror
We're shaking hands in Northern Ireland

We're roaring for a while – we are
We're mixing our heroin with cocaine
We're getting weaker hits for bigger prices
We're slitting skin for seventy quid

We're all working in offices
We're drinking Starbucks and wearing Gap

We're getting LA tattooed on our necks

We're moving now
We are
We're moving now

We're taking off our rings
We're injecting into our groins at this stage

We're taking a ten percent cut
We're talking about leaving

We're robbing and selling people to feed our habits
We're really fucking dying sick

We're paying off our sons' debts
We're using our guns like toys

We're spreading out
It's countrywide
We're crying about not seeing our children
We're trying to be better
We're putting other people first

We're watching people nodding off on YouTube
We're taking shits in lane ways
We're buying weed in shops
We're drinking more than we ever have
We don't know how to stop

We're living on the streets
We're getting our dole cut
We're contracting Hepatitis C

We're knocking it all down
We're operating the bulldozers
We're having wakes for buildings
We're tasting dust in our mouths

We're documenting our past
We're putting our gardens at the front
We're not living on top of each other
We're shaking hands with politicians
We're making murals about Hope

We're missing a generation

We're feeling this huge sense of loss
We're trying to forget
We're thinking it doesn't affect us

We're feeling this huge sense of loss
We're talking about our memories
We're watching it all crash down around us
We can't believe it's happening again
We're worrying about what we're leaving behind us

We're strung out on methadone
We don't know if we want to stop

We've accepted
We've separated
We're being fragmented
And screaming about feeling fragmented
And this is what we're up against

We feel this huge sense of loss

And we've lost
We have lost

We're starting again
We're starting again

TRADE
BY
MARK O'HALLORAN

Trade premiered on 29 September 2011, at the Dublin Theatre Festival, with previews on 27 and 28 September.

OLDER MAN	Phillip Judge
YOUNG MAN	Ciarán McCabe

Directed by Tom Creed
Designed by Ciarán O'Melia
Produced by Philip McMahon

It had previously received a public reading at Project Arts Centre, Dublin, on 10 December 2010. On this occasion it was presented as part of Queer Notions, a festival of theatre and other performances by thisispopbaby. This reading was also directed by Tom Creed. Older Man was played by Liam Carney, Young Man by Robbie O'Connor.

A cheap B&B in Dublin's North Inner City. The room is small and shabby. A queen-size bed with polyester quilt covers. A window onto a yard. The last of the light has almost gone from the sky and it colours the room blue into black. It is late autumn. There is no lamp on and the room is illuminated only by sodium light bleeding in from the yard or from the door to a small ensuite which is slightly ajar. There is an eighteen-year-old boy here. He stands alone for a moment, small in the shadows. He is wearing sports clothes and a baseball cap. There is a forlorn look on his face or an absence. Occasionally he comes back fully into the space and moves about. There is the sound of running water from the bathroom. Someone is cleaning themselves.

YOUNG MAN: You finished nearly?

OLDER MAN: *(Off stage.)* What?

YOUNG MAN: You done?

OLDER MAN: *(Off stage.)* Hold on.

YOUNG MAN: It's just cause it's nearly fucking half past like.

OLDER MAN: *(Off stage.)* I know…

YOUNG MAN: Yeah, well.

OLDER MAN: *(Off stage.)* Wait.

    Beat.

YOUNG MAN: *(To himself.)* Sake.

    Beat. The YOUNG MAN sits on the side of the bed. He sits silent. Eventually an OLDER MAN enters from the bathroom. The YOUNG MAN doesn't look up or acknowledge the OLDER MAN. The OLDER MAN is in his late 40s. His collar is loose as he has been washing himself. We can see that he has been in an altercation. His face carries an injury to the nose. It is not serious. There are some spots of blood on his shirtfront. He is also holding a toothbrush in his hand. He stands not far from the bathroom door awkwardly. He beholds the YOUNG MAN.

OLDER MAN: Clean now anyways. Done. Better.

YOUNG MAN: Yeah?

OLDER MAN: *(Explaining why he washed.)* A bit of blood just. Gone.

Beat.

OLDER MAN: She thought I was mad at the door I'd say. Do you think?

YOUNG MAN: I don't know.

OLDER MAN: She won't call anyone will she?

YOUNG MAN: She's grand.

OLDER MAN: Used to it maybe.

YOUNG MAN: Yeah.

OLDER MAN: People.

Beat.

YOUNG MAN: Is it sore your nose?

OLDER MAN: What not no. He caught it with his swing just. It's grand. I been hit harder in my day you know.

YOUNG MAN: Who done it?

OLDER MAN: No one.

The OLDER MAN realises he still has a toothbrush in his hands.

OLDER MAN: This.

YOUNG MAN: What?

OLDER MAN: Yeah. I suppose I look like a right fucking knob standing here with this in my hand and my face in bits.

YOUNG MAN: No.

OLDER MAN: Odd even.

YOUNG MAN: Maybe.

OLDER MAN: Yeah.

Beat. The OLDER MAN feels awkward, exposed or ridiculous. He looks at the brush in his hand again.

OLDER MAN: I'm kind of funny about teeth me this.

YOUNG MAN: Yeah?

OLDER MAN: I can't feel clean if I can't wash them just. Carry that with me everywhere then.

He remains standing.

OLDER MAN: Always been funny about my teeth. Washing them about ten times a day I do. Always at the dentist. The hygienist then as well.

YOUNG MAN: Right.

OLDER MAN: Yeah. Wouldn't like to lose them just.

Beat.

OLDER MAN: Should stop getting my gob punched in that case I suppose you could say.

Small beat. They both smile. The room is still. The OLDER MAN looks at the toothbrush again.

OLDER MAN: She's an awful cunt anyways.

YOUNG MAN: Who?

OLDER MAN: The hygienist but you're as well.

YOUNG MAN: Right.

OLDER MAN: I'd hate to like to think there was smells or that there. From my mouth. I'm mad like that. I imagine. I'm stupid.

Pause. He puts the toothbrush away in his jacket.

OLDER MAN: *(Meaning the hygienist.)* Exactly. Awful fucking job.

Beat. The OLDER MAN is perhaps upset.

He steadies his nerve.

OLDER MAN: Apparently they're always killing themselves.

YOUNG MAN: Who?

OLDER MAN: Dental hygienists. I heard, women ones.

YOUNG MAN: Oh.

OLDER MAN: Yeah women ones the worst they say. Don't know why that is. Maybe cause they hate themselves apparently or everyone else hates them or something.

Beat.

OLDER MAN: I don't know how true that is now I just read that.

Beat.

OLDER MAN: Wish my one would kill herself.

Small beat. The OLDER MAN tries to smile or laugh but may be close to tears.

OLDER MAN: Yeah. No.

YOUNG MAN: Are you alright?

OLDER MAN: I'm alright. I think.

YOUNG MAN: What happened?

OLDER MAN: Nothing no. You're good to see me.

YOUNG MAN: Yeah.

The OLDER MAN looks at the YOUNG MAN.

OLDER MAN: *(Softly.)* Take off your hat.

YOUNG MAN: What?

OLDER MAN: Just.

YOUNG MAN: Covering me hair sort of.

OLDER MAN: Just please.

Pause. The YOUNG MAN takes off his baseball cap. He does perfunctory fixing of his hair. It has been very badly bleached and is heavily waxed forward. It may make him look younger and more vulnerable.

YOUNG MAN: *(Softly.)* There.

OLDER MAN: Thanks.

Beat. The OLDER MAN could almost be close to tears. He stands very still and awkward. He pulls himself together almost.

OLDER MAN: *(Meaning the YOUNG MAN's hair.)* Who done that on you?

YOUNG MAN: Me mate.

OLDER MAN: *(Light.)* Not much of a mate.

YOUNG MAN: Practising she was.

OLDER MAN: Right.

YOUNG MAN: She's in a salon.

OLDER MAN: *(Almost laughing.)* Really?

YOUNG MAN: Started just.

OLDER MAN: God fucken help us.

YOUNG MAN: Though all she ever does in there is sweep up or sit on her hole.

OLDER MAN: And you let her at you?

YOUNG MAN: I know.

OLDER MAN: Yeah.

YOUNG MAN: *(He trails off.)* She's a fat fucken…

Beat.

OLDER MAN: Can't really see it that well anyways with the lamp there not on.

YOUNG MAN: Will I turn it on?

OLDER MAN: Do you want it on?

YOUNG MAN: I don't know.

OLDER MAN: I don't give a fuck either way now if I'm being honest. You can just leave it off or you can just…

Beat. The moment hangs. The YOUNG MAN eventually leans over and turns on the lamp by the bed. He may feel slightly exposed by this action. The OLDER MAN is still standing stranded.

OLDER MAN: There.

YOUNG MAN: What?

OLDER MAN: Yeah.

Small beat.

OLDER MAN: Your hair *is* sort of, it's kind of fucked.

YOUNG MAN: I know.

OLDER MAN: It looks sore.

The YOUNG MAN smiles and fixes his hair again.

YOUNG MAN: I could kill her I could.

OLDER MAN: It's not that bad though but. You just look a bit, you know.

YOUNG MAN: I know.

OLDER MAN: Like a knacker.

Beat. The phrase has landed harder than the OLDER MAN had intended.

OLDER MAN: Sorry. I didn't mean…

YOUNG MAN: No.

OLDER MAN: I was just being funny. I'm a fucken edjit really is what. I should shut up.

YOUNG MAN: You're alright.

OLDER MAN: My mouth.

Beat. The OLDER MAN may move closer to the YOUNG MAN.

OLDER MAN: You hot?

YOUNG MAN: What?

OLDER MAN: You alright?

YOUNG MAN: The radiators?

OLDER MAN: Yeah.

YOUNG MAN: It's nice it's grand.

OLDER MAN: It is.

Beat.

YOUNG MAN: It was cold before earlier.

OLDER MAN: Was it?

YOUNG MAN: Yeah in town.

OLDER MAN: You were around?

YOUNG MAN: I was around and it was cold.

OLDER MAN: I was inside all day. Most of the day. Before I called you before… I stayed in bed late and then.

Beat. The OLDER MAN looks at the YOUNG MAN questioningly.

OLDER MAN: *(Low.)* Were you working or…

YOUNG MAN: What?

OLDER MAN: Just…

Beat. The room is very still again.

OLDER MAN: Take off your top, your jacket, if you want, if you're hot. Do you want a drink?

Beat. The YOUNG MAN takes off his tracksuit top. The OLDER MAN watches him closely.

YOUNG MAN: I don't know.

OLDER MAN: I have cans there in my bag. Only cheap auld Polish shite but…

The YOUNG MAN looks at him.

OLDER MAN: I didn't know what to get you, what you drink, but those were going then so I got them.

Short beat.

OLDER MAN: If only, now, if you want just only.

Beat.

OLDER MAN: Do you want?

YOUNG MAN: *(Softly.)* Yeah so.

OLDER MAN: So go on so. They're there for you. You can take them with you after then or…

Small beat. There is a recyclable shopping bag in the room holding the beer. The YOUNG MAN gets up and gets a can.

OLDER MAN: I got six or eight or something.

YOUNG MAN: You having one?

OLDER MAN: I will. I'll join you anyway.

The YOUNG MAN takes a couple of cans and delivers one to the OLDER MAN. They are close now. The OLDER MAN and the YOUNG MAN open their cans. They both drink.

YOUNG MAN: I'm trying not to be drinking.

OLDER MAN: Me too as well yeah. Cheers.

YOUNG MAN: Cheers.

They drink.

OLDER MAN: Chin-chin as the man said.

YOUNG MAN: What?

OLDER MAN: There. Us.

They clink cans. The silence is thick around them.

OLDER MAN: Not bad.

YOUNG MAN: No. It's nice, they are.

OLDER MAN: It's shite. It's nice. It's OK. Yeah.

Beat.

OLDER MAN: We can relax before…

Beat. They drink.

OLDER MAN: I'm glad to see you anyways.

YOUNG MAN: Thanks.

OLDER MAN: I didn't think I'd see you again after the last time.

YOUNG MAN: Oh?

OLDER MAN: I thought I didn't want to just.

YOUNG MAN: Right.

OLDER MAN: I nearly even deleted you even.

YOUNG MAN: Yeah?

OLDER MAN: Yeah. Only I didn't cause I couldn't. My new phone is a Samsung and I'm fucking baffled by it. I'm more used to Nokia mostly. My daughter tries to teach me sometimes but I'm stupid with machines like. The internet and that. She just dies laughing at me then and it was her made me get the fucken thing in the first place. Calls me a dope. Only joking just. Can barely use the fucken remote control me. So I never got to delete you.

Beat. They drink.

OLDER MAN: I needed to. To see you.

Beat.

YOUNG MAN: Why?

OLDER MAN: Just mad shit just.

YOUNG MAN: Yeah?

OLDER MAN: I haven't been myself. I don't know. I been lonely or something.

The silence resumes. Again the OLDER MAN stands and is on the point of tears perhaps. Again he steadies himself.

OLDER MAN: So how you been keeping and anyways?

YOUNG MAN: Yeah you know.

OLDER MAN: I know.

Beat.

OLDER MAN: And you alright?

YOUNG MAN: Yeah.

OLDER MAN: Yeah good yeah.

Beat.

YOUNG MAN: Only I'm not at home any more.

OLDER MAN: Oh?

YOUNG MAN: No.

OLDER MAN: Why?

YOUNG MAN: No why. She's just, I was sick of her, me ma. I'm done with her. She's mad.

OLDER MAN: Right.

YOUNG MAN: Drinking and that. Throwing slaps. She's a cunt really.

Beat.

OLDER MAN: So where you now?

YOUNG MAN: Nowhere really. I was staying with my girlfriend first in her place. But then the baby was crying all the time and I was coming in late and she didn't want me drinking or anything even so I went.

OLDER MAN: OK.

YOUNG MAN: Fighting always.

OLDER MAN: Not good.

YOUNG MAN: No.

OLDER MAN: With a baby not good anyways.

YOUNG MAN: I know.

OLDER MAN: So.

YOUNG MAN: So I'm staying with mates now. Kipping down with mates. With one mate just. But.

OLDER MAN: Yeah?

YOUNG MAN: With him. But it's not forever that.

OLDER MAN: Alright.

YOUNG MAN: He has a place.

OLDER MAN: Yeah.

YOUNG MAN: He has a place now. But I'm only for a while with him. And I don't know then.

OLDER MAN: Right.

YOUNG MAN: He's a fucking asshole mostly but he's alright.

OLDER MAN: And you're alright?

YOUNG MAN: I'm alright.

OLDER MAN: Good.

YOUNG MAN: Get my own place then maybe sometime.

OLDER MAN: Good man.

Very long beat.

OLDER MAN: So what's your baby?

YOUNG MAN: What?

OLDER MAN: Is it a boy or a girl?

YOUNG MAN: A she.

OLDER MAN: And what she called?

YOUNG MAN: Why?

OLDER MAN: No why. You don't have to say. I'm just asking just…

Beat. The YOUNG MAN looks at the OLDER MAN.

YOUNG MAN: *(Softly.)* Chloe.

OLDER MAN: Oh?

YOUNG MAN: Yeah.

OLDER MAN: Chloe.

YOUNG MAN: I picked it.

OLDER MAN: It's nice.

Beat.

YOUNG MAN: Chloe.

Beat.

OLDER MAN: You're young for a baby.

YOUNG MAN: It was an accident.

OLDER MAN: I know yeah

They both smile.

OLDER MAN: You love her?

YOUNG MAN: Who?

OLDER MAN: *(Smiling.)* Chloe.

YOUNG MAN: Of course.

OLDER MAN: Of course.

YOUNG MAN: She's lovely. The little thing. She cries a lot.

OLDER MAN: Does she?

YOUNG MAN: Wah!

OLDER MAN: I know.

Beat.

YOUNG MAN: She's twenty-three weeks nearly.

Small beat.

YOUNG MAN: I gave up smoking when she was born.

OLDER MAN: Good man.

YOUNG MAN: Just.

Beat. They drink.

YOUNG MAN: She's lovely Chloe is but I hardly get to see her now. My girlfriend never wants me there.

OLDER MAN: I see.

YOUNG MAN: And then she blames me for not being around. She's a cunt too sometimes Lorraine. She hates me nearly.

OLDER MAN: But she had a baby for you.

YOUNG MAN: That's why maybe.

OLDER MAN: What age is she?

YOUNG MAN: Same as me, younger. Eighteen, seventeen.

OLDER MAN: Yeah?

YOUNG MAN: Yeah.

Beat.

YOUNG MAN: But I still give them money when I can sometimes. I'd do anything for her if I could.

OLDER MAN: I know.

YOUNG MAN: I do this.

OLDER MAN: Yeah.

Pause. They both drink silently.

OLDER MAN: Quiet, we're quiet.

YOUNG MAN: Just.

OLDER MAN: I know.

Beat. The YOUNG MAN looks at the OLDER MAN.

YOUNG MAN: Who slapped you?

The OLDER MAN is pained. He looks at the YOUNG MAN.

OLDER MAN: I just done something.

YOUNG MAN: What?

OLDER MAN: Nothing. Just fucked things up for myself.

YOUNG MAN: How?

OLDER MAN: Not too mad now. I didn't fucken murder anyone or that. So you can relax. Just…

YOUNG MAN: OK.

OLDER MAN: I'm just a fuck-up.

YOUNG MAN: Oh?

OLDER MAN: I am. That's all.

Long beat.

OLDER MAN: *(Cheerfully changing the mood.)* And I lost my job there as well. Since I seen you.

YOUNG MAN: Right.

OLDER MAN: Yeah. Fucken…

Beat.

OLDER MAN: It's hard to believe that just.

YOUNG MAN: When?

OLDER MAN: Gone.

YOUNG MAN: Oh.

Beat.

OLDER MAN: They had some scutty little fuck in a suit come in and tell me. We been taken over by some crowd from Norway or Sweden or somewhere. Scandinavia apparently which is news to me. Yeah. And now half of us is gone and the other half has to work twice as hard. Bang.

YOUNG MAN: Right.

OLDER MAN: That's the way of things anyways. Cargo.

YOUNG MAN: Sorry.

OLDER MAN: Thanks. All falling to fuck.

YOUNG MAN: Yeah?

OLDER MAN: Yeah for certain. Broken. But we keep going.

YOUNG MAN: Yeah.

OLDER MAN: *(Almost angry.)* We keep fucken…

Beat.

OLDER MAN: And it could be worse now I suppose. I mean we never remortgaged or nothing. We don't think like that, us. So the house is paid for and my kids is paid for but still but. And my wife works so…

YOUNG MAN: Yeah.

OLDER MAN: So we could be worse so.

Beat.

OLDER MAN: I just always had that job just. Even when things was bad before. I never worried.

YOUNG MAN: Oh.

OLDER MAN: I been in there since I was sixteen. Loved it sort of. Fucken dull alright but that suited me. I'm dull fucken dull you know. The docks. The port. And I loved it there I do. It's neat ordered and all.

YOUNG MAN: Right.

OLDER MAN: And I know they fucked it up a bit with building shit everywhere but the port is still the port. It's hidden there behind all the blah. Still looking out on the world.

Beat.

OLDER MAN: It's like we're all being put back in our box or something isn't it?

Small beat.

OLDER MAN: And now I don't know what I'll do now.

YOUNG MAN: Oh?

OLDER MAN: Yeah. I'm done.

Long beat.

OLDER MAN: Here's me giving you all this now.

YOUNG MAN: That's alright.

OLDER MAN: I'm an awful mouth.

YOUNG MAN: No.

OLDER MAN: I am. I'm sorry. I should shut up or something.

Beat. The OLDER MAN *looks at the* YOUNG MAN.

OLDER MAN: I was worried about you, you know.

YOUNG MAN: Oh?

OLDER MAN: No reason now. I been thinking about you. I couldn't stop.

YOUNG MAN: Why?

OLDER MAN: No why. Not bad now. Since the last time. Since then. Since we met even. I like you. I was worried about you. Thinking if you're safe.

YOUNG MAN: I'm grand.

OLDER MAN: I see.

Beat.

I *dreamed* about you.

Beat. The OLDER MAN *feels awkward again.*

OLDER MAN: You're looking at me now.

YOUNG MAN: No.

OLDER MAN: He's a fucken nut job you're saying.

YOUNG MAN: I'm not.

OLDER MAN: Go on.

Beat.

OLDER MAN: Can I tell you this?

YOUNG MAN: What?

Beat.

OLDER MAN: I dreamed about you.

YOUNG MAN: Right.

OLDER MAN: I did. I do.

YOUNG MAN: What?

OLDER MAN: Fucken stupid.

Beat.

OLDER MAN: I dreamed and this might sound crazy now so you can call the fucken funny farm yeah and I'm never one to dream either so you can write this one down too. Maybe boring dreams about work maybe. Shipping orders or packing containers and really boring shit with lists. Like that. But this dream was different. This dream I was talking to you, yeah.

YOUNG MAN: Right.

Beat.

OLDER MAN: Yeah. I *dreamt* I was holding you. Holding on to you. The both of us easy. Only next thing it changes and I don't know how it starts. Maybe you rock forward or maybe you want it but we're falling in a lurch like down a set of steps. A big steps a stairs and we're falling into the dark and I let you go then cause I can't hold on. I can't hold on and I let you go then and you disappear down this down. And I'm hardly falling now at all I'm stopped and standing but you just keep falling farther. And I want to help you I do but I can't. I can't reach out. I can't reach down. And then I wake then. And I'm crying. I'm crying cause you're gone cause you're *dead* maybe. I'm crying. There. Then. Like that. That's it. That's all.

Beat. The OLDER MAN tries to recover himself. The YOUNG MAN is perhaps disturbed.

OLDER MAN: Mad.

YOUNG MAN: Yeah.

OLDER MAN: And it wasn't once this.

YOUNG MAN: No?

OLDER MAN: This was loads of times this. Five or six times. More. And nearly always the same and it upsets me no end. It's stuck in my head now and I feel responsible. I find it hard to sleep then sometimes.

YOUNG MAN: Sorry.

OLDER MAN: No it's nothing. It's just me. It's my head and I'm the one.

The OLDER MAN is deeply moved. He stops speaking. The moment hangs.

OLDER MAN: So I haven't been myself just and my wife now doesn't know what's going on. She thinks I need help or counselling or something and I think she thinks I'm losing my mind. Which is a worry.

Beat.

OLDER MAN: Yeah. So that's why I called you then just. I thought I'd like to see you.

YOUNG MAN: Right.

OLDER MAN: I thought I'd like to see that you were well, you were alright. And then that's done then. I'd leave you alone then I think.

A very long pause. Eventually the YOUNG MAN puts down his can.

YOUNG MAN: *(Meaning sex.)* We going to do this?

OLDER MAN: Not yet I think.

YOUNG MAN: You want to?

OLDER MAN: Wait.

An long awkward pause. The OLDER MAN is in deep silence. The YOUNG MAN is perhaps anxious to leave.

YOUNG MAN: I better go then.

OLDER MAN: What?

YOUNG MAN: If we're not doing nothing.

OLDER MAN: Where are you going?

YOUNG MAN: *(Making up an excuse.)* I'm meeting someone.

OLDER MAN: *(Standing.)* Who?

YOUNG MAN: *(Standing too.)* It's late.

OLDER MAN: It's not late.

YOUNG MAN: Just.

OLDER MAN: I'm paying.

YOUNG MAN: I know.

OLDER MAN: So sit fucking down.

YOUNG MAN: What?

OLDER MAN: Please.

Small tense beat.

OLDER MAN: Please. We'll start in a minute in a while… Sit.

There is a stand-off. The YOUNG MAN may leave. He stares at the OLDER MAN.

OLDER MAN: I'll pay you more.

YOUNG MAN: How much?

OLDER MAN: A hundred.

YOUNG MAN: Yeah?

OLDER MAN: Yeah. A hundred. Sit down.

The YOUNG MAN does not know what to do.

OLDER MAN: You can buy something nice for Chloe then.

Beat. The YOUNG MAN eventually sits.

OLDER MAN: Thanks.

The OLDER MAN remains standing.

OLDER MAN: Am I creeping you out here is that it?

YOUNG MAN: No.

OLDER MAN: I'd say I am.

YOUNG MAN: You're not.

OLDER MAN: I can't believe I am talking all this shit like this here even. That I'm here like this even. I don't usually talk. I mean I talk but I don't usually say nothing ever.

Beat.

YOUNG MAN: What do you want to do?

OLDER MAN: Wait. For a while wait just… Alright?

YOUNG MAN: Alright.

OLDER MAN: We relax.

Beat.

OLDER MAN: Are you finished your drink?

YOUNG MAN: Yeah.

OLDER MAN: Here.

The OLDER MAN hands the YOUNG MAN another can. They sit. The OLDER MAN looks at the YOUNG MAN.

OLDER MAN: I want to look at you.

YOUNG MAN: Oh.

OLDER MAN: I want you to take off some more of your clothes?

YOUNG MAN: What?

OLDER MAN: Your top just if you want. Is that OK?

YOUNG MAN: It's grand.

OLDER MAN: Open your can there.

YOUNG MAN: No.

The YOUNG MAN stands and takes off his top. There is a type of vulnerability to this action. A masking bravado.

He stands for a moment bare. His body is attractive. Eventually he sits.

OLDER MAN: Oh.

The OLDER MAN stares at him for a long moment. The YOUNG MAN becomes a little unnerved by this.

YOUNG MAN: What?

OLDER MAN: Nothing. Lovely you're lovely.

Beat.

OLDER MAN: When I first seen you first. You remember?

YOUNG MAN: What?

OLDER MAN: In them toilets there.

YOUNG MAN: Yeah.

OLDER MAN: I was afraid of you.

YOUNG MAN: Yeah?

OLDER MAN: Yeah. I was afraid of you but I wanted to touch you. My heart was fucken thumping. I like looking at you.

Beat. The YOUNG MAN looks hard at the OLDER MAN.

OLDER MAN: *(Almost chuckling.)* If people saw me here now this they wouldn't believe me.

YOUNG MAN: No?

OLDER MAN: No not at all. Yeah. Fuck.

He laughs short. Beat.

OLDER MAN: Do people know you do this? Does anyone?

YOUNG MAN: Not many.

OLDER MAN: Exactly. Your girlfriend?

YOUNG MAN: No.

Beat.

OLDER MAN: *(Meaning homosexuals.)* I'm not one of those you know.

YOUNG MAN: I know.

OLDER MAN: You're not one of them either.

YOUNG MAN: No.

OLDER MAN: Yeah exactly. I mean I see them all the time everywhere I do. On the telly permanently. With their clothes. With their clothes and their fucken…

YOUNG MAN: Yeah.

OLDER MAN: With all that.

YOUNG MAN: I know.

OLDER MAN: And they have no idea.

YOUNG MAN: I know.

OLDER MAN: They don't have families.

YOUNG MAN: No.

OLDER MAN: They don't have children.

YOUNG MAN: I know.

OLDER MAN: They don't know what it's like.

YOUNG MAN: Yeah.

OLDER MAN: Not for us what it's like. I'm not them.

Beat.

OLDER MAN: So what am I do you think?

YOUNG MAN: I don't know.

OLDER MAN: You can say.

YOUNG MAN: I don't know.

OLDER MAN: Do you hate me?

YOUNG MAN: No.

OLDER MAN: Thank you.

Beat. The YOUNG MAN looks at the OLDER MAN and eventually decides to speak.

YOUNG MAN: There was a lad in school with me. Ahead of me he was. Jason Connolly. A big bastard and mad as well and we used to go mitching together and it was just gas just and no one gave a fuck about us really. Jason and me.

Beat.

YOUNG MAN: And one day we was up around Ballybough and then down by Fairview park then messing, hanging around like. And I must have said something cause me and Jason had a few words then. We was locked and he hit me a few slaps and he fucked off then so I was left there alone. Crying I think drunk. And this man stops. In the park just. This man. An auld fella. Starts talking all funny. Sort of weird shit about women and that. Had a car he had. So I went with him just. That was all. He gave me money and I was just laughing my hole off I was. I didn't care. I was 14. It was easy.

Beat. The OLDER MAN is disturbed by this.

OLDER MAN: And do you never be afraid now?

YOUNG MAN: I can look after myself I can.

OLDER MAN: I know.

Beat.

YOUNG MAN: Some people is just dirty bastards just.

OLDER MAN: Yeah.

YOUNG MAN: I know them. I can spot them.

Beat.

YOUNG MAN: There was this one fucker once. This lad. He went about shouting a bit. Tried holding me down by the neck. Saying things.

OLDER MAN: And what did you do?

YOUNG MAN: Gave him a few digs. Told him I was going to stab him. Told him I was going to shame him.

OLDER MAN: Yeah?

YOUNG MAN: Yeah. He stopped then. Let me up. Started crying he did.

OLDER MAN: Right.

YOUNG MAN: The fucken asshole.

Small beat. The YOUNG MAN opens his beer.

YOUNG MAN: I'd like to make loads of money.

OLDER MAN: I know.

YOUNG MAN: For Chloe. For when she's older.

Long pause.

OLDER MAN: My son it was who slapped me.

YOUNG MAN: Oh?

OLDER MAN: Oh yeah.

YOUNG MAN: Why?

The OLDER MAN sits.

OLDER MAN: We're not close. Obviously. We never been. Don't know whose fault that is. My fault. His mother's fault maybe. I was always the giving out one you see. Shut up you and that. That was my part. Old-fashioned but that's us.

Beat.

OLDER MAN: And I'm good with my daughter now. She's different. She loves me I think. But not him, I don't know him. He's rough.

Beat.

OLDER MAN: *(With difficulty.)* If he wasn't my son now and he is. I'm only saying. He looks the head of me the poor fuck. But if he wasn't and I met him in *life...* I don't know that I'd like him you know. I wouldn't. I know that.

Beat.

OLDER MAN: I wouldn't like him as a person you know. He's hard. And I'm only saying this now just.

YOUNG MAN: You're alright.

OLDER MAN: Same age as yourself maybe. Older. Is that an awful thing to say that?

YOUNG MAN: I don't know.

Beat

OLDER MAN: Yeah. And that pains me now that does. Looking at him. I love him I do, I have to. But I don't know him. I don't like him. He doesn't know me. No.

Long pause.

OLDER MAN: Is your dad with us?

YOUNG MAN: What?

OLDER MAN: Is he dead or?

YOUNG MAN: No no. He's alive he's grand.

OLDER MAN: And you like him?

YOUNG MAN: He's me Da.

OLDER MAN: You love him?

YOUNG MAN: Why?

OLDER MAN: No why. Just.

Beat. The YOUNG MAN decides to speak.

YOUNG MAN: I do. He's a fucken tart sometimes though. He's funny.

OLDER MAN: Oh?

YOUNG MAN: Always sniffing around after women. He loves them he does. Says he wants to come back as a lesbian next time round.

OLDER MAN: Yeah?

YOUNG MAN: He's always saying shit like that. He's funny.

Beat.

OLDER MAN: And does he help you?

YOUNG MAN: What do you mean?

OLDER MAN: He helps you?

YOUNG MAN: I don't know.

OLDER MAN: He should.

Beat. The YOUNG MAN thinks.

YOUNG MAN: He has another family now like. He left me Ma a long time ago. When me and my sister Nadine was small. He left me and Nadine there with her, my mother, and she's a mad fucken… I don't think he should have done that. And that annoyed me for a while about him but he's a good laugh he is sometimes.

OLDER MAN: OK.

YOUNG MAN: Lives in Cherry Orchard now. I never hardly see him never. Sometimes in town sometimes or when I was living in my Nan's. We'd go drinking.

Beat. The YOUNG MAN thinks.

YOUNG MAN: Your Da?

OLDER MAN: What?

YOUNG MAN: Where's he?

OLDER MAN: My old man is dead.

YOUNG MAN: Right.

OLDER MAN: He's dead a year.

YOUNG MAN: Oh.

OLDER MAN: That time I first met you he was just gone.

YOUNG MAN: I'm sorry.

OLDER MAN: No. He was an old bastard. I don't miss him.

Beat.

OLDER MAN: I think about him but I don't miss him. I wonder am I turning into him sometimes you know.

YOUNG MAN: Yeah?

OLDER MAN: Apparently we all do.

YOUNG MAN: Fuck.

OLDER MAN: Exactly.

Beat.

OLDER MAN: Will you take off some more clothes?

YOUNG MAN: What?

OLDER MAN: You can take off your shoes, your sweats if you want.

YOUNG MAN: Do you want me to?

OLDER MAN: I want you to.

YOUNG MAN: OK.

OLDER MAN: Leave on your smalls just, your boxers. Let me look at you. I don't want a show or anything.

The YOUNG MAN takes off his runners and his tracksuit bottoms. He stands in his underpants and socks only. He fixes himself. He is beautiful to look at. The OLDER MAN watches him as if in a trance.

OLDER MAN: You're young.

YOUNG MAN: Yeah.

OLDER MAN: You can be here easy. Sitting here yourself just.

YOUNG MAN: What?

OLDER MAN: I can't be like that. I sit here now and I'm old. I wish I wasn't. I wish I could be different. I wish I could be young again. You're beautiful.

73

Long beat.

OLDER MAN: When my father died yeah?

YOUNG MAN: Yeah?

OLDER MAN: My father was all straight lines. This and this and this. You know?

YOUNG MAN: Yeah.

OLDER MAN: And he was permanently fucken church and morals and he terrorised everyone in our house then. And I took more than my fair share. I was the oldest. I was his greatest disappointment it seemed in life like.

YOUNG MAN: Right.

OLDER MAN: Yeah. And he was probably right.

Beat. The OLDER MAN steadies himself.

OLDER MAN: So when we had his funeral then. And he went sudden now like. I mean one minute talking shite and the next thing he's down and bang he's gone.

YOUNG MAN: Right.

OLDER MAN: Yeah. In front of me this was. At my Mam's place when I went over to visit him, cause I went over twice a week when no one else did and he was still a cranky old cunt.

Beat.

OLDER MAN: And he dropped then and I couldn't save him. I couldn't bring him back and I tried, I don't know why. In the galley kitchen there. He was just gone and there was a broken plate on the floor there beside him small. Ridiculous.

Beat.

OLDER MAN: And all that's took its toll then. This year and after. Before I met you.

YOUNG MAN: Right.

OLDER MAN: And then I met you. When I met you. You were like a shining thing.

Beat. The YOUNG MAN is confused or disturbed by this statement.

OLDER MAN: Is that a stupid thing to say?

YOUNG MAN: I don't fucken know.

    Beat.

OLDER MAN: But at my Dad's funeral then anyway. After his funeral. I found out this thing. I heard this thing. I was told.

YOUNG MAN: What?

OLDER MAN: I guessed. There was a woman in the church there at his funeral. And I'd known her from around our area. From the local pub and that. And she wasn't married. About that much away from being a slapper really but holds her own she does and she drinks. But there was something in the way I seen her there. The way she looked and the way she was crying in the church there. And a few weeks later I seen her again in our local and I'm a bit pissed so I goes over and I sits down at her table and she looks at me, 'oh,' like you know. Valerie her name is Val. So I asks her straight out simple sitting there and she tells me. Like that. Yeah.

    Beat.

OLDER MAN: He'd been banging her for years it seems. Twenty years, more. That far back. And she loved him the fucken edjit she said and that was all. He used promise he'd leave me Mam when the kids was done and that and she believed him then and she settled for it and that was her life. And I felt sorry for her there I did. Yeah. Another one of his fuck-ups. That was all. Fuck him.

    Beat.

OLDER MAN: Left me complicated he did. Like this. Confused.

    Beat.

YOUNG MAN: You alright?

OLDER MAN: Me? I am yeah I am.

YOUNG MAN: You sure?

OLDER MAN: Yeah. Are you cold?

YOUNG MAN: No.

Beat. The OLDER MAN stares at the YOUNG MAN sitting semi-naked before him.

OLDER MAN: When I think about all that, all he did, I'm not angry you know.

YOUNG MAN: No?

OLDER MAN: I don't mind anyone fucken anyone you know. It's nature isn't it?

YOUNG MAN: Yeah.

OLDER MAN: Exactly. Men do that. We're animals. So I'm not angry at that.

YOUNG MAN: No?

OLDER MAN: Not at all. I mean it didn't make me love the cunt for sure. No.

YOUNG MAN: Right.

OLDER MAN: Exactly. But do you know what it made me?

YOUNG MAN: What?

OLDER MAN: It made me afraid.

YOUNG MAN: Oh?

OLDER MAN: Yeah.

Beat.

OLDER MAN: It made me afraid that no one knew him only in bits. That he lived a life and no one knew him fully. Not his children, not his wife, not even himself. That all he was at the end was an accumulation of fucken lies. That he never lived, he was of no consequence, nothing. He failed and he fucked us all up and then he died.

Beat.

OLDER MAN: Isn't that hard?

YOUNG MAN: It is.

OLDER MAN: It's awful. I hate it and it makes me afraid.

Beat.

OLDER MAN: I have a wife like.

YOUNG MAN: I know.

OLDER MAN: I know.

> *Beat.*

OLDER MAN: And I don't want to be like him, like that.

YOUNG MAN: I know.

OLDER MAN: I don't want to go and be gone and have people putting me together different after. I want to be straight out.

YOUNG MAN: Yeah?

OLDER MAN: Yeah. For certain.

> *Beat. The OLDER MAN looks at the YOUNG MAN.*

OLDER MAN: That's why I done it.

YOUNG MAN: What?

OLDER MAN: I told him.

YOUNG MAN: Who?

OLDER MAN: My son.

YOUNG MAN: What did you tell him?

OLDER MAN: This.

> *Beat.*

OLDER MAN: I'd had a hard weekend of it this weekend drinking. With me brother-in-law Noel. He's just fell out of his marriage and I was keeping him company and he's a fucking dog like.

YOUNG MAN: Yeah?

OLDER MAN: Anything now. So I was kind of disgusted with myself. When I woke up. Sick.

YOUNG MAN: Right.

OLDER MAN: He says things, Noel does, and he sickens me but I never contradict anyone and I should.

YOUNG MAN: OK.

OLDER MAN: He hates people I think.

YOUNG MAN: Right.

OLDER MAN: He's a fucking asshole. And I just sit there then. Listening.

Beat.

OLDER MAN: Dying I was. When I woke. And I'd been thinking that dream again.

YOUNG MAN: Oh.

OLDER MAN: Yeah.

Beat.

OLDER MAN: Sick and my son there and my wife was working.

Beat.

YOUNG MAN: So?

OLDER MAN: So we start up the usual shit me and him, my son. And we're chipping away at each other. And we don't know each other. And I want us to stop. I want us to just talk. To try even. And I don't know why but I felt like I was about to climb out of myself you know.

Beat.

OLDER MAN: So I told him then.

YOUNG MAN: What?

OLDER MAN: Everything. I told him everything.

YOUNG MAN: What?

OLDER MAN: How I met you. What we did.

YOUNG MAN: Who?

OLDER MAN: You. That. I told him all that. And I was calm now. I wanted him to know me.

YOUNG MAN: I don't understand.

OLDER MAN: I know but I just wanted to be honest. From now on. I just want to be good. To be good and moral. I think I'd have died if I didn't.

YOUNG MAN: Fuck.

OLDER MAN: I know.

Beat.

OLDER MAN: I told him what we did. All. What we do. The fucken and that. And he looks at me like I don't know.

Beat.

OLDER MAN: I told him I loved you. I told him I loved you more then I loved him. I told him that.

YOUNG MAN: Why?

OLDER MAN: Cause I do.

YOUNG MAN: You don't.

OLDER MAN: I meant I only I cared for you only. I talk to you.

YOUNG MAN: So?

OLDER MAN: So he goes for me. He tries to batter me. He's crying.

YOUNG MAN: Fuck.

OLDER MAN: And then I rang you then. There. After I left.

Beat.

OLDER MAN: Pulled the whole fucking thing around my ears I have. Haven't I? Now I don't know what's worse. Having done what we do. Or having said it out loud.

Very long pause.

OLDER MAN: Can we start.

YOUNG MAN: What?

OLDER MAN: This. Can we do this. I won't talk anymore.

Beat. The YOUNG MAN stands now confused.

OLDER MAN: What?

YOUNG MAN: Why did you say that?

OLDER MAN: What?

YOUNG MAN: That you love me.

OLDER MAN: Cause I do.

Small beat.

OLDER MAN: I care about you. I want to help you.

YOUNG MAN: You don't know me.

OLDER MAN: Nearly.

YOUNG MAN: No.

OLDER MAN: Oh.

Beat.

YOUNG MAN: This is just this. It isn't real. It's money.

OLDER MAN: Yeah?

YOUNG MAN: That's all.

OLDER MAN: Right.

Beat. The OLDER MAN is a little broken.

OLDER MAN: I'll pay you still.

YOUNG MAN: I know you will.

OLDER MAN: How much?

YOUNG MAN: You said a hundred.

OLDER MAN: Yeah.

Beat.

YOUNG MAN: What do want me to do then?

OLDER MAN: The same. Like before.

YOUNG MAN: OK.

OLDER MAN: Fuck me and that.

YOUNG MAN: OK.

Beat.

OLDER MAN: And I'll leave you alone then I swear. I'll try.

Beat.

OLDER MAN: Only first though.

YOUNG MAN: What?

OLDER MAN: I want to hold you first.

YOUNG MAN: Yeah?

OLDER MAN: I want to hold you just. Just a minute just.

YOUNG MAN: Right.

OLDER MAN: Is that OK?

YOUNG MAN: Yeah.

OLDER MAN: Thank you. Thank you.

> *The OLDER MAN moves to the YOUNG MAN.*
> *He holds onto him. He cries. Blackout.*

THE ART OF SWIMMING
BY
LYNDA RADLEY

*This script contains information and material from
the archives of Mercedes Gleitze.*

With the permission of, and kindly supplied by, her family.

The Art of Swimming was produced by Playgroup and first performed at the Arches, Glasgow, on 26 and 27 September 2006.

Performed by Lynda Radley
Music composed and performed
by Michael John McCarthy

Directed by Tom Creed
Designed by Claire Halleran
Lighting Designed by Tom Creed

It was subsequently performed at the following venues and festivals:

Cork Midsummer Festival, Half Moon Theatre, Cork, June 2007

Kinsale Arts Week, Municipal Hall, Kinsale, July 2007

Edinburgh Festival Fringe, Traverse Theatre, Edinburgh, August 2007

Dublin Fringe Festival, New Theatre, Dublin, September 2007

Bewley's Cafe Theatre, Dublin, February 2008

Amsterdam Fringe Festival, Compagnietheater, Amsterdam, September 2008

The English Theatre, Sculpture Museum on the Sea, The Hague, April 2009

Citizens Theatre, Glasgow, May 2009

It won the Bewley's Cafe Theatre Little Gem Award and was nominated for the Fishamble New Writing Award at the Dublin Fringe Festival 2007, was short-listed for the Meyer-Whitworth Award in 2007, and was nominated for a Total Theatre Award for Innovation at the Edinburgh Festival Fringe 2007.

1.

Stage directions are in bold.

The narrator's voice is in plain text.

Mercedes' voice is in italics.

> **Preset: A gramophone plays popular music of the 1920s and 30s. Various boxes and bric-à-brac are upstage, piled together.**
>
> **I walk on stage, cross to the gramophone and switch it off.**
>
> **(Thereafter music is played live on accordion, typewriter and laptop from among the boxes.)**
>
> **During the following I takes stones and shells from a drawstring bag and set out a small square, big enough only for me to stand in.**

Good Evening Ladies and Gentlemen and welcome to my performance. In order for it to work, I will need you to sometimes imagine that I am Mercedes Gleitze: the first British woman to swim the English Channel. This I did in 1927, aged twenty-six, and it took fifteen hours and fifteen minutes.

If it helps you to have a more fulfilling theatrical experience, you can imagine that I *did* decide to spend the exorbitant amount of money they were asking for in the second-hand clothing shop where I found an authentic period swimming costume – you know, one of the ones that comes down to here (**indicating thighs**) and looks like something a wrestler might wear. It was navy blue and made out of cotton jersey.

> **I am wearing a black vest and black trousers. I have rolled up the trousers creating an approximation of the costume described.**

I am taller than *I* am, obviously, and broader, with a long mane of dark hair. I am famed for my beauty as well as my talent.

I say:

I step into the small stone square.

(The sound of breathing and the sea) *In the open sea you have no idea what's coming next. You must make your peace with currents and tides. You must learn how to track them. You have to swim straight, but you cannot waste too much energy on looking up, so you learn blind how to navigate a straight, liquid line. You must learn how to swim in the dark.*

You can think only miniscule thoughts – Stroke. Pull. Stroke. Pull. Stroke. Pull. – Don't think and there's nothing to distract you from the cold. Think too much and your mind will find a way to convince you to stop. So you focus on direction, navigation, drinking, urinating, pacing, hours, minutes, and seconds. Your inner engineer must travel internally; monitoring each temperature change, feeling each fluctuation, assessing the quality of each breath. Each stroke. Pull. Stroke. Pull. Stroke. Pull.

You speak to your lungs and you say, 'You are bigger than this.'

You speak to your heart and you say, 'Don't beat faster, slow down.'

You speak to your spine and you say, 'Keep rotating.'

You speak to your legs and you say, 'Keep kicking.'

You speak to your arms and you say, 'Keep pulling.'

You speak to your joints and you say, 'Look, you can have your revenge when I'm old.'

Each time your mind wanders towards the pain you must pick it up and pluck it away from the brink like a wayward child.

Every time an image of failure comes to you, you must cast it back into the blue.

If you feel the swell of early celebration you had better check yourself because your strokes will have turned sloppy and you're breathing too fast.

You just have to be, letting your conscious mind take care of the machine and your subconscious float to the surface like a cork.

You just have to swim.

I step out of the square and address the audience.

(**Fairground music**) Imagine that you are an audience. You are an audience at Blackpool Tower Circus in the early 1930s. World War One is a receding memory. World War Two hasn't happened yet. You are surrounded by glint and gilding the likes of which you have never seen before. You are probably poor, but not as poor as the poorer poor who can only imagine being here.

During the following I bring out a small step-ladder. I also fetch a metal bucket and remove a circle of red satin from within it. This is spread on the floor in front of the ladder, and I place the bucket in the centre of this circle.

Tonight you have seen many exciting entertainments. Some of you may choose to imagine yourselves as children. You may feel sick with sweetness or excitement. With tears in your eyes, you may be remembering the face of a clown which terrified you earlier; the fear now solidifying into a lifelong phobia. Perhaps you just felt sexual stirrings brought on by the slitherings of an acrobat in an improper costume. Maybe you are feeling an acute pang of inadequacy caused by feats of the strong man, and now you are boring your wife and dampening your children's imaginations by explaining to them that it is all just a sham. You may be sitting there wishing that the bear *had* bitten down on its tamer's neck. You may now be craving a pony that you will surely never find under the Christmas tree. You may be bored.

Suddenly, rain pours down from overhead, and the ring fills with water as huge fountains gush downwards.

I reach into the bucket and pull out a watering can with which I pour water into the bucket.

There is a collective intake of breath as a swimming pool is formed.

The ringmaster says: *And now Ladies and Gentleman, Boys and Girls, in an exhibition of scientific swimming I present to you the first British woman to swim the English Channel, the first person to swim the Straits of Gibraltar and the world record holder for endurance swimming at forty-six straight hours: the talented, the powerful, the beautiful Miss Mercedes Gleitze. Bathing costume worn by Miss Gleitze kindly supplied by JF Orry Ladies Department, Blackpool; for all your swimming needs.*

Imagine I'm the closest thing to a celebrity that you have ever seen.
Now imagine that this carries me up to a diving platform high above you. I take up position.

I climb to the top of the ladder and stand looking into the bucket.

I say:

Gegrüßet seist du, Maria, voll der Gnade,
der Herr ist mit dir.
Du bist gebenedeit unter den Frauen, und gebenedeit ist die Frucht
deines Leibes, Jesus. Heilige Maria,
Mutter Gottes,
bitte für uns Sünder jetzt und in der Stunde
unseres Todes.
Amen.

Now imagine that that bucket of water is the circus ring swimming pool and I am about to break its flickering surface.

2.

I climb down. During this segment I bring forward a small, old-fashioned, folding table. I carry a leather-covered box to the table. When I open it I discover swimming logs, an old photograph and a folded cloth.

Still damp, she signs the many photos and scraps of paper you bring to her: mementos that will be loved and looked at for a while. Before they slowly lose their significance. Before she slips out of memory and is forgotten. She retires, marries a sheet metal engineer of Irish extraction, settles down and becomes a philanthropist, setting up a home for the poor. During the Second World War she once more lives through the eerie duality of her German parentage and British citizenship, especially when she receives a letter from the war commission telling her that *The Mercedes Gleitze Home for Destitute Men and Women* has been destroyed by enemy bombing. She has three children, grows older and, in 1981, she dies.

These mementos, now mori, these photographs and autographs, are occasionally excavated from behind ornaments on the mantelpieces of dying grandparents, or unearthed from the hiding places of children who have long since grown up. Someone makes a decision: to throw them away or to keep them. To look up this exotic name on the internet or to assign the found object to another box on another mantelpiece where the image of Mercedes inside patiently awaits another grieving grandchild eager to know more about the dead relative they spent the last few years ignoring. The celebrity that once filled Blackpool Tower Circus with raucous applause and indefinable wonder survives in sporting legend, the *Oxford Biographical Dictionary* and in the memories of her family and friends.

I found her in Cork City Library in the summer of 2005. A beautiful woman wrapped modestly in a towel smiling demurely at me. She was surrounded by civil servants and the caption underneath said that she just had swum for thirty hours in a baths which has long since disappeared from Eglington Street, Cork. That was all: her name, the date (1930) and the feat. A few nights before I had found myself constructing sentences around the idea of long distance swimming while falling asleep. And then this beautiful woman inexplicably appears in a book of old photographs. And I'm a botanist collecting samples. I'm a butterfly collector pinning down wings. I hang what I imagine on the bones of her biography. I'm a scientist trying to create a formula for this name: Mercedes Gleitze.

I carefully and meticulously unfold the cloth and spread it over the table.

3.

**I bring out an old-fashioned picnic basket and place it
on the table. When opened, the lid of the basket reveals
a seascape with a tiny kite made of cheese suspended
from a wire at one edge of the lid.**

I say to her:

From aged eighteen months to ten years you lived with
your grandparents in Herzogenaurach, Germany, but at
age ten your mother travelled to Germany to take you
home. You returned to your birthplace of Brighton where
you were reunited with your sisters, your father and the
sea. (**Fairground music**) You lived at the gable end of a
row of terraced houses and you could see it through the
window of your small attic bedroom. You inhaled it on
your walk to school. It clung to the clothes on the washing
line. You could smell it on your skin. While your mother
helped you to improve your English you learned, without
learning, how to walk into a wind but stay steady on the
rocks, how deep is too deep and not to tense when you
float. Come summer you watched with fascination as
families poured out of London trains on sultry afternoons.
You wondered at the wonder that appeared on their faces
with that first look at the horizon. You observed behind a
wry smile as they cried over kites lost to the wind, as they
reddened, as they headed out when they should have been
coming in and as they were led indoors just when the air
was ripe for adventures, as they sank, as they swallowed
water, as they had their ears clipped and their legs smacked
and their noses wiped.

And you watched with a different look on your face as the
very presence of the ocean opened up to them a world of
seaside indulgence that you had never known: a world of
ices, lemonade and picnics, afternoon tea and high tea,
pink biscuits and clotted cream scones. Your mother never
spread a blanket on anything other than a bed. You ate
indoors around the table, on the floral table cloth. There

was no sand in your sandwiches. (**Using the picnic things I have made a sandwich: when I lift it up, sand leaks out**)

You do not remember the first time you felt the sea swirl around you, but you do remember the first time you swam.

You were still small and not allowed to wade in without an adult. But many of your friends had been swimming for years, had been taught by their fathers. You thought that you had seen enough to know what to do but didn't wish to skip procedure. For weeks Heinrich had been promising to teach you but he was a busy man: a journeyman baker. So you waited – you are good at waiting – and you played with Jimmy from number one hundred and twenty-five who had toy soldiers. (**A toy soldier is placed amid the landscape of the picnic**)

(**During the following more soldiers emerge**) Together you had been employing his mother's washing bucket in an attempt to recreate your new favourite Bible story: Moses parting the waves, over and over again. Those soldiers who were usually the goodies became the Israelites and managed to stay dry. Those soldiers who were usually the baddies became the Egyptians and were given a drenching. (**I drop a soldier in my tea**) Some of them were never the same again. (**More soldiers are taken out and two opposing armies dot the landscape**) As you watched them float down the gutter and into the hairnet Jimmy had stretched over the drain to prevent unnecessary loss of life, you wondered if this would happen to you when you swam. If Papa let go would you just be swept away? The secret was kicking, Jimmy said. He said you had to kick against the water and that's what kept you going. He administered a kick to your backside to illustrate his point.

You practised in bed, on your stomach. It bunched up the sheets but it made you feel better.
It always made you feel better to be prepared.

When the fateful day arrived, you set your seven-year-old face into the best Moses grimace you could manage and you waded in until the water was waist high. Before your father could even put his hands out to cradle your small body in this new posture, before he could coach you to keep your head up for now, before he could again give a warning about jellyfish, you were off.

(**The sound of breathing**) She lifted her feet, she took a deep breath, she half dived half fell into the water, and she began moving her arms and legs the way she had practised. Rather than punishing her arrogance, rather than spitting her back out, rather than invading the little girl's body, the sea made room for her, embraced her and allowed her travel through it. Heinrich had trouble keeping up. He jogged alongside making encouraging noises and wondering, yet again, at the ability of this child to surprise.

The picnic things have been tidied away. I close the lid of the basket and hold it like a suitcase. Only the toy soldiers remain on the landscape created by the cloth on the table.

When the war broke out in 1914, your father, like 30,000 other German nationals, was interned. Your mother returned the rest of the family to Germany but you were desperate to go back to the country you now called home. The first time you thought about swimming the English Channel was when you hatched a plan to walk and swim back to England during World War One. You simply looked at a map and resolved to walk to Holland, cross that country until you reached the sea's edge and then follow the Dutch coastline south until you encountered that part of the French coast where the Channel is at its narrowest. Then you would simply swim home. Your teenage self had no concept of the true measure of that distance which looked so manageable on a map. You just knew which side of it you wanted to be on. Why was that? Where did that fierce, seemingly unwarranted loyalty come from? You made it as far as an island off the coast of Germany but the idea of swimming the Channel remained. A decade later, you were still trying.

4.

I return the picnic basket to the pile of objects upstage. During the following I gather the soldiers, one by one:

In 1875 Captain Mathew Webb became the first person to swim the English Channel and he is, in a way, responsible for so many failures. The portly possessor of a fine handlebar moustache, he swam the channel in a costume of red silk while smeared in porpoise oil. Afterwards, his presence at the London Stock Exchange brought business to a close. A triumphal arch was erected in his home of Shropshire, he embarked on a lecture tour and licensed his name for merchandising. A spendthrift who liked to show his friends a good time, he often found himself short of money and was forced to perform a number of commercial stunts, including floating for sixty hours in the whale tank at the Royal Aquarium in Westminster. Fortunately, there were no whales in there at the time. Eventually, in poor health and running seriously low on funds, he decided to swim across the top of Niagara Falls. He was rowed out to midstream wearing the same silk trunks as he had when swimming the Channel. He dived into the river and was instantly grabbed by the force of the current. He held his own for a while but was eventually dragged under. His last words to the boatman were: 'If I die, they will do something for my wife.'

I drop the soldiers into the bucket of water.

In 1909 his elder brother unveiled a memorial. The inscription it bears reads: 'Nothing great is easy.'

I unfold the table cloth, revealing a map of the channel which falls to the floor.

5.

I bring out a rope knotted throughout at small equal intervals.

(**The sound of breathing and the sea**) *There is always something unnatural about finding yourself standing on a beach at two o'clock in the morning and realising that you are about to take your clothes off and wade in, but particularly in October, on the north coast of France. I won't put my feet down again for many hours, but putting my feet down will mean success.*

I don't survey the vista, or scan the horizon or any of that because it's pitch black and there's a heavy drizzle falling. From my vantage there's no way to tell where the sky ends and the sea begins.

I feel ready. For the first time in all of my attempts I am going to allow myself to go further than is actually safe for me to go. I feel prepared to push myself to the edge of my capabilities, beyond what is reasonable.

But I don't know how long I can keep this feeling up, and now this misty rain has swept down from nowhere... They ask me if I'm sure. I say, 'This is the weather we've got. It's neap tide. It's calm. The currents are good. It's already October. We need to go now because soon it's going to be too cold again, and I can't wait till next year.'

'I know the way,' I think, 'I've traced it seven times before.' And the porridge I had for supper last night tugs at my stomach and says, 'Not quite.'

At 2.55 a.m. I begin.

I step onto the cloth and into the map.

There's nobody to see me off: Mr Allan – the guide in charge of charting the course – and the fisherman – who will steer it – are both on board the boat. I gave the signal for Allan to start the clock and walk in; the most unnaturally natural thing I know to do.

I push the rope through my hands, a knot at a time.

The first few hours are difficult. There's always a gnawing anxious feeling and that isn't helped by the strong currents off the French coast. They've been my downfall when I've tried swimming in the opposite direction. Sometimes it's like swimming but standing still. You can be five hundred yards from shore and find it impossible to make it. Or you can be swept towards Belgium, or south towards Brittany. Swimming in the opposite direction I'm trying to use these tides to my advantage, but it means I have to push hard from the beginning. I don't like going out strong.

It's like being back in those early days of training in the Thames. I'm not really in my body. I'm not travelling from limb to limb and from organ to organ, checking status, giving pep talks. I'm in my head, going over each of my seven previous attempts, remembering what went wrong, agonising over stupid mistakes and feeling the weight of exhausted disappointment. 'Remember to pace yourself or you will get too tired by the end.' 'Don't allow the currents to beat you, swim through the waves.' 'If the weather changes the weather changes, there's nothing you can...'

Dry mouth, no hunger, can actually hear the clock ticking even though Allan's got the stopwatch on the boat. Last year Gertrude Ederle came over from America and became The First Woman. She did it in fourteen hours and thirty-nine minutes on a second attempt, and she was only nineteen.

And I catch myself in these moments: 'Thinking like this isn't going to help. The more you agonise the more likely you are to make the same mistakes all over again, or different ones, and you won't even see them coming because you'll be too busy failing.'

At intervals Allan allows me to catch up to the boat. He bends over the side muttering times and tides and instructions. Careful not to disqualify me by touching me, he throws me grapes and honey, or strong tea, or cocoa. Stretching out on my back, I feed like some performing seal. I struggle to push the liquids down. I feel no hunger but I know I need to eat. I don't usually taste anything, but I feel the warmth and I feel the food, feel what it does.

The rain seems to be closing in around me. I no longer have any sense of where I've swum from and where swimming to. I'm in the middle of nowhere and it seems like the most ridiculous thing in the world. The rain falls heavier. An ambivalent dawn is breaking.

It's light now and I do begin to slow and I do begin to hurt, as I knew I would. My arms have gone completely numb. The water temperature is dropping. My lungs are burning and the cold is beginning to invade my marrow. I need to sprint to bring my temperature back up. 'Take it easy.' 'You can do this.' 'Just one last concentrated push that's all you need.' 'Stroke, pull, stroke…' I am so wrapped up in an anxious attempt to compose myself that I don't hear the fisherman's signal, or the shouts from the guide boat. I lift my head to breathe and from out of the rain there's the prow of a steamer only five feet away. I stop. (**I drop the rope**) *I barely remember to tread water and I swallow a gulp full of the Channel, but somehow it passes me by, just. Its swell knocks me backwards. I shout, 'I'm alright!' and start swimming again.*

I begin again to pull the rope through my hands.

I'm losing a lot of fluid. The sea is salty and my sweat is salty and it's mixed with the lard and Vaseline on my skin. In the shipping lanes it's choppy and I begin to feel sick. I swim through what seems like a universe of jellyfish, trying not to hold my breath with fear. One of them stings me on my left calf. It doesn't hurt, which is to say the cold hurts more. I feel like a machine. I feel out of control.

And then I am suddenly aware of the presence of something else out there besides myself. It's a sound, or sounds. At first I think I'm hallucinating and then I realise that it's coming from the guide boat. They must have brought a gramophone on board and now they've wound it up for this final stretch.

(**I sing**) *Show me the way to go home.*
I'm tired and I want to go to bed.
I had a little drink about an hour ago
And it's gone right to my head.

I pick up speed. I shift gears from breaststroke to over-arm and I begin the sprint towards the shore which I can just about make out in the distance.

(**Singing**) *Show me the way to go home*
Show me the way to go home
Show me the way to go
Show me the way to go
Show me the way
Show me the way
Show me
Show me
Show
Show
Show

The last knot has passed through my hands.

When I crawl up the beach I don't feel anything but relief. Fifteen hours and fifteen minutes. I have just become the first British woman to swim the English Channel. I collapse and can't be woken for two hours. It's a dreamless sleep.

6.

I step out of the map and fold the cloth.

(**The sound of a typewriter**) Like a lot of us, before
she finally succeeded Mercedes found it necessary to
be held down by a day job. She worked as a bilingual
shorthand typist in Westminster, and trained to be a long
distance swimmer in the Thames. For a while now I've
been working for a property development company in
Glasgow, and staring at my laptop in my bedroom in the
student district. The symptoms of such a life include: a
lot of looking out the window when you should be doing
something else, a lot of talking about Channel swimming
to people you meet on social occasions and a lot of clock
watching and becoming obsessed with time, figures,
distances, feats…

I sometimes imagine us as colleagues, Mercedes and I,
fellow working girls in the typing pool; sitting at opposite
desks and covering for each other in front of some smarmy
boss who calls her 'Toots' and me 'Ginger'. When nobody
else is around, I ask her how the swimming is going and
tell her that I'm sure she'll make it across eventually. At
elevenses, she asks me how the writing is going and tells
me that she's sure I'll figure her out eventually. The rest
of the time we both keep our heads down and dream of
the sea. She keeps herself to herself, slightly wary of my
interest in her. I am afraid to ask too many questions;
afraid that what I have already concocted will be ruined by
the truth.

Of course once she had her first big success, Mercedes
left it all behind for a life of sponsorship, touring and
endorsements.

After her Channel crossing, for reasons that we will come
to, Mercedes kept detailed logs of all further swims and
asked locals to sign declarations and write accounts of her
accomplishments. These testify that she became the first

person to swim the Straits of Gibraltar twenty years before the first recorded crossing by a man took place.

During the following, I waltz around the stage referring to the swimming logs I have gathered from the table.

(Fairground music)

She also swam:

– The Wash: a square-mouthed estuary on the northwest margin of the east coast of England.

– Lough Neagh: the largest freshwater lake in Ireland, fifteen miles wide, known for its extremely rough and windy conditions and formed, according to legend, when Fionn Mac Cumhaill scooped up a portion of land to fling at a Scottish rival.

'There was a dense fog which made conditions very difficult… During the route selections were played by a gramophone kindly provided by Mr McCully the jeweller of Antrim and the people who came by boat to witness what is Miss Gleitze's crowning triumph discoursed a lot of popular songs and otherwise encouraged her. She swam absolutely unprotected and unaided…and landed without any assistance.'

– From Port Stewart in Northern Ireland to Moville in the Republic, across the mouth of Lough Foyle: the only place in the world where The South is north and The North is south.

– Between the Aran Islands where:

'the night was one of the most beautiful which has been witnessed on the Bay this year… She commenced with the trudgeon stroke and having got well clear of the land, changed to the breast stroke which is the most favoured by her for long swims… Miss Gleitze suffered very much in the early hours from the cold and occasionally complained of pains, and at one point her husband considered the advisability of taking her out of the water. However, she would not hear of this, the suggestion seeming to act as a spur, and she increased her pace… About 10 a.m. the crew of the pilot boat, rowing boat and Miss Gleitze herself, joined in a decade of the Rosary, the effect being most impressive.'

Around the Isle of Man in stages: a distance of over 100 miles. Legend has it that the Isle of Man is in fact the lump of earth Fionn Mac Cumhaill threw at his Scottish rival.

The Hellespont from Europe to Asia Minor, famously swum by that other champion of sea swimming, Lord Byron.

'A chilly dawn, with the north wind chasing the smoke-like clouds across a grey-blue sky, a ruffled sea, that wonderful crispness in the air which put fresh life into our veins, this was the morning that greeted us as we assembled to act as witnesses to Miss Gletize's swim.'

– Wellington Harbour in New Zealand.

– from Cape Town to Robben Island both ways; becoming the first person to complete the double.

And The Firth of Forth where:

'At 11.53 she entered the water…wearing a rosary round her neck… She wore no goggles or bathing cap but had a veil over her face to keep back her long hair and to protect her eyes from the salt spray… The local police did splendid work but were hopelessly outnumbered by the frenzied crowd numbering some 12,000. Thus ended the greatest of all Forth swims, accomplished by a mere girl of twenty-seven years… She came, she saw, she conquered.'

7.

During the following I gather all the objects still left downstage – the table, the rope, the stones etc – and return them to the pile. Only the ladder and bundled up cloth remain.

The first few days after you finally make it pass quickly. You sleep a lot. Your limbs ache and you are hungry almost all of the time, but in between are these moments of absolute elation, absolute joy and a feeling of proving yourself. That you have been right to keep trying; that all that time training and trying and failing and training harder and trying and failing again haven't been wasted. You are already looking for the next challenge and have your eye on the Gibraltar Straits, principally because it hasn't been done, not by anybody. At this moment you feel you could accomplish anything.

There are newspaper men knocking on your digs' door in London and offers coming in for sponsorship and endorsements. You have the wonderful realisation that you might never need to be a typist again. If you keep a smart head on your shoulders, you can probably be a professional swimmer for as long as your body holds up, but that might only be a decade at most, so you will have to take your opportunities where you find them.

But then, just a few days after your swim, the newspapers print that a woman named Dorothy Logan has made a successful Channel crossing too. She claims to have broken Ederle's record, and for some reason that you can't quite fathom, this news makes you feel sick to your stomach. **(I go to the ladder as if about to lift it but instead take the cloth from where it lies folded on the top rung and hold it to me.)** You've never met Logan, though you have heard her name mentioned a few times, but never in connection with a Channel attempt. You didn't think anybody else would try making a crossing this late in the year. None of the fishermen at Folkestone spoke of another swimmer wanting to rent a boat or a guide…

Sure enough, a few days later she reveals herself a hoax. And then doubts are cast on the truth of your swim, made worse by the fact that the only witnesses are Mr Allan and the fisherman who, it is argued, could both be seen to have a vested interest. Or might have been paid off.

Now the knocks on your digs' door are getting louder and more insistent: 'Miss Gleitze would you care to comment on the truth of the rumours?' 'Miss Gleitze how do you intend to answer your critics?' 'Miss Gleitze are you going to do it again?'

I turn up the music and keep the curtains closed. I already know what I have to do, but I want to delay the inevitable for a few more hours. My body knows I am about to sell it out, and my muscles seem to ache more on purpose. I have a sweet cup of tea and a frustrated cry, pull myself together, pick up one of the cards that has been shoved under the front door, telephone the number on it and say, 'All right, I'll do it again.'

I pick up the ladder and move it centre stage. I address Mercedes as if she is at the top of the ladder.

A date is set for what they are calling your Vindication Swim. It will take place on October 21st 1927. There are things I need to ask. You were stubborn and you felt slighted and wanted to be vindicated. But you weren't stupid. You must have realised that already the temperatures had significantly dropped to the low fifties. Surely you knew that the risk of hypothermia was greatly increased? Were you spurred on by your success and did that cloud your judgement, making you feel invincible? Or was it what I want to believe: that you knew there was a significant chance you wouldn't make it but you still wanted to at least try?

(**The sound of the sea, building**) *We set out at 4.21 a.m.,
later than I would have liked, but it's not just my decision anymore.
There are hundreds of people here; officials and journalists and
spectators. People who are willing me to succeed and people who
are sure I will give up. It makes me nervous. I am grateful for
the interest and the enthusiasm and for all the good luck wishes
I receive, but as I stand here about to go in again, I wish for the
quiet and the solitude of that previous morning.*

*It's cold. It must be some of the coldest water I have ever swum
in. The pain is almost unbearable at times and then it gets to a
point where I can't really feel much of anything at all. Far from
welcoming this, I know that it's a bad sign. 'Sprint girl, sprint to
get your temperature back up.' And I do for a while, but as soon as
I return to a regular pace my stroke rate drops until sometimes it is
as low as ten strokes per minute. And of course the slower I get the
colder I get, and the colder I get the slower I get, and the colder I
am the more my mind is affected.*

Is being an athlete like being a performer? Did you have
your little routines, your mantras and superstitions; a way
you liked to do things? Were they an attempt to maintain
the illusion of control?

*I try praying. 'Gregusest seist du Maria…' I vary my strokes –
breast stroke to over arm – but then I can't stand putting my face
in water this cold because it makes me want to gasp, so I change
back again.*

Did you look up and catch the worried looks on the faces
of your family and supporters? You were an experienced
long distance swimmer who had failed to make this
crossing many times before. Did you know somewhere
inside that you had set yourself an impossible task, or is it
really true that people like you possess some sort of strange
ability to ignore reality and persuade your body into
compliance? Were you afraid?

*There are well wishers travelling in boats alongside me, playing
music and singing songs. At first I listen to them and it's a*

welcome distraction, but then it gets to a point where I just want them to be quiet. I just want it to be me and the sea. I want to be able to be inside my own head and to be inside my body and to swim and be left alone. I have been swimming for over ten hours now and I can feel myself slipping away. Great waves of tiredness are passing over me and it feels like the music is lulling me to sleep. So I muster up as much strength as I can and I shout to the guide boat, 'For Pete's sake, tell them to play something lively.'

Not that it makes any difference. At various times it is suggested that I should get out of the water, but I won't let them persuade me. 'No, I am not going to give up willingly.' I have made a deal with Mr Allan that he is only allowed to pull me out if he feels that it's no longer safe. I know that he will keep his word.

'Stop thinking about failure. You've gone this far and now you know what success feels like. Think about that.' I push and my body tries to respond. My legs want to keep kicking, and my arms want to keep pulling, but my heart is beating much, much too slowly.

I begin to slip into unconsciousness and I feel myself being hoisted on board the boat.

At 2.45 p.m. you were reluctantly pulled out of the water, seven miles short of your goal. You failed. The reporters, doctors and experts on hand were amazed at your ability to withstand the cold, at your endurance and at your fitness and decreed that you must have been telling the truth first time around. According to all, it was a victory in defeat. What was it to you? Were you crushed by your collapse and did you have to muster up courage to get back into the water? Or had you perhaps thought this might happen? Were you angry that it was only now, only when you had put your life at risk, that you were believed? Maybe you were heartened by the public's willingness to take your word for your previous swim?

I let go of the cloth, placing it with the other objects.

There are things I don't know, but there are things that have been recorded. Just as news of your vindication swim hit the papers, a chap by the name of Hans Wildorf, co-founder of Rolex, had just patented the first waterproof wristwatch and he wrote asking if you would wear it on your person as you swam. It was a good deal and you agreed. The Rolex Oyster was marketed as The Wonder Watch that defies the elements, with your endorsement of course:

'You will like to hear that the Rolex Oyster watch I carried on my Channel swim proved itself a reliable and accurate timekeeping companion even though it was subjected to complete immersion in hours of sea water at a temperature of not more than fifty-eight and often as low as fifty-one degrees. The newspaper man was astonished and I of course am delighted with it.'

It kept going, though you could not.

You proved yourself well and truly by swimming the Straits of Gibraltar the following year, with a detailed log and over fifteen signatories who all testified that you did it unaided. You *were* vindicated. You did go down in history as the first British woman to swim the English Channel.

I sit on the ladder.

For me a long distance swimmer is someone remote; detached from everyday life. I'm a terrible swimmer. I didn't properly learn until adulthood. Chlorine makes me sneeze. Years of playing a wind instrument made my lungs big enough to swim a width without taking a breath, and so I never learned how. I will never swim the English Channel. But it was the solitude and the faded limelight that attracted me to your story. And since I began trying to track you down, it is that same solitude that has presented the biggest challenge.

Having lived a life of endurance, fame and remoteness you became a recluse. You had travelled the world, swimming in many of its oceans and lakes. You had performed endurance feats in swimming pools and exhibitions of scientific swimming in the circus, but when your body finally did have its revenge, you chose to retreat inwards once more. You portioned up this part of your life and packed it away within yourself. And when you died, you took most of your memories with you.

All that remains are the logs of your swims, programmes and photographs found boxed up in your attic. They have shown me a glimpse of the space around a person who can never really be known or recreated.

I found her in Cork City Library in the summer of 2005, but when I returned in 2006, the book of old photographs from which she smiled demurely at me could not be found. It felt like Mercedes was courting celebrity all over again.

Imagine that I'm the closest thing to a celebrity that you have ever seen.

Now imagine that this carries me to a diving platform high above you.

I climb to the top of the ladder.

I take up position.

I say:

(**The sounds of breathing and the sea, building and then retreating**) Imagine smearing your body in a mixture of lard and Vaseline to keep out the cold.

Imagine the exhilarating bite of the sea on a winter's morning.

Imagine cold, relentless sheets of rain pounding down while the sea churns around you.

Imagine fighting a rising tide.

Imagine being dragged off course and having to swim harder, and faster, for longer.

Imagine maintaining your resolve through repeated failures.

Imagine not seeing them as failures.

Imagine wading in from empty beach on a moonless night, and knowing that you will swim through that night, and all of the following day.

Imagine the clock which never has bad days, which never gets tired, constantly ticking.

Imagine your aching muscles which you must ignore and control.

Speak to your lungs and say, 'You are bigger than this.'

Speak to your heart and say, 'Don't beat faster, slow down.'

Speak to your spine and say, 'Keep rotating.'

Speak to your legs and say, 'Keep kicking.'

Speak to your arms and say, 'Keep pulling.'

Speak to your joints and say, 'Look, you can have your revenge when I'm old.'

Imagine crawling up a beach so completely spent that your body shuts down into unconsciousness.

Imagine the release of realising that you have succeeded at last.

Imagine accomplishing your greatest ambition and then having it doubted because of the actions of a charlatan.

Imagine having to do it all over again.

Imagine what it's like to go from being a shorthand typist to a world record breaker.

Imagine knowing you could hold fifteen hours of swimming in your lungs.

Imagine holding fifteen hours of swimming in your lungs.

Imagine travelling around the world, making your money through elaborate performances of feats of endurance.

Imagine what it is like to go from being a vaudeville star to a mother and a wife.

Imagine turning your back on a talent that inspired awe in others.

Imagine sinking into solitude.

Imagine slipping into old age and obscurity.

Imagine watching your fame fade away, as you keep the curtain closed and the music turned up.

Imagine the deep sleep of satisfaction as you remember it all.

I climb down.

Imagine finding this life in a library on an ordinary Thursday afternoon. And saying to yourself: 'Remember to breathe.'

Lights Fade.

PINEAPPLE
BY
PHILLIP MCMAHON

For Mam, Jen, and Dad who will always be with us.

Commissioned and produced by Calipo Theatre and Picture Company.

Pineapple premiered at the Droichead Arts Centre on 29 April 2011 in a production by Calipo Theatre Company in association with the Drogheda Arts Festival

Written by Phillip McMahon
Directed by David Horan

Cast:
PAULA: Caoilfhionn Dunne
DAN: Nick Lee
ANTOINETTE: Janet Moran
ROXANNA: Jill Murphy
STEPH: Niamh Glynn

Production Design by Paul O'Mahony
Lighting Design by Sinead McKenna
Sound Design by Ivan Birthistle & Vincent Doherty
Costume Design by Emma Fraser
Produced by Collette Farrell & Lara Hickey

Characters	Off-Stage Voices
Paula, 26	Olivia / Paula's Neighbour
Roxanna, 16 / Paula's sister	Jean / Paula's Neighbour
Dan, 28-30	Nicola / Paula's Neighbour
Antoinette, 32 / Paula's best friend	Patsy / Antoinette's Father
Steph, 16 / Roxanna's best friend	

The main action takes place in Paula's kitchen. A tumbledown room littered with toys and piles of laundry. The rest of the action takes place in a mucky area between places; a no-man's-land.

ACT ONE

SCENE ONE

A mucky field. ROXANNA and STEPH hang around nothing in particular, sipping on Bacardi Breezers.

ROXANNA: I can't stand fuckin' Pineapple. I says to your man; I says – *You Paki cunt, pay your Bacardi bills and get some 'lemon lime' or some 'watermelon' or somethin'.*

STEPH: Makes your spunk taste good.

ROXANNA: What?

STEPH: Pineapple.

ROXANNA: What?

STEPH: Makes a fella's spunk taste…sweeter like.

ROXANNA: Says who?

STEPH: Read it somewhere.

ROXANNA: That's disgustin'!

STEPH: Just sayin'.

ROXANNA: Well shut up sayin'…me stomach is turnin'!

The girls swig their Breezers.

It's fuckin' borin' round here.

STEPH: Is right.

ROXANNA: We'll fuckin' die here.

STEPH: Breslin says that from the minute we're born, we're dyin' – just depends how long it takes each of us.

ROXANNA: Dope.

STEPH: Then Charlene O'Neill pushes her glasses up 'er snout – asks Breslin if he clocks himself as an optimist?

ROXANNA: Scarlet for her…

STEPH: Is right! Then Breslin gets into a serious deep and meaningful; spouting some shite about the ability to be an optimist while still accepting the facts of life. It was bore-fuckin'-central. That chat'd put you to sleep quicker than a Venn Diagram; but sure be the time they'd finished the bell was bangin' so it wasn't all bad.

ROXANNA: Fitzy been knockin' about?

STEPH: What?

ROXANNA: Fitzy?

STEPH: I was in town Friday and Saturday, wasn't I?

ROXANNA: Right.

STEPH: Stayed out all weekend nearly. Said I was in yours…

ROXANNA: Your Ma not know I was away?

STEPH: Talkin' to the wall, you do be.

ROXANNA: Right.

Pause.

STEPH: What's it like over there?

ROXANNA: Brilliant.

STEPH: Is it yeah?

ROXANNA: Just bigger. Better like.

STEPH: And the fellas?

ROXANNA: Massive.

Pause.

STEPH: Was you out much?

ROXANNA: Nah.

STEPH: At all?

ROXANNA: Me aunty is *real* strict; fuckin' weapon she is…but she'd to stay out one night, 'cos some auld one she minds was sick, or dyin' or somethin'.

So it was just me in the gaff with Simon; me cousin. He works in Tesco or somethin'.

And we're sat in front of fuckin' *Family Fortunes*. All ready for bed I was, in me pyjamas, and Simon pulls on me pony tail.

He's a bit of a sap, but he's sound like.

So I reefed him back. Like *reefed* him.

And I musta hurt him, 'cos he was all…bruised pride or… you shoulda seen the face on 'im…and he clatters me/

STEPH: /Fuck.

ROXANNA: Not like…anyway *(Points at her ring.)* I send a sovereign his way, but he catches me.

Grabs me real rough.

Pins me down; elbow on me chest and the breath all caught in me throat…and he…kisses me Steph.

Me cousin.

Works his tongue through me teeth; all spit and hot air…

STEPH: –

ROXANNA: So I kiss him back; 'cos it doesn't mean anything, ye know?

And he's all gentle now; the soft couch and the TV.

And he's shakin'; his hand and his top lip.

And he draws his fingers across me stomach; like he's writin' his name or…

The stretch of elastic then; cold hands, and me no knickers…his face on fire…eyes burnin…

STEPH: Paedophile eyes. Tell me you stopped him.

ROXANNA: Course I did.

Get your fuckin' fingers outta me lunch box!

Fucker gets all flustered then. Simple fuck.

'Cos the horn is wearin' off or maybe 'cos it clicks in his tiny mind that he was about to finger his sixteen-year-old cousin; and he catches me by the throat like a dog – chokin' me.

I turn out the big guns then. Boo-hooin' for mercy. Drip drip on the aunty's good shag.

Works a' coarse.

He's all, *Oh Fuck.*

Catchin' his breath or his thoughts or…

Holdin' his head like a looper.

Oh Fuck.

The accent on 'im.

Throws himself round the room, *Oh-in* and *fuck-in.*

Simon, I says, *Chill out ye sap, it's cool.* And you'd swear I just donated me life's savin's to his favourite charity 'cos he's all grateful. Thanks me, and shakes me hand - the fuckin' eejit – says he wants to take me into town for a straightner.

I'd to be at the doctors first thing is the thing, but he's all – *no bother, no bother* – says it's him taking me. Makes no difference if I'm hung over or not, once his Ma's none the wiser; *mum*, he calls her.

So we drive into town and he pays for everything, and we get pallatic on *WKD* 'til six in the mornin'…and I'd to be up again at nine!

PAULA enters. She is in her kitchen. She is in a different scene to the two girls.

STEPH: Is this in London?

OLIVIA: *(Off-stage and in Scene Two.)* Paula?

ROXANNA: No, Leeds.

STEPH: You lucky bitch.

SCENE TWO

PAULA's kitchen. A voice of a neighbour is heard offstage. PAULA opens her kitchen window wide and leans toward the open space.

OLIVIA: *(Off-stage.)* Paula?

PAULA: Fuckin, what?

OLIVIA: Paula Lyons, do you think I've nothin' better to do than roar at your bleedin' kids all day? I won't have a blade o' fuckin' hair left with them.

PAULA: Playin' is all.

OLIVIA: If that shoppin' trolley passes my window the once more…

PAULA: Get over it. Fuckin' curtain twitcher.

OLIVIA: You get over it; d'you hear me? You get the fuckin' boat over it. See that trolley…you want the guards called…

PAULA: You might get more satisfaction out of Tesco love.

PAULA's focus changes to her kids playing below.

Aaron get off that hedge…'cos it's a hedge! *(Pause.)* I'm warnin' ya, do not walk in this flat head-to-toe in muck 'cos I'll reef ya, d'ya hear me? *(Pause.)* Fish-fingers, why? *(Pause, changing tone.)* Ah Aaron, go after Jason before he goes near that road. *(Pause.)* 'Cos he's your brother, that's why!

Flustered, Antoinette enters with bags of shopping from Lidl. Her fingers are crushed by the plastic.

ANTOINETTE: Paula quick…me fingers…quick.

PAULA untangles the bags from ANTOINETTE's fingers.

Fuck sake.

Pause.

It's like shoppin' in bleedin' Beirut. I swear to god. Lash on that kettle, will ya? I've a card of Kit-Kats in one of these bags…

PAULA is away in her thoughts.

Paula?

PAULA: What?

ANTOINETTE: The kettle? I'm bleedin' gaspin'.

PAULA switches the kettle on.

Passed Jean on the way up. She's after balloonin'. It's either twins or cream cakes…I says it to her an' all: 'It's either twins or cream cakes,' I says. Ragin' she was. They'd first-aid kits in Lidl, I got ya one.

PAULA makes tea.

Roxanna's home?

PAULA: *(Only half hearing.)* What? *(Out the window.)* Aaron, don't have me come down to ya…

ANTOINETTE: Roxanna, she's back.

PAULA: Yeah.

ANTOINETTE: Just saw her cutting across the shops.

PAULA: Right.

ANTOINETTE: Not a bother on her.

PAULA: Right, yeah.

PAULA and ANTOINETTE sit in silence.

ANTOINETTE: Bold as brass.

PAULA: How are you getting home?

ANTOINETTE: Not going 'til later!

Pause.

Bus I suppose. Unless me aul' fella comes through with a lift – pox bottle. Sooner see me cartin' fuckin' shoppin' and baby on a bus than drop us up the road.

PAULA: It's the getting back I suppose.

ANTOINETTE: It's the fuckin' petrol is what it is. Tight cunt. See what he says when he drops Stacey over.

PAULA: Your Ma has her?

ANTOINETTE: Don't talk to me…

PAULA puts tea on the table. ANTOINETTE tears a packet of Kit-Kats open with her teeth.

Says she'll take the bus up in the mornin'. I've me carpets coming first thing and ye know yourself, they could be all day fittin' them and Stacey'll only be under their feet. So she's comin' up anyway. I got a load of biscuits in and ham and all. I even got these Cappuccino's that you just pour water in to; chocolate powder an' all. They sound gorgeous.

PAULA: For your Ma?

ANTOINETTE: No, you thick, for the carpet fitter!

PAULA: You on the lookout for a culchie?

ANTOINETTE: I'd take a culchie over the pricks around here any day.

Pause.

Bit of luck me Ma might give me a dropsy for the carpets.

PAULA: Were you talking to her?

ANTOINETTE: What? *(as in 'who?')*

PAULA: Roxanna.

ANTOINETTE: Crossing the muck with your one Steph. Called her like – little bitch heard me an' all – kept walkin' but.

PAULA: Right, yeah.

ANTOINETTE: The neck a' young ones these days.

Pause. PAULA is preoccupied.

There's blacks moved in beside me.

PAULA: –

ANTOINETTE: Right next door.

PAULA: And what?

ANTOINETTE: What?

PAULA: Were you in with them or what?

ANTOINETTE: Waved to *her* – your one. Nodded back. Didn't wave or nothin' – I says I won't call her a snobby cunt just yet…on account of the fact she's probably up to her eyes gettin' her own place sorted.

PAULA: Everyone's movin'.

ANTOINETTE: Rake of kids. *Chocolate drops*, I says to meself. Sure who else would I be talkin' ta?

PAULA: Jean got 'er place, was she sayin'?

ANTOINETTE: You jokin'? She could hardly get a word in edgeways with the battered sausage hangin' out of her mouth. Young-one's a glutton. Like, there does be cravin's and then there does be pure piggery.

PAULA: *(Lightly.)* Shut up you/

ANTOINETTE: She even pregnant? *D'you* ever see a fella climb those stairs?

PAULA: *(PAULA calls out the kitchen window.)* Jean?! *(To ANTOINETTE.)* Ask her yourself.

ANTOINETTE: *(Lightly.)* Fuck off you!

PAULA: Jean?!

JEAN: *(Off-stage.)* What?

PAULA: Antoinette wants ye.

JEAN: What love?

ANTOINETTE: *(To PAULA.)* You're dead. *(To JEAN, out the window)* Paula was saying you got a place?

JEAN: A duplex! Was I not sayin'? I was leggin' it, sorry; starvin' I was.

ANTOINETTE: *(To PAULA.)* Fat cunt. *(To JEAN.)* You delighted?

JEAN: *(To a child.)* Kevin, fuck off away from me for two minutes!! *(To ANTOINETTE.)* I just can't wait to have enough rooms to be able to hide from these fuckin' kids.

PAULA: *(To ANTOINETTE.)* I'm surprised the kids are not hidin' from *her.*

ANTOINETTE: *(To PAULA.)* Hidin' the bleedin' food from 'er.

JEAN: Ran inta your sister there. Was she sayin'?

PAULA: Haven't seen her love.

JEAN: She's some mouth on 'er.

PAULA: You're no saint yourself.

JEAN: She's home inanyways?

PAULA: She hasn't darkened this door.

JEAN: Enjoy the peace while it lasts sweetheart. Anyway – I'll leg it – there's a packet of Custard Creams starin' me out of it here.

Pause.

PAULA: Did Rox say she was calling over or what?

ANTOINETTE: Are you deaf or somethin'? I wasn't talkin' to 'er.

SCENE THREE

ROXANNA and STEPH. The Wasteland.

STEPH: They don't even ask for ID. Like, the lads know the bouncers by name an' all.

ROXANNA: They sound like muppets.

STEPH: Ah, they're a laugh, and it's town like…beats this shit hole any day.

Pause.

They buy me drinks and everything…all night.

ROXANNA: *(Considers.)* I suppose. I'll come out the next time.

Pause.

STEPH: Here?

ROXANNA: –

STEPH: Did it…hurt…when you did it with Fitzy?

ROXANNA: When?

STEPH: The first time.

ROXANNA: No. Why?

STEPH: At all?

ROXANNA: No, it never did.

STEPH: It's just that Alan, one of the lads, says he wants to fuck me.

ROXANNA: Right.

STEPH: Tonight like. Said it real casual.

ROXANNA: Right.

STEPH: I fancy his mate Trevor more, but I want to get it over with ye know?

ROXANNA: It's pure easy.

STEPH considers this.

STEPH: And what's the story with Fitzy now, are yiz still doin' it?

ROXANNA: Says he still fancies me…even after everything. Says he fancies me more for being so strong.

Pause.

STEPH: It's just that I fancy your man's mate more. Trevor is his name.

ROXANNA: So?

STEPH: I suppose.

ROXANNA: It's the experience you want. Fellas want ya knowin' your way round…

STEPH: Never thought of that.

Pause.

ROXANNA: I was sick all day.

STEPH: Were you drinkin' or…?

ROXANNA: No. Few *Breezers* is all.

STEPH: Say it to your Ma?

ROXANNA: Are *you* wise?

STEPH: What about Paula?

ROXANNA: She'll only have me tormented about Leeds.

STEPH: She's your sister! She cares…

ROXANNA: 'Still a head wrecker but.

Pause.

What does he look like this fella?

STEPH: Alan? *You'd* probably say he was bet down. I don't know. He's twenty. He's a job an' all…so…he's money like.

ROXANNA: Well make sure he spends it.

STEPH: Too right.

ROXANNA: That's the trick with fellas; give them nothin' for nothin'.

Music rises. Each character inhabits the stage. An introduction of sorts; opening titles. ROXANNA, ANTOINETTE, STEPH and PAULA all stand as music plays over. Last to appear is DAN.

SCENE FOUR

PAULA's kitchen late at night. PAULA, ANTOINETTE and DAN. All are tipsy but not drunk. DAN is a stranger.

ANTOINETTE: *(About her carpet.)* It's like beige all through the hallway and the same in the sittin' room. Biscuit I think your man called it. Anyway, he was a wreck. He had some lino but, in the back of the van and he says he'd lay that as a nixer, for fifty quid…in the kitchen. I put me sad face on and me Ma paid for it. Fifty wasn't bad but?

PAULA: That's grand in'it?

ANTOINETTE: He says to me – *If the shop is on to you, say nothin' about the lino.* – Proper bogger he was. I told him not to sweat it. I says – *Your secret's safe with me mister.* Mortified he was; robbin' bastard.

DAN: Is there any booze goin'?

PAULA: What?

DAN: A can or a whiskey or somethin'?

PAULA: It's not a bleedin' party you're at.

DAN: *(To ANTOINETTE.)* Is it not?

ANTOINETTE: I never said party exactly. I said, *let us in your taxi.*

DAN: I live the complete other way.

PAULA: That's Antoinette for ya.

ANTOINETTE: Don't start all that – *That's Antoinette for ya* – I won't be havin' any of that. Antoinette nothin'…

Pause.

Sure lash the kettle on, we have a cup o' scald now we're all here.

PAULA: *(To DAN.)* Do you want tea?

DAN: Seriously?

ANTOINETTE: *(To PAULA.)* I do. So chop chop.

PAULA: Don't get smart with me Antoinette…I'll scald ya with the cuntin' kettle.

DAN: Will I fuck off then?

ANTOINETTE: Unless you fix washin' machines?

DAN: What?

ANTOINETTE: Paula needs her plumbing seen to.

PAULA: *(Laughs.)* Shut up you, makin' a show o' me! Inanyways sweetheart – unless me calculations are wrong, your own pipes are a bit rusty.

ANTOINETTE: You bitch! I'm talkin' about your bleedin' washin' machine. Is it on the blink or wha'?

PAULA: You what? Me…? Oh – it is yeah. *(To ANTOINETTE.)* See *you*…confusin' me…

ANTOINETTE: Rusty pipes? The neck a' you.

DAN: Right I'll leg it then.

ANTOINETTE: Sit down there – we're only buzzin' off ya. What are we Paula?

PAULA: Exactly. Don't be gettin' your knickers in a squiz. *(PAULA moves to the fridge.)* I've a couple of Smirnoff Ice in here somewhere – left over from the Communion.

ANTOINETTE: *(To DAN)* Party! What did I tell ya?

DAN: Do I look like a Smirnoff Ice type?

ANTOINETTE: No but you look like you're making your communion, so shut up and sit down.

PAULA hands DAN and ANTOINETTE a Smirnoff Ice with a straw in each bottle.

DAN: *(About his clothes.)* This is all my best gear by the way. Is it that bad? Ah you's are winding me up. It's not fair. I'm a bit dozy with a beer on me.

ANTOINETTE: A bit?

DAN: *(About the clothes.)* This is me seriously making an effort. I was trying to make a good impression or whatever…

PAULA: Were you now?

DAN: I was out with a girl, wasn't I?

ANTOINETTE: Oh my god – you were on a date?

PAULA: Tonight?

ANTOINETTE: You were, weren't ya?

DAN: Don't look so surprised.

PAULA: And?

DAN: Well I'm sittin' here, aren't I?

ANTOINETTE: You bombed like a sack of shit, did you love?

PAULA: A date? Cringe.

DAN: It was going okay. I was being funny, *(To ANTOINETTE.)* shut up! She was havin' a good time I reckon. It was a blind date yoke – through a mate at work – one of those… but yeah, we were havin' fun. I took her for dinner – you know, nothin' fancy or anything, just a place at the back of a pub and I had the – I dunno – some sort of skewer thing and she had a prawn cocktail thing to start and then she went on to have a Sea Bass and I was thinkin', you know – that's a lot of fish – but she *had* said something about being a part time vegetarian, so maybe she only eats seafood. Anyway it comes to like – just before the bill comes and she – now just before I tell you, I actually don't care right – but she farts at the table/

PAULA: What?

DAN: /and I laughed, 'cos I thought it was funny, or cute – I didn't care basically – we all do it. But she leapt up out of her seat and legged it to the jacks – and I'm sat there not knowin' whether I should pay the bill or what, because I know *your* crowd can be quite sensitive about that, so I waited…

ANTOINETTE: Go on…

DAN: Well she comes back and says that she's sick – like dodgy food or something, and I'm all up for complaining to the kitchen or the waiter or whoever but she's – Grainne's her name – she just says that it's best to be at home if she's not well…then I say that maybe she just needs to sit on the jacks for a bit. You know, like, trying to be sound – but she was like a rocket then; out the door – no mention of the bill or anything…

ANTOINETTE: Scarlet Church!

PAULA: *(To DAN.)* Sounds like you got blown out.

DAN: What?

ANTOINETTE: Dumped, if you will.

DAN: Ah – I wasn't that into it anyways. I've got trust issues with vegetarians. Part time or otherwise.

Pause. DAN's tone changes. He swigs his drink maybe.

Fuck it I suppose. You win some, you lose some.

Pause. His tone picks up again. He raises his drink in a toast.

Cheers.

The girls clink bottles with DAN.

Who's Communion?

PAULA: You what?

DAN: The booze…

PAULA: It was only a few bottles, for anyone callin' in or anything…

ANTOINETTE: Little Aaron. Mr Bling. Gorgeous he was.

PAULA: Get a life you – there was nothin' bling about him. The bleedin' height of good taste, so he was.

DAN: You've a kid?

PAULA: Two.

DAN: They here?

PAULA: Out with their Da.

DAN: Is he due back? I don't want any trouble.

ANTOINETTE: Relax – you've more chance of catchin' the Virgin at Knock.

PAULA: As in – No.

ANTOINETTE: He no longer – what's the word for it – 'resides' here? That's it. The fucker no longer resides here.

ANTOINETTE jumps up to use the toilet.

Hang on there now 'til I wet me sponge. Say nothin' 'til I come back right…

ANTOINETTE exits. PAULA and DAN sit in silence for a second.

DAN: They'll be all over this in work now – the news will trickle in via your woman – I'll be made out to be some sort of insensitive pig.

DAN burps. PAULA smiles.

Shit, sorry. It's this fizzy muck you have me on.

PAULA: You're grand. We all do it right?

DAN: That is exactly what I said! We do all do it – *fart away sweet heart* – That's what I should have said. She'd have probably keeled over. I mean in fairness, a fart, who gives a fuck? It's funny.

PAULA: It *is* funny.

DAN: It's very fuckin' funny. And if you can't laugh then what's the…? Ah, I dunno.

Pause.

She definitely said party you know; outside the pub – I wouldn't just…

PAULA: You're grand.

DAN: Well I wouldn't.

PAULA: It's okay.

DAN: I'm just a bit dozy with a beer on me.

PAULA: Yeah.

PAULA stands awkwardly. DAN stands and moves to her as if to kiss her.

What's this?

DAN: What?

PAULA: What are you doin'?

DAN: I just had it in my head…

PAULA: Jesus. Fellas! Yiz are as predicatable.

DAN: Sorry. The drink and the hour.

PAULA: It's home time.

DAN: What?

PAULA: The party's over.

DAN: You wouldn't send a fella out in that?

PAULA: You'll get a taxi on the main road.

DAN: It's Baltic out!

PAULA goes to leave the room.

PAULA: Hang on there…

She exits.

DAN: I've been to worse parties by the way. In case you're wondering – I had a good time.

PAULA re-enters with a big man's jacket.

PAULA: Take this or you'll freeze.

Pause.

Take it.

He reluctantly takes the coat from PAULA.

DAN: I was only…I don't know. I'm sorry.

PAULA: I know yeah, but it's late. *(About the jacket.)* You can keep that.

SCENE FIVE

The next morning. ANTOINETTE sits in PAULA's kitchen reading a magazine.

JEAN: *(Off-stage.)* Paula?

ANTOINETTE ignores JEAN calling from upstairs.

Paula?

ANTOINETTE gets up and closes the window.

ANTOINETTE: *(To herself.)* Fuck off. Heifer.

ANTOINETTE goes back to her magazine. ROXANNA enters looking queasy.

Wonders will never cease, what?

ROXANNA: Where's Paula?

ANTOINETTE: Corpo.

ROXANNA pours a glass of water, but thinks better of it and rushes to the toilet.

(About the Corpo) Waste a' time. They doe wan' t' know. There's no talkin' to Paula but. She's not exactly close friends with common sense is she? Distant cousins if anything…pen pals.

The sound of vomiting in the next room. ANTOINETTE's face creases in disgust. ROXANNA enters.

Was that you, ye dirty bitch?

ROXANNA rummages through PAULA's biscuit tin come medicine box.

ROXANNA: Have you pain killers Antoinette?

ANTOINETTE trawls through her bag.

ANTOINETTE: I've Feminax…any use?

ROXANNA: Me head is liftin'.

ANTOINETTE: You're not supposed to be drinkin'. That's rule number one; I know that much. What is it…recovery an' all that. Drink'll pull the bleedin' stomach out of ye.

ROXANNA: Mind your business. I'm sick.

Pause. ANTOINETTE hands ROXANNA the pills.

ANTOINETTE: You glad to be home?

ROXANNA: It was only a long weekend.

ANTOINETTE: Still.

ROXANNA: Same shit, different day here.

ANTOINETTE: *And* there.

ROXANNA: Give it a rest, will ya? You're like an aul'one.

ANTOINETTE: It's a kickin' you want.

JEAN: *(Off-stage.)* Paula?

Pause.

Paula?

ROXANNA throws the window open.

ROXANNA: She's fuckin' out.

JEAN: *(Light hearted.)* Roxanna ya pox. I'll tear the bleedin' hair outta ya, you curse at me again. Where's your sister?

ROXANNA: Is it the 'O', the 'U' or the 'T' you don't understand?

ROXANNA closes the window.

Dozy gee-bag.

ANTOINETTE: Were you over with Fitzy or…?

ROXANNA: What of it?

ANTOINETTE: Drama in his garden is all. Passin' last night.

ROXANNA: You've too much time on your hands.

ANTOINETTE: Couldn't miss it. Big hoo-hah. Half the road was out.

ROXANNA: It'd suit you to mind your business.

ANTOINETTE: Has the little fucker even called you?

The hall door slams. PAULA talks from the hallway.

PAULA: Taxi driver's after overcharging me I think. What's six from twenty?

PAULA sees ROXANNA. They stare at each other for a second.

ROXANNA: Fourteen…

PAULA: Me brain is dead. Yeah, and he handed me back twelve. Twelve from twenty is eight.

ANTOINETTE: Was he foreign?

PAULA: No. He was Irish. Know him an' all. I'll catch him again, the robbin' swine.

Pause. PAULA and ROXANNA take each other in.

Howaya?

ROXANNA has tears in her eyes.

ROXANNA: I've a pain in me head.

PAULA: It's okay.

ROXANNA: The fuckin' bitch locked me out. I was like a knacker climbin' in the toilet window. I'd to take me skirt off just to fit through the yolk. She's touched in the head Paula. Goes on this mornin' as if nothin' happened. She's a psycho. Woke up with a lump on me nut from where I whacked it off the sink…well the tap actually. Felt nothin' last night; but this mornin', I felt it fuckin' tenfold. Have you any Solpadeine?

PAULA rummages through a biscuit tin filled with medicines and tablets.

PAULA: I must'a had the last one.

PAULA leans out her window and shouts.

Jean? *(Pause, no response.)* Jean? *(Pause, no response.)*

ANTOINETTE: Talk about choosin' your moments. She hasn't bleedin' stopped all mornin'!

PAULA: Nicola?

NICOLA: *(From offstage.)* What?

PAULA: Have you painkillers?

NICOLA: Just Anadin, why?

PAULA: Roxanna got a bang of a tap!

NICOLA: She home?

PAULA: Safe and sound. Will you send us down two?

NICOLA: Course I will. Have you any DVDs down there? I'm bored off me tits!

PAULA: I've *Nemo* and *Rush Hour 3*. Send Kayleigh down.

NICOLA: C'mere, ask Rox what's goin' on over in Balcurris?

PAULA: With what?

NICOLA: The Fitzy's gaff. Guards trolling it all day.

PAULA looks to ROXANNA.

ROXANNA: One o' the brothers prob-ly, or the Da, I dunno.

PAULA: *(To NICOLA.)* She doesn't know sweetheart.

NICOLA: Ah – yiz are useless!

PAULA comes in from the window.

ROXANNA: Don't be broadcastin' me bleedin' business!

PAULA: You'd rather suffer?

ANTOINETTE: Any joy with the corpo?

PAULA: *(Sarcastic.)* Mm. They says take me pick of any gaff the length and breadth of the city.

ANTOINETTE: That was decent o' them…and there was you expecting a no!

PAULA: Bastards.

PAULA looks at the mess surrounding her.

This place is fallin' to bits.

ANTOINETTE: I wouldn't do a tap to it if I was you. No way. I wouldn't even wash the windows – not that you do inanyways mind.

ROXANNA: Somethin' will come up Paula. It has ta.

PAULA: I can't carry on like this – we'll rot here. It's no good.

ROXANNA: Somethin' *will* Paula.

PAULA kisses ROXANNA's forehead. The voice of ANTOINETTE's father is heard from out on the street.

PATSY: *(Off-stage.)* Antoinette?

ANTOINETTE: Stick on that kettle Rox.

PAULA and ROXANNA throw a look to ANTOINETTE.

What?

ROXANNA: Your poor Da.

PAULA: Shift your arse.

ANTOINETTE: I never says to him what time to come over. I'm no more ready to move than you are. Leave him.

PATSY: *(Off-stage.)* Antoinette?!

ANTOINETTE: Poor Da nothin'. He never even said he was droppin' me home. It's Saturday bleedin' night. He's only over here 'cos he wants rid of Stacey. You've no idea of him.

PATSY: *(Off-stage.)* Antoinette?

ANTOINETTE: *(To PAULA.)* What?

ANTOINETTE leans out the window.

I heard you the first time. I'm wipin' me bleedin' arse. Giz a minute.

She comes in from the window.

He's a torment.

ANTOINETTE moves to the hall to get her coat.

I'd sooner sit here with yous than on that buildin' site on me tobler.

PAULA: Ring us after, yeah?

ANTOINETTE talks as she leaves the flat.

ANTOINETTE: Ragin'.

The hall door slams and the flat is suddenly quiet. PAULA moves around the kitchen with a cloth, wiping surfaces.

ROXANNA: Where's Aaron and Jason?

PAULA: With *him*. Says his auld one's giving him stick 'cos she never sees them. Told him that's his doin' and not mine. Came over yesterday, full of the joys of spring after winning a tonne on a horse; fuckin' eejit. You'd swear he just won the lotto, wavin' it in the air. I didn't even let him past the door; told him he better spend every last cent on those kids.

Pause.

ROXANNA: They must wreck your head all the same.

PAULA: You get used to it.

ROXANNA: Still…they must.

Pause.

PAULA: You *did* do the right thing in Leeds.

ROXANNA: Did I?

PAULA: You're only a baby yourself.

ROXANNA: An' what?

PAULA: You've a second chance now. You can start over.

ROXANNA: Yeah.

PAULA: You won't know yourself. All brand new. You can get back into it now: school and the whole lot.

ROXANNA: Don't start Paula.

PAULA: It's your time you wanna be takin'…your body an' all that…but a second chance; that's all I'm sayin'.

ROXANNA: Me Ma says I'm disgustin'. Says she can't face lookin' at me; what I done and what I did. Says she can't sleep with the thoughts of me.

PAULA: That's/

ROXANNA: /Wants me took to a priest.

PAULA: As if those fuckers would understand – No way.

ROXANNA: Will you ring 'er?

PAULA: What?

ROXANNA: Ma. Will you put her straight? She might listen to you.

PAULA becomess uncomfortable.

PAULA: Stay over here for a bit, yeah? 'Til she calms down.

ROXANNA: Right.

PAULA: Text her an' say you're mindin' the kids or helpin' me out or somethin'.

ROXANNA: Yeah okay.

PAULA: Leave her give her mind a rest.

Pause.

ROXANNA: I'm not going to no priest.

Pause.

PAULA: Antoinette brought up a load of pirates. We get a kebab tray and drag out the duvets?

ROXANNA: I can't. I've to go on a message.

PAULA: It's too quiet with the kids gone. You know what I'm like.

ROXANNA: I can't Paula. I've to find Fitzy.

PAULA: Jesus Roxanna.

ROXANNA: I promised him.

PAULA: And what about when he promised you. When he said he'd take you to Leeds?

ROXANNA: He had his reasons.

PAULA: Cowards invent reasons. I know that only too well. Fellas have reasons and excuses drippin' off them.

ROXANNA: Not Fitzy.

PAULA: Stay with me sweetheart.

ROXANNA: He loves me Paula.

PAULA: Fellas are dogs. Learn that. It's all love and – *I'd do anything for ya* – until you're in your moment of need and

he's either there beside ya or he's not…and Fitzy wasn't.
He's not.

ROXANNA: What about his needs? The things he needs?

PAULA: You've obviously been watchin' too much television.
Your brain is tapped. His needs? Listen; fellas have an
amazing talent of gettin' exactly what they want *and* need.
Don't you worry 'bout that. But your needs, young one.
Your needs! Let that be your number one concern from
here on in.

SCENE SIX

*PAULA's kitchen. Night time. DAN stands in the kitchen holding the
big jacket. He has a black eye. PAULA is gathering ice into a tea towel.*

DAN: I did all that last night. I'm fine, honestly.

PAULA: It looks sore but.

DAN: He caught me lovely, the fucker. Don't feel bad or
anything.

PAULA: What?

DAN: Well when I left here I'd to jog it was so cold, and then
finding the 'main road' was all a bit *Where's Wally*…and
then…once I'd finally flagged a taxi, a couple of boys
emerged from the fog shouting, 'you've skipped the queue
love.'
Pause.

The fuckin' queue? It was a dual carriageway.

PAULA: They take your money or anything?

DAN: Seemed happy enough with the aul' dignity ye know? I
think I even offered to *share* the cab – it was *that* cold – I'm
a sap really…I woke up laughing – I'm a fuckin' eejit.

PAULA: *(Laughs.)* I'm sorry…I can just picture you though.

DAN: I thought the coat would've helped me blend in. I think I
might have even attempted an accent. *(Attempts an accent.)*

Alright boys? That's when he landed one on me. *(laughs)*
Come to think of it, I'd have punched me.

They laugh which turns into dead silence. Long pause.

So…I wanted to drop the coat off – just 'cos it harbours
bad memories for me basically – and er…just 'cos I wanted
to say I was drunk last night but I wasn't…

PAULA: The jacket's for the bin anyways. But thanks.

*PAULA takes the jacket from DAN. He hovers in silence for a second
searching for something to say that might keep the conversation going.*

DAN: *(Taking a chance.)* Make us a cup of tea, will you?

PAULA: Are you takin' the piss?

DAN: I've come all this way.

Pause. PAULA relaxes.

PAULA: Sit down.

DAN: My granddad worked on these places, was I saying that?
We used to drive down here when we were kids. The old
man would park over by the shopping-centre and marvel
at his work.

PAULA: Lucky you.

DAN: Who needs the funfair when you can get a two-hour
lecture on the inner workings of a tower block? Every last
detail divulged; the design process, the execution. In the
summer he'd even go as far as drawing diagrams in the
dust of his bonnet. Then it was up the back roads to the
airport for an ice cream and a look of the planes heading
off. We were…spoiled.

PAULA: –

DAN: I'm Dan by the way.

PAULA puts tea on the table.

PAULA: I know, yeah. Sure we were…

DAN: Nah – you never asked. You or your mate.

PAULA: Oh right – I'm Paula.

DAN: I know yeah. Paula and Antoinette. Double trouble…

ROXANNA enters with STEPH.

PAULA: What's wrong?

ROXANNA looks to DAN.

ROXANNA: Cem over to say I'm stayin' in Steph's tonight.

PAULA: No. Sorry.

ROXANNA: What?

PAULA: Sorry Steph. No offence or nothin'…

STEPH: No.

ROXANNA: What ya talkin' about?

PAULA: You're stayin' here tonight. Now go meet Fitzy, or whatever you have to do…but your sleepin' here, d'ya hear me? Or else you're goin' home. They're the options.

ROXANNA: Fuck sake.

PAULA fishes for a tenner in a bag.

PAULA: Stick the kids coats on an' take them for a burger or somethin', I've no dinner made. Get you and Steph somethin' too.

STEPH: Thanks Paula.

ROXANNA: Are you mad? I'm not takin' no bleedin' kids nowhere. Do I have skivvy tattooed on me forehead?

PAULA: Roxanna, I'll pull bleedin' lumps out o' you if you keep up your lip. Me Ma might take it off you, but I won't. Now if you wanna stay here, in my flat, then you play by my rules…do ya hear me? Do you hear me?

ROXANNA: You'd've more bleedin' freedom in *Mountjoy.*

PAULA: Keep goin' the way you're goin' an' you'll soon find out.

STEPH: Come on Rox, you're makin' a show of us.

ROXANNA takes the tenner.

ROXANNA: Fuck sake.

ROXANNA looks at DAN as she leaves.

What are *you* lookin' at?

PAULA: Get out before I lamp ye.

The girls exit.

DAN: She's a charmer.

PAULA: You might wanna mind your own business.

ROXANNA and STEPH walk straight out of the previous scene and into the next. They are in the wasteland with the kids, whom we never see.

SCENE SEVEN

The wasteland.

STEPH: Mr Breslin pins up a chart of a woman's body, and with a ruler he starts pointing at the bits. He kicks off with the breasts, as he calls them…draws an X on the nipple, and says that for those that don't know, a woman's breast produces milk. We were pissing ourselves laughin' but he was sweatin' too much to notice. Then he coughs and moves down…starts naming parts like they're on his shopping list; vagina, cervix, fallopian tube, ovary, uterus…then Orla nudges me and points at Breslin's package…the fucker is only hard – the creep. So I nudge Charlene and she points it out to Karen who pulls an orange out of her bag and aims it at Breslin's knob. She's some aim, the jammy bitch. He yelped like a stuck pig. Class dismissed. The fuckin' laugh.

Pause.

All the girls were askin' for ye…

ROXANNA: *(Calls to the kids.)* Aaron fuck off. We're talkin'.

STEPH: When you coming back an' all. How you doin', an' all that.

ROXANNA: I haven't changed me number.

STEPH: Still. They says hello an' all.

Pause.

ROXANNA: Fitzy's brother hung himself.

STEPH: I know. Sure Karen lives next door to them.

ROXANNA: Oh yeah.

STEPH: What over?

ROXANNA: Went over earlier but the Da says for me to stay away; it's just family.

STEPH: Did they say what it was over?

ROXANNA: He owed money to some young fella in a gang I think. Money for yokes or somethin'.

STEPH: Shit.

ROXANNA: Somethin' stupid. Three hundred quid or somethin'.

STEPH: It has to be over somethin' else?

ROXANNA: Maybe. He was a fuckin' loser an' all. The labour wouldn't let him sign on or anything…so he was dealing yokes…like, not even dealing them; buying them and addin' a euro or takin' them himself. He was a dzope. He'd come home mad out of it…tellin' Fitzy how much he loves him an' all. In the mornin' but, it was all different. Wouldn't look at Fitzy…like…wouldn't even be in the same room as him. Always made out like Fitzy was wasting his time doin' his course.

STEPH: Still.

ROXANNA: What?

STEPH: He's dead like.

ROXANNA: And wha'?

The girls swig their Breezers.

STEPH: What about Fitzy?

ROXANNA: Wants ta be left alone.

STEPH: *That's fellas*, as Paula would say.

Long pause.

ROXANNA: And what about your man?

STEPH: It wasn't… He stuck it in and went at me like mad but I wasn't feeling much. It was small like. It was uncomfortable I suppose, but it wasn't…it was just grand.

ROXANNA: Well don't let him and his tiny mickey put you off! Go after your man Trevor now. They're all mad for it I bet.

STEPH: Not sure like. Your man Alan made a bit of a hoo ha when we were leavin' the pub. High fivin' the lads an' all, saying that he was taking me home to doggy the hole off me.

ROXANNA: Urgh. Pig. And did he?

STEPH: No he didn't. Just wanted to kiss and cuddle mostly.

ROXANNA: Fuckin' eejit!

STEPH: I can still taste his breath; all beer and smokes.

ROXANNA: Still – one down.

STEPH: Totally.

ROXANNA: *(Calling.)* Aaron…Jason… Fuck off home. It's freezing out.

Pause.

I said, go home.

STEPH: Should we have got them the chips?

ROXANNA: Size o' them.

STEPH: Ah, they're gorgeous but.

ROXANNA: Money went on Breezer's inanyway.

STEPH: We walk over?

ROXANNA: Do I look like their bleedin' mother?

Pause.

STEPH: This over Fitzy then?

ROXANNA: Fuck Fitzy. Fuck Paula. Fuck fuckin' everyone. They can all fuck off. Tryin' to run me bleedin' life.

STEPH: Masters, or rather mistresses of our own destiny is what Breslin says.

ROXANNA: Fuck Breslin. Fuckin' ride him already and give us all a bit of peace.

STEPH: Your man Alan didn't text me or anything. I don't want him to, but he said he would.

ROXANNA: He sounds like a dope. If he texts, text back and ask him if he knows where to get the mornin' after pill. Make him sweat.

Pause.

STEPH: He has a girlfriend.

ROXANNA: So?

STEPH: Yeah, I suppose.

ROXANNA: You're hardly lookin' to marry him.

STEPH: Bury him more like – Yoke.

Pause.

ROXANNA: Fitzy's brother had a one year old, did you know that?

STEPH: –

ROXANNA: A little baby girl. One year old. And he was able to bail out on her. Just like that.

Pause.

Thing is; she'll always have that now – that little baby. Her whole life she'll carry that with her.

SCENE EIGHT

PAULA rummages for some clean clothes. She holds dirty T-shirts in her hand. DAN stands awkwardly.

DAN: Can I do anything?

PAULA ignores him. She darts into another room. We hear her talking to the boys.

PAULA: Put that on ya. Now. *(Pause.)* Well you's shouldn't have walked home on your own. *(Pause.)* Well you should've told her no. Anything could've happened to yiz. Yiz have me up the walls.

PAULA re-enters. She stops to take a breath. She might cry.

DAN: They're home now…

Pause.

PAULA: What?

DAN: It's okay.

DAN holds PAULA into him like he might kiss her if she let him. It only lasts a second before she pulls away.

PAULA: I could murder Roxanna; leaving them roam the streets on their own.

DAN: There's a good reason I bet.

Pause.

I'll touch on. I'm in the way.

PAULA: Yeah.

DAN moves to exit.

Or hang on. I dunno. *(Frustrated.)* Fuckin' hell…

DAN considers and sits down maybe.

DAN: Go easy on yourself. They're home.

PAULA: There's days when I won't even let them outside you know. Days when I hold them up in here…the three of us…it's cruel in its own way…but it's the only way to know they're safe sometimes.

DAN: That's no way to live either.

PAULA: Sometimes it is. There's no rules.

DAN: You must miss your fella?

PAULA: The owner of the coat?

DAN: The extra set of hands.

PAULA: He wasn't any use to us.

DAN: Times like this.

PAULA: He wouldn't work or do anything. In the end he said he was depressed, but I think he picked that up off the telly. We're all *something*…but we get on with it.

DAN: The father of your kids…that has to count for something.

PAULA: He wasn't a father. He was half a man.

DAN: Still…

PAULA: Remembered for Christmases and birthdays for all the wrong reasons…

I'd me tree set up this one Christmas, and I'd got all these handmade decorations at the market. Your wan must have stroked them out of Arnott's, they were that nice…all snow globes and angels. None of that stringy glittery shite anywhere.

The boys helped me dress it.

Aaron would have been four or five and Jason…sure he was still in nappies…

And I remember askin' Git if he wanted to help…get into the Christmas spirit, or whatever.

'Fuck off and leave me alone,' he says, 'Do I look like Santa's little helper?'

He thought he was funny…fuckin' eejit.

He was a bit of a smoker, Git. He never touched any other drugs, but he was a fucker for the hash. Never in front of the kids…I'd'a had his life…but he was a smoker, yeah.

Christmas Eve, I'd managed to get the kids down early. They'd had their bath and they looked gorgeous in their matching pyjama's that *(Points at the door)* Antoinette got them – she was next door at the time – and I remember looking at them asleep and thinking, 'That's me. That there is what I've achieved.'

I wrapped all the presents.

About eleven I'd everything done.

Git was stoned on the couch.

I opened a can for meself. I never drink beer. Only at Christmas. I love the first sip…that's when you know all the madness is over and you can start to enjoy it then.

I'd only had one can, and I hadn't even heard the door go.

They were just standin' in the sitting room. In no hurry and certainly not afraid.

Only three of them…and just young fellas…eighteen, if even.

I started to shake Git, but he was in 'Lala' land.

One of the young fellas put his finger to his lips and made a fist with his other hand.

The other two started gathering up the presents.

'Git,' I says, 'wake up, ye fuckin' eejit.'

The young lads just laughed… It was too easy for them.

'Your tree is gorgeous missus,' one of them says, lifting it from its stand. But it gets caught at the plug and he's stuck as to what to do, so he yanks it.

His mates are at the door then, arms full of presents, 'leave the tree ya fuckin' queer,' but he's got it in his head now. He keeps yankin' the bleedin thing and me good decorations are getting tossed all over the shop.

So I picked up an unopened can and hopped it off his head.

Only for his mates broke their holes laughing he'd have probably punched me…and they just danced out the door with all the things meant for my little ones.

Pause.

So do I miss him…me ex-fella…the father of me kids…the half a man…no…I don't.

Pause.

DAN: Were you married?

PAULA: Are you mad?

DAN: Small mercies.

PAULA: When he was locked or stoned he'd start mouthing off – new start, this and that – make somethin' of ourselves, this an' that. But sure, he'd have it all forgot by mornin'. He had a knack of meaning nothing of what he said.

Pause.

I suppose he did us a favour by walkin'.

DAN: *You* didn't…?

PAULA: The first sign of trouble and he was out the door. Very fond o' sayin' he had options – and right enough, he did in the end.

DAN: Well he's missing out. I'd love to be a Da. *(Pause.)* Sure the day is young yet…

PAULA: You don't have anyone…?

DAN: To make pregnant? I don't. Not at the moment.

PAULA: Well if you're not married, what's wrong with ya?

DAN: I bottled it.

PAULA: What?

DAN: I didn't rock up at the church.

PAULA: Stop!

DAN: It's true. School mates, friends, work people…they were all there, hats at the ready…my family, her family… But I just couldn't…I had this knot in my stomach that was just saying, *No.*

PAULA: Did you not have, like, years to think it through?

DAN: I know. I did. She was a lovely girl, but she didn't make me feel anything but ordinary, you know? I'm not looking for fireworks every time I look at someone, but I do want to feel…something. I want to be excited.

PAULA raises an eyebrow.

Not in that way! Well actually, yes, in that way too…but in loads of ways…

PAULA: But waiting 'til the day? I mean…

DAN: I'm not proud of it. But an hour later and we'd have spent our lives miserable or trying to get out of it.

PAULA: What did she say?

DAN: *Thanks.*

PAULA: Shut up!

DAN: She sent me an email. She hasn't spoken to me since – but she actually said thanks and went on to list the reasons why we shouldn't be together – and she was petty enough at times but she spoke loads of sense too – like she was more straight talking and sensible in those few lines than she had been in eight years of going out, so I was like – *good for you* – and at the end of the mail she wrote in CAPS the main reason she was glad we didn't get married…

PAULA: Yeah?

DAN: Because *she* didn't love me.

PAULA: Fuck.

DAN: And I was like – *snap* – and *good* – because it means that we did the right thing. And it made me wonder then why I asked her and why she said yes – but then we do that kind of thing all the time because it's easier, isn't it – than being on your own?

PAULA: I don't know.

DAN: Am I talkin' too much?

PAULA: No.

Pause.

DAN: I bumped into her sister in a club last time I was home and she took great drunken pleasure in telling me that Elaine was engaged again. And even though I didn't love her – that was still a kick in the balls.

A light goes on in the hallway. PAULA's ears prick up.

PAULA: I'll only be a second.

PAULA leaves. Offstage we hear her talking to the kids.

I know you're asleep baby. I'm just wiping your face 'cos you're piggy...now, close your eyes if you're asleep.

Pause.

I'm puttin' you into my bed with me, okay sleepy? In with me tonight.

Pause.

I know she did... She is bold, I know. I'll get you the chips tomorrow. Close your eyes now okay, and I'll be into yiz in a little minute. *(She laughs.)* Close them!

PAULA enters the kitchen. The gentle tumble of the washing machine is heard. Noises from the street. A siren. They look at each other. They really look at each other. DAN moves to PAULA. He kisses her.

SCENE NINE

ROXANNA enters. She's drunk. She switches on the kitchen light to reveal PAULA waiting at the kitchen table.

ROXANNA: What?

PAULA slaps ROXANNA across the face.

ROXANNA: They ran off on me Paula.

Throughout the next exchange PAULA has the red mist around her. When she is physical with ROXANNA it should look uncomfortable for the audience and really painful for ROXANNA. PAULA grabs ROXANNA by the hair.

PAULA: I will have your tiny fuckin' life before I let you do anything to those kids, do you hear me? Let me guarantee you that, I will cut your throat the minute my boys are scratched as a result of you.

PAULA has ROXANNA by the hair, her other hand is over her throat or face.

ROXANNA: *(Crying.)* You're hurtin' me Paula. I'm sorry. I'm sorry...I am.

PAULA: My kids could have been dead.

ROXANNA: I'm sorry.

PAULA: Do you even hear that? They could have been dead because of you. Your flesh and blood. You're horrible. I can't even look at you. You have me heart torn out.

PAULA releases her grip on ROXANNA who is crying.

ROXANNA: There's just stuff going on is all Paula; with Fitzy.

PAULA: I don't want to hear your excuses.

ROXANNA: His brother hung himself.

Pause.

PAULA: I wouldn't even know whether to believe you. The lies fall out of your mouth.

ROXANNA: Fitzy's brother hung himself Paula. He's dead.

PAULA: Well that's a crying shame. That's heartbreakin', but it's no excuse.

ROXANNA: He won't see me.

PAULA: Grow up Roxanna.

ROXANNA: I'm serious Paula.

PAULA: I warned you about him, and I told ya not to come crying to me over the scumbag.

ROXANNA: He's not replyin' to me messages and his auld fella says I've not to go near the house.

PAULA: If the brother is dead, then that's the why. Have some cop on.

ROXANNA: He promised he'd be there for me Paula. No matter what.

PAULA: That's fellas!

ROXANNA cries.

ROXANNA: Not Fitzy.

PAULA: What about him saying he'd take you to Leeds?

ROXANNA: He couldn't go Paula. He couldn't face it.

PAULA: But he let you face it on your own? What kind of a man is that?

ROXANNA: He couldn't face it 'cos he didn't want me to do it.

PAULA: Well that's very fuckin' easy for him to say. Did it occur to him to think about that when yiz were lyin' down?

ROXANNA: He *wanted* the baby Paula. He said that when I told him I *was*, he started having dreams about it; about a little baby and about me…the three of us…and a house of our own…a family like.

PAULA: You're sixteen, you thick bitch. You can barely look after yourself.

ROXANNA: He needs it Paula. It's the only thing keepin' him goin'.

PAULA: What d'you mean, he needs it? Needs what?

Pause. ROXANNA is quiet.

PAULA: No Roxanna.

ROXANNA: Sorry.

PAULA: Love – no. No.

ROXANNA: I couldn't do it. Not on Fitzy. He wanted it so badly. He said it would help him get out of his gaf and the whole lot. He's miserable Paula. He's so sad.

PAULA grabs ROXANNA tightly.

I'm sorry. It's still in me.

SCENE TEN

DAN and PAULA arrive home after a daytime date. They look fresh having stepped in out of the cold. DAN catches up with PAULA. He kisses her. She kisses him back, slightly uncomfortable.

DAN: We should head further afield next time.

PAULA: Sure Dolly-er is on the doorstep nearly. Any further and the day'd be gone.

DAN: I mean like a weekend somewhere – something short – my old dear has a cottage in Sligo that she's always trying to get me down to. There's a door needs fixing…

PAULA: Sligo?

DAN: Well it's not Paris, but it's a fine house – just needs a bit of TLC. It has a little pathway down to the beach and fuck all else for miles. No traffic, no noise – no interruptions. Just nothing.

PAULA: Would you not go mad?

DAN: With the quiet? No. Everything just slows down. It's brilliant.

PAULA: You'd only be there and it'd be time to come home. What would be the point?

DAN: A few hours up the motorway is all.

PAULA: It sounds lovely an' all – but sure, I haven't been *anywhere*. Not in ages.

DAN: So?

PAULA: It's not that easy.

DAN: It's a weekend in the sticks.

PAULA: Still.

DAN: I'm not asking you to emigrate.

PAULA: I have to collect the kids.

DAN: I'll get them. I said I would.

PAULA: Right. Thanks.

DAN makes to leave.

DAN: I'd just like to take you somewhere. That's all.

PAULA: And I have responsibilities. I know that's boring but – that's the way it is.

DAN: We'll take the kids with us. Whatever you want.

PAULA: It's not about the kids. Roxanna needs people around her right now.

DAN: You can't watch over her twenty-four-seven.

PAULA: She needs me. End of story.

DAN: She has you wrapped around her little finger.

PAULA: She's a fuckin' teenager – she's pregnant…

The hall door slams.

PAULA: Rox?

DAN: Roll out the cotton wool…

ANTOINETTE enters.

PAULA: What do you want?

ANTOINETTE: Lovely!

DAN: I'll go so.

ANTOINETTE: The accent on 'im. See you love.

DAN: Paula?

PAULA: What?

DAN: I'm going.

ANTOINETTE: I think she heard ya love. It's only the three of us here.

DAN: Yeah. See you.

DAN exits.

ANTOINETTE: I love it when they're moody.

PAULA: What?

ANTOINETTE: What? I got you credit.

PAULA: You don't get your scratch 'til tomorrow?

ANTOINETTE: Found fifty outside Dunnes didn't I? Says I better get rid, before it burnt a hole in me pocket.

PAULA: *Dunnes*? I thought we were going tomorrow?

ANTOINETTE: I got the chance of a lift off…bleedin'…Adeola. And sure you were off gally-vantin'.

PAULA: Off who?

ANTOINETTE: Your wan. Me neighbour. She's downstairs waitin' on me. You wanna see the kids in the back o' the car; four black ones and Stacey…it's like one of those parralolly unilolly *(She means parallel universe.)* yokes… says I to Adeola, *(Speaks as if ADEOLA is deaf.) – space time continuum. –* Says she to me – *I've no idea what your talkin' about* – I says – *I'm not far behind you love.* – ah yeah…she's sound as a pound.

PAULA is a little taken aback.

PAULA: Well, that's good. That's great isn't it.

ANTOINETTE: He got his taxi's worth in the end what?

PAULA: What?

ANTOINETTE: Your man, Dan. Oh that rhymed – I'm at that all day. Me nerves.

Pause.

Dots called over last night.

PAULA: Right?

ANTOINETTE: Yeah. Called over to see Stacey an' all.

PAULA: First time for everything.

ANTOINETTE: Yeah. That's what I says.

PAULA: Musta been no free tables at the snooker hall?

ANTOINETTE: He'd a drink on him.

PAULA: Waster.

ANTOINETTE: Swore on his life it was just one. Crossed his heart. Bein' all merry. All jovial an' all.

PAULA: Yeah?

ANTOINETTE: Gave him his dinner then.

PAULA: You're touched.

ANTOINETTE: Stacey was conked out on the couch.

Pause.

It was him what said it was like old times.

PAULA: Did he now?

ANTOINETTE: *Cast your mind back* – he says.

PAULA: Easy for him to say.

ANTOINETTE: That's what I says.

PAULA: Too easy.

ANTOINETTE: Yeah.

PAULA: Prick.

ANTOINETTE: *Cast your mind back* – he says – *You and me used to make a great team. We used to be somethin' special us.*

PAULA: Cringe.

ANTOINETTE: Big time.

PAULA: One drink me hole.

ANTOINETTE: *Ge'rup out of that* – I says to him – *I've no need to cast me mind back. I've a child as a daily reminder.*

PAULA: D'you say that to him?

ANTOINETTE: And the rest. Up the walls he had me. Spoutin' all sorts of shite. How he loves me an' all. How he just couldn't cope an' all, but that he always thinks about me and all this shite.

PAULA: And *you* gave him his dinner?

ANTOINETTE: Just kept sayin' he loves me.

PAULA: Yeah?

ANTOINETTE: Like, nearly cryin' he was.

Pause.

Over and over – *I love ye.*

PAULA: And what?

ANTOINETTE: Me heart was broken when he was goin'. Kissing me in the garden, like we'd only met or like we were in love or somethin'. Holdin' me into him – kissin' me like his life depended on it.

PAULA: And then leggin' it.

ANTOINETTE: I love him Paula.

PAULA: And when was that ever enough?

ANTOINETTE is crying maybe.

ANTOINETTE: I love him and I hate him – am I mad?

PAULA: Dots is a waster love. Out and out. Just count up the times the fucker had the police at your door, or the bleedin' eyes robbed out o' your head? All for that selfish fucker to satisfy himself. Love isn't nearly enough – and I know you *do*, but you're too good for that shit. You're better than that.

ANTOINETTE gathers herself.

ANTOINETTE: A good slap is what I need.

PAULA: Well that can be arranged. You want a sup a' rosey?

ANTOINETTE: No – I better bleedin' go…your wan downstairs has a bit of temper on her…she warned me not to be too long. Says I – *Adeola, not bein' funny or nothin', but don't lose the run of yourself sweetheart.* She didn't understand me but… sure who would, says you…I better be gone…

PAULA: You don't want to stay for a while then? Egg and chips?

ANTOINETTE: I better go while I've the chance of a lift. I'll never make it on the bus.

PAULA: You're miles away.

ANTOINETTE stands by the door.

ANTOINETTE: I know. *(Pause.)* See ya love.

PAULA is left in the empty flat.

SCENE ELEVEN

ROXANNA and STEPH are at the Wasteland. DAN and PAULA are in PAULA's kitchen. This scene plays out in two places at once. The time is the same in both. It's a sort of split-screen scenario, but all should inhabit the space equally and maybe feel on top of each other. ROXANNA and DAN having played out different scenes will end up in the same scene.

DAN stands awkwardly with a bottle of champagne.

DAN: Where are the kids?

PAULA: *(Points upstairs.)* Sleepover in Jean's.

They share a look. It's their first time alone in the flat.

STEPH: *(About the baby.)* What does it feel like?

ROXANNA: Nothin'.

Pause.

Like an alien. It feels disgutin'.

DAN: I'm sorry.

PAULA: What for?

DAN: For arguing with you yesterday. I don't know.

PAULA: You're touched. You think that was a row? Don't be soft…

He produces a bottle of champagne.

DAN: Well let's call it a row. That way we get to drink this and make up.

PAULA: Oh yeah?

They kiss.

STEPH: Your man Trevor is a lovely kisser.

ROXANNA: What about the Alan one?

STEPH: Fuck him. Your man Trevor drove all the way out here. Took us up the airport.

PAULA and DAN kiss or are close throughout the next section.

ROXANNA: Did you fuck him?

STEPH: Wanted to, but there was other cars there. He got a bit cranky then so I pulled him off to shut him up.

DAN: What?

PAULA: Sorry. I'm…

DAN: It's okay. I'm the same.

PAULA: Really?

DAN: It's been a while.

PAULA laughs.

I mean, I remember how it's done. Don't worry about that; but I'm a bit out of practice.

PAULA: Me too.

DAN: It's okay.

They kiss.

STEPH: This young one messaged me on Facebook the other mornin' calling me a tramp an' all.

ROXANNA: That yoke is for simpletons.

STEPH: Sayin' she's gonna pull the head off me.

ROXANNA: As if.

STEPH: Turns out she's a baby for Trevor.

ROXANNA: That's her tough shit.

STEPH: I says it to him an' all – he's real honest – and he says that the baby is his, but that she tricked him some way and that he doesn't really see her any more.

ROXANNA: So what is she bangin' on about?

STEPH: Some shit about the bond between them. The glue, or somethin'…

ROXANNA: Well…fuck *her.*

STEPH: You will come out with us won't ya? The laugh like.

ROXANNA: If I can ever get passed Paula.

STEPH: Do you want some of this?

ROXANNA: What is it?

STEPH: Breezer – from me Ma's large bottle.

ROXANNA: The last one made me blow chunks.

STEPH: So?

PAULA pulls away from the kiss.

PAULA: Sorry…

DAN: No.

PAULA: Will I get glasses so? *(For the champagne)*

He nods. PAULA moves to get glasses.

DAN: How is Roxanna?

ROXANNA: We were stood talkin' about names.

PAULA: Off chasing that scumbag probably.

PAULA's mood changes.

ROXANNA: He's all set on a girl. Reckons fellas have no sense. I don't care what it is...I'm just glad that I'm havin' it now. Aoife he wants...but I think that sounds real hickey, like Doreen or somethin'. I told him I wanna call her Shannon...or if it's a boy I wanna call him Dale. Fitzy says – what, as in Dale Farm ice-cream? – thinkin' he's funny... so I says – No, like Dale Winton – just to wind him up 'cos he hates gays.

DAN: Paula.

ROXANNA: Anyway, it was great just to see him. I was startin' to forget what he looks like.

PAULA: What?

STEPH: So he wants the baby now?

ROXANNA: Says it's the only thing keeping him goin'.

DAN: You don't know that this kid is no good.

ROXANNA: Says he can't forgive himself over Tommo but.

PAULA: A bit of experience and you can spot them. The signs.

ROXANNA: There's a row about to break. Fitzy is all geared up for a scrap.

DAN: Give him a chance maybe. You never know.

STEPH: What over?

ROXANNA: Nothin'. His dead brother. Broken hearts. Over nothin'.

PAULA: He had his chance.

DAN: There's no value in willing him to fail either.

PAULA: Look out there. All you see is stories of big hearts and broken promises. Fellas that promised us the earth but when it came to it, they were gone.

DAN goes to kiss her apologetically.

Don't.

She leaves the room.

ROXANNA: I says to him – do you love me – an' all.

DAN picks up the champagne bottle.

…looking for a fight, 'cos me head has been wrecked over him…so I stuck that to him – do you love me – and he says…

DAN pops the champagne and drinks from the bottle.

…he says that I'll never be able to imagine the places that he's been in his head. He says but, that even when it got really dark for him, all up in his head…that he could still see me and the baby.

DAN in the kitchen with empty champagne bottle, drunk.

STEPH: I've to leg it. Me auld fella will batter me.

STEPH gets up to leave.

ROXANNA: The only thing keepin' him goin' he says.

STEPH makes to leave.

STEPH: Were you ballin'?

ROXANNA: *(Calling after her.)* Cryin'? Get a life. It *was* like me heart could breathe again but.

ROXANNA and DAN are suddenly in the scene together.

Where's Paula?

DAN: Telly Room.

ROXANNA leaves the room and comes back seconds later.

ROXANNA: She's asleep.

DAN: She'll be back now.

ROXANNA: I said she's asleep you fuckin' eejit. You've to go home now.

DAN: *(Calls.)* Paula?!

ROXANNA: Did yiz fuck?

DAN: What?

ROXANNA: *(Annunciating the word.)* FUCK. Tonight. Did yiz do it?

DAN: Give your mouth a rest.

ROXANNA: I just want to know if you stuck it in me sister, and if you did, which I'd put money on it that you did – 'cos why the fuck else would you be stalking her – so like – I'm just wondering was she any good?

DAN: If you were mine, I'd...

ROXANNA: If I was yours? Your what?

DAN: You want manners put on you.

ROXANNA: A good kickin'?

Pause.

A slap? A good seeing to, is that it?

DAN: It's a strange creature you are.

ROXANNA moves closer to DAN.

ROXANNA: That's it, isn't it? You wanna give me a good seeing to?

Pause.

Fuck me sister and then fuck me. Make a night of it.

DAN: You have your sister and every other clown round here wrapped around your little finger. It's not right. I'd fuckin' have you, *(meaning, "your life")* that's for sure.

ROXANNA: Would you now?

ROXANNA moves closer to DAN. Her mouth is dangerously close to his.

Have me then.

DAN: There's a badness in you.

ROXANNA moves closer to DAN. She lowers her voice as she speaks to him.

ROXANNA: You think I'm sexy, don't you?

DAN: Enough.

ROXANNA: What it must be like to fuck a sixteen-year-old; that's the fantasy in'it?

DAN puts his hand on ROXANNA's waist to hold her or hold her back. He is sitting but she is standing. They are almost at the same level.

DAN: You're only a young one.

ROXANNA: And you a man. Big man like ya.

DAN: I pity you. Getting yourself into all sorts.

ROXANNA: You'd have me. That's what you said.

ROXANNA's lips move towards DAN's. He doesn't stop her.

A good seeing to.

SCENE TWELVE

PAULA is dressed in funeral attire, she leans out the kitchen window talking to JEAN.

PAULA: You won't know yourself with stairs an' all.

JEAN: *(Off-stage.)* It's just one more fuckin' thing to clean what?

PAULA: You said it!

JEAN: Was there many there?

PAULA: Packed to the hilt. Kids mostly. Teenagers.

Pause.

When you off?

JEAN: Two weeks. Can't bleedin' wait.

PAULA: You'll be a new woman on the Southside!

JEAN: I'll be a lady what lunches! *(Change of tone.)* Fuck…I'm burnin' bleedin' toast up here…

ANTOINETTE, ROXANNA and STEPH enter with bags of chips. They are all dressed in black having been to a funeral.

163

ANTOINETTE: You'd swear someone took a shit in that lift. Thank fuck I'm out of this kip, that's all I'll say…

PAULA: I doubt that somehow. Rox, put plates under those chips.

ROXANNA and STEPH put out plates.

STEPH: There was loads of rides there today, wasn't there?

ANTOINETTE: Get a grip, it was full of knackers.

PAULA throws ANTOINETTE a look.

What? D'you want me to lie. It was full of scum. That's the truth of it.

PAULA: You're hardly from royalty yourself.

STEPH: Did you see Bucko?

ANTOINETTE: With the diamond yoke in his ear?

STEPH: Total ride! And Fitzy's older brother was smokin' hot in that suit…and even Fitzy…he's spoken for of course… but still…

ROXANNA is away in her thoughts. PAULA is buttering bread and handing out tea.

ANTOINETTE: You could dip each and every prick at that funeral in gold and I still wouldn't touch them.

PAULA: Don't mind Antoinette. Her taste in men isn't as impeccable as she makes out.

ANTOINETTE: I know a waster when I see one.

PAULA: Even when you're servin' him up his dinner?

ANTOINETTE: You what?

PAULA: *(Meaning the girls.)* Give them a break is all.

ANTOINETTE: 'Sake.

The four girls get stuck into their chips and tea.

PAULA: *(To ROXANNA.)* Were you talkin' to *him*?

ANTOINETTE: I thought you said to leave her be?

PAULA: Shut up you.

STEPH: Was ye?

ROXANNA: His Ma wouldn't shake me hand or nothin'.

ANTOINETTE: Over what?

STEPH: Sure he only told them, didn't he?

ANTOINETTE: There's only so much bad news a mother can take I suppose.

PAULA: *(To ANTOINETTE.)* Are *you* thick?

ANTOINETTE: What? You can't say fuckin' boo in this kip.

ROXANNA: Collared him outside and he was just in bits. Says the young fellas who were after Tommo was textin' him, sayin' they were thrilled he was dead…it saves them a job an' all.

PAULA: Scumbags.

ANTOINETTE: Every last one of them.

ROXANNA: His heart is broken but.

STEPH: He was roarin' cryin' when I saw him. He was in bits.

PAULA: That's the way of it.

STEPH: Up in the back fields last night the brothers had a fire lit. Crowds of youn' fellas out. They'd a car at the bottom of the pitch, the fire climbin' out the windows…and the kids all out collecting wood for them. Palettes and tyres… like ants they were…and the brothers tanked up. Whiskey and vodka from the bottle; the flames catching their tears, and their faces…roaring from the heat; all orange and red…and them not far from the depths of hell.

PAULA: You've a long way to come back from somethin' like that.

STEPH: And the songs they were singin'. Hardshaws huggin' each other and cryin' into the ground. Thugs, screamin' o' the injustice. Wolfe Tones, and the Dubliners. Rebel songs an' all. Songs about freedom, or whatever they could get heads to. Their voices breakin' with the whiskey and the hurt. Broken hearts trun on the fire…and Tommo, they says, dancin' in its glow.

The women are all quiet. Long pause.

PAULA: Your child did that and your life'd be over. She'll never move from that now, that auld one.

ANTOINETTE: Your 'what's his name' was there today.

PAULA: What?

ANTOINETTE: Your man. Down the back he was; throwin' his beady eye over the whole affair.

PAULA: Dan?

ANTOINETTE: Couldn't take his eyes off *you.*

PAULA: At the church?

ANTOINETTE: *(Sarcastic.)* No – at the chipper.

PAULA: I haven't heard a peep from him in days.

ANTOINETTE: He was there alright. Glad Eye O'Hara.

ROXANNA: He was lookin' at me.

Pause.

PAULA: What?

ROXANNA: Dan. He was lookin' at me. In the church.

Pause.

PAULA: Why would he be lookin' at you?

ROXANNA: Why d'ya think?

Long pause. ROXANNA stares at PAULA.

'Cos of Fitzy, I suppose. His brother.

Pause.

ANTOINETTE: It's a bit much all the same. Like, coffin chasin' to get your attention. It's a bit creepy.

ROXANNA: He *is* a creep.

PAULA: Excuse me?

ANTOINETTE: I think he is a bit, is he?

PAULA: What is it *you* don't like about him Antoinette; the fact that he's got a job? Or his ability to hold a conversation?

ANTOINETTE: Desperation more like.

PAULA: Careful now sweetheart; your track record doesn't quite give you license to judge.

ROXANNA: She's only ragin' 'cos no fella will go near 'er.

PAULA: Oh, they'll go near her alright. It's staying near her that's the problem.

ANTOINETTE: Do you think I come down to this dump to take abuse?

PAULA: It's only a dump when it suits ya.

ROXANNA: And you know where the door is...you use it often enough.

ANTOINETTE: I could say the same for you young one.

ROXANNA: I'm family.

ANTOINETTE: Yeah…and blood is not the only thing thicker than water.

PAULA: Are you plannin' on being a gee-bag all day?

ROXANNA: Try all year.

ANTOINETTE: What?

PAULA: I've no time for your bitchin' today.

ANTOINETTE: Who's bitchin'?

PAULA: Either shut your mouth or go on home.

ANTOINETTE: You kickin' me out?

ROXANNA: How did you guess?

PAULA: *(To ROXANNA.)* Shut up you. *(To ANTOINETTE.)* I'm givin' you options.

ANTOINETTE: I get fuckin' more respect from the strangers livin' next to me than I do off me own mates.

PAULA: Here we go –

ANTOINETTE: You'd wanna stop to catch yourself. Holier than bleedin' thou. D'you think my life revolves around whatever it is you think I should or shouldn't be doin' on any given day? It'd serve you well now to remember the times I've held the weight of you in this kitchen, cryin' over Git and the kids, cryin' over your auld fella, god rest his soul, or your aul' one who can't stomach the sight of ye.

PAULA: Give over and sit down.

ANTOINETTE: I've a pain in my hole with you makin' a thick o' me. Sneerin' when you should be supportin' – *Why did you move out so far? Why are you givin' Dots his dinner? Why are you not just like me?* – Because I'm gettin' on with it. I'm doing something. I'm not standin' still – unlike some people.

ANTOINETTE storms out.

PAULA: Is she for real?

The hall door slams.

STEPH: Will I go after her?

PAULA: Leave her.

ROXANNA: She's a guaranteed boomerang.

PAULA turns on ROXANNA.

PAULA: That mouth of yours will be the end of the lot of us. You just don't fuckin' let up sometimes.

Very long pause. The air is thick with tension.

STEPH: *(Whispers to ROX.)* Will we go?

ROXANNA: Paula? *(PAULA doesn't answer)* Paula?

PAULA: What?

ROXANNA: I'm sorry right.

PAULA doesn't answer.

ROXANNA: Paula. Me Ma rang me.

PAULA stops what she's doing.

PAULA: And what?

ROXANNA: Wasn't gonna pick up, but the day that's in it you know?

PAULA: –

ROXANNA: She sounded wrecked on the phone. Like, not cryin' or nothin' but her voice was shakin'…like she was holding on to somethin'…

PAULA: You should go down to her.

ROXANNA: *You* should.

PAULA: You need to tell her what's going on. It's only right.

ROXANNA: She says to me face that I'm disgustin'…like an animal or somethin'…she said that…wanted the priest to make it all better…holy water from the kiddy fiddler for a quick fix. Fuck her.

PAULA looks sad.

PAULA: You can't spend your life avoiding 'er. It's *her* grandchild.

There's a knock at the door. PAULA exits to answer it.

ROXANNA: You talkin' to me or yourself?

STEPH: We goin' out or what? Me head is bleedin' wrecked with the two of yiz.

ROXANNA: Say nothin' 'til I sort it.

PAULA can be heard in the hallway just before she enters.

PAULA: Jason, no! Sit in there now 'til the cartoon is over; we're talkin' in here…

PAULA enters with DAN.

DAN: How are ya?

STEPH smiles and ROXANNA looks away.

PAULA: Dan said hello to yiz.

ROXANNA: Yeah, we're not deaf? Howaya.

STEPH: Hiya.

DAN: How are *you* Roxanna?

PAULA leaves the room.

ROXANNA: Bored, and you?

Slight pause.

DAN: I've been better.

ROXANNA: Haven't we all.

DAN: You haven't been saying anything to upset Paula, have you?

ROXANNA: Like what?

DAN: Like, lies.

STEPH: You're *real* serious mister.

ROXANNA: I don't tell lies.

DAN: I hope that's true.

STEPH: He's a bit of a ride, in' 'e.

ROXANNA: He is I suppose – and a great kisser…I hear.

STEPH: Oh!

PAULA re-enters.

PAULA: What? *(Beat.)* Roxanna, their coats are on. Will you drop them up their nanny Grogan for me? He's takin' them swimmin' of all things.

ROXANNA: No.

STEPH: Come on; we get out of here, it's borin'.

PAULA: As a favour, please.

STEPH: Ask her now if you can stay at mine.

PAULA: What?

STEPH: We were gonna go the pictures an' stay in mine.

PAULA: *(To ROXANNA.)* Can you not go the pictures and come home here?

ROXANNA: I'm not going anywhere. It doesn't matter.

PAULA: Fuck sake. Just go! Jesus Christ! Drop them over and go to Steph's. Go on. Go out. The face on ye. Jaysus.

DAN: *(To ROXANNA.)* I doubt she'll offer twice!

STEPH: Come on now before she changes her mind. Are you mental?

ROXANNA: 'Sake.

ROXANNA gets up to leave. PAULA moves to the hall to gather the kids and STEPH moves with her, leaving ROXANNA and DAN alone.

ROXANNA: I wish you'd ever fuck off.

DAN: You're a nasty piece of work.

PAULA calls from the hall.

PAULA: Roxanna?

ROXANNA: Comin'.

DAN grabs ROXANNA by the arm maybe.

DAN: People get sick of burdens very quickly. Remember that.

PAULA enters.

PAULA: Today please.

ROXANNA: *(Acting all innocent.)* If you want me to come home tonight I will?

PAULA strokes ROXANNA's hair.

PAULA: No love. You chill out. It's been a tough day all round.

ROXANNA looks to DAN, then exits. PAULA and DAN stand close to one another.

DAN: I thought we could talk.

PAULA: I thought we might have seen the last of you.

DAN: Oh?

PAULA: It's been a few days.

DAN: I was flat out with work and that.

PAULA: Oh right.

DAN: Yeah.

PAULA: You were at the church today?

DAN: I had thought to call up and see if the boys needed looking after but then I thought that you all might need some space and then I wasn't sure then, and sure by then

I'd over-thought the whole affair so I just slipped in the back of the church.

PAULA: But no phone-call?

DAN: Yeah. I don't know.

ANTOINETTE is standing at the kitchen door.

ANTOINETTE: Your hall door was open.

PAULA: You come to your senses?

ANTOINETTE: Me phone.

ANTOINETTE retrieves her phone from the table.

PAULA: Sit down there.

ANTOINETTE: It's just that I promised Adeola I'd mind her little brown bunch on account of her going the bingo… so…I…I've to…

PAULA: You're being a wagon.

ANTOINETTE: I get nothin' but abuse in this gaf and you…all this…all the girls are talkin' about you and bleedin'… *(DAN)*

PAULA: So what? Let them talk.

ANTOINETTE: And I get a roasting for offerin' Dots up a fuckin' pork chop.

PAULA: You sat here crying your eyes out 'cos you say you love Dots – but he's a toe rag. Am'n I only trying to protect you.

ANTOINETTE: A hypocrite is what you are…

PAULA: I don't love Dan.

DAN looks uncomfortable.

That's the difference. Get that into your brain.

Pause.

ANTOINETTE: Me Ma says I've to give me own area a chance or I'll never settle in.

PAULA: And what?

ANTOINETTE: Nothin'. I just…I just won't be knockin' about as much…

PAULA: Right. Well…that sounds about right I suppose.

ANTOINETTE: It's just with Stacey an' all. She needs to start makin' her own friends…

PAULA: Yeah.

ANTOINETTE: Yeah…well…anyway…

PAULA: What?

ANTOINETTE: Nothin'.

ANTOINETTE leaves.

PAULA: She'll have changed her mind by tomorrow…that's Antoinette for you…

Pause. DAN looks dejected.

What?

DAN: Fuck sake Paula.

PAULA: *That* was about Antoinette.

DAN: Cut me some slack.

PAULA: I'm sorry. But we're not in love, are we? Like – not yet anyway.

DAN kisses PAULA. He's nervous.

DAN: I don't know.

PAULA: You're going soft.

DAN: It's just Roxanna…

PAULA: I know. I don't know what to be doing with her. How to help her. But I know what's going on in her mind because I was there too, you know? That was *me* too.

DAN: Has she said anything about me?

PAULA: Like what?

Pause.

DAN: Can I tell you something?

PAULA: I can't take any more surprises.

DAN hesitates. He could say anything.

DAN: It's just to say that I don't love you either.

PAULA laughs maybe.

But that I could. I definitely could.

PAULA and DAN kiss passionately. DAN lifts PAULA onto a counter top, they kiss as they undress each other.

SCENE THIRTEEN

The dead of night. PAULA's kitchen. DAN falls over a pile of washing looking for the fridge in the dark. He pours himself a glass of milk by the light of the fridge. There is a thunderous knocking on the door. Startled, DAN flicks on a light. The knocking continues. A voice is heard through the letterbox.

DAN: Paula? You awake there?

DAN leaves the room to answer the door.

DAN enters the kitchen with STEPH in tow. Her lip is cut.

DAN: Sit down there. I'll get some water.

PAULA enters all sleepy. STEPH is crying.

PAULA: What in the name of jaysus?

STEPH: I'm sorry. I couldn't go to me own house. I'd a been kilt. Young one sendin' me messages an' all sayin' she was gonna reef me…

PAULA: Where's Roxanna?

Pause.

STEPH: I was tryin' to phone you but your phone was off.

PAULA: What?

STEPH: They took her to the hospital.

PAULA: A fuckin' pregnant girl as back up. Are you thick?

DAN: Save your energy Paula.

DAN puts his hand on PAULA's shoulder. She pulls away.

PAULA: She's only fuckin' a baby herself.

Sounds rise; an ambulance, a telephone. Lights go dark.

SCENE FOURTEEN

The stage is empty. ROXANNA and STEPH are the first to inhabit their space at the muck. PAULA enters the kitchen. She moves around it, folding washing and checking on the kids out the window. STEPH and ROXANNA sit apart saying nothing.

PAULA: Aaron…Aaron… Take that roller skate off him…'cos it's dangerous…Jason… *(Paula laughs)* I'm not messin' with ya…put the boot down or I'll streal ya…yiz are not funny, the two of yiz…

DAN enters.

DAN: Your door was open.

PAULA comes in from the window.

PAULA: *(Signalling the window.)* The boys…

DAN: How are ya?

PAULA: Getting on with it. You?

DAN: I'm okay. I slipped the lads some sweets there on the way up – young Jason said you'd string me up for it.

PAULA: They won't eat their dinner.

DAN: Well I made them promise, didn't I?

PAULA: Right.

DAN: A man-to-man kind of thing.

PAULA: God help us.

Pause.

DAN: Did you get my messages?

PAULA: What?

DAN: I was feeling like a bit of a desperado, calling and calling, but I didn't wanna just drive over in case you needed your space – Roxanna or whatever. But I left a tonne of messages for you – and some of them quite good actually – so I'm hoping you got them. It's just I never heard back and it's been a fortnight.

PAULA: It's been hectic.

DAN: I decided that two weeks was the threshold of politeness for a house call. So here I am.

PAULA: We've been up to ninety is the thing.

DAN: I got that part – yeah. But in fairness I think hectic is just another flavour in this place so it's no excuse really.

PAULA: Do you want tea or something?

DAN: No Paula. I don't want tea. Jesus.

PAULA: Are you gonna stand there, or…?

DAN: I don't know…

DAN sits down.

Things went okay in the hospital after? You should have let me stay. I wanted to.

PAULA: I could kick meself for not seein' that comin'.

DAN: They're teenagers. It's what they do.

PAULA: Mm.

DAN: How could you have known?

PAULA: I took my eye off the ball.

DAN: That's rubbish.

PAULA: It's what my old dear said when she arrived. She couldn't help herself – it wasn't in her to let things be, even for one night.

DAN: So she went in? I knew she would. It's family.

PAULA: Oh she was thrilled. Beside herself she was. Rubbing a set of rosary beads like some sort of Bond villain. Oh she came in alright – and just in nick of time according to her. The whole scenario was like a living, barely breathing example of everything she'd ever warned us about. Violence and teenage pregnancy – all we were missing was some needle marks and she'd a' had a hat trick.

DAN: Mother's love being right. You gotta let that slide.

PAULA: *I* took my eye off the ball.

DAN: But Roxanna – the baby – Steph?

PAULA: All alive – yes.

DAN: That's good.

PAULA: It's just with all these roads meetin', you know – at the once. It's too much.

DAN: I'm a bit dense when it comes to cryptic crosswords. Do you wanna flesh that one out for me?

PAULA: Your timing.

DAN: Oh fuck off. It's like you've no idea what you're even saying. If you like someone, you just go for it. There's never going to be a good time for you.

PAULA: If you like someone?

DAN: What's the other option – deny yourself a shot at happiness? 'Til when? And what if there are no more chances when you finally decide that the timing suits ya?

Pause.

PAULA: I went into a church yesterday.

DAN: –

PAULA: It's thick really. I don't believe in god or any of it, and priests make me sick to me core…but I dunno – habit, or…peace and quiet…something.

I went in anyway and there was a rehearsal for a communion on – a little girl's school – all excited – racin' through their prayers and the cocky ones stickin' their tongues out for the imaginary bread.

Gorgeous, the lot o' them.

I sat at the back; the stations of the cross on all sides.

I'm right beside number four – *Jesus meets his mother.*
And she looks a kind sort Mary – like we know she was prone to a few lies – but a kind cut to her – and I get to thinkin' about my Ma, and how she believes all this shit – these fairytales – they're not even stories to her; they all happened! Each and every one.

And all this while Rox is around the corner in the hoppo… and I get to thinkin' about our Da – and what a kind sort he was – all gentle and soft – and I'm crying then, you know – 'cos of the event itself – Rox and Steph; the baby – and also because I hadn't clapped eyes on my mother in a year – and that was a shock in itself…or…me emotions were…

And I wished then that the Da was around to look after all this.

You know when you miss someone so much that it's like someone's ringin' your heart out like a dish cloth?

And – er – yeah – it occurs to me too that er – you know – you remember people how you want to, don't ya? Good or bad. 'Cos our Da, you know – he was the kindest fella to us – perfect he was – but he was cruel to me Ma – yeah – he was a violent sort I suppose you'd say – just not to us.

And she said it to me the other night.

Like fair balls to her, because the woman is a shite communicator – but yeah…she says like…at some whacky hour of the mornin' – she says that she resents us for lovin' him more than her.

Pause.

And you can't argue with that. The fella used to hurt her. And we were never around for her.

And she says that the rosary beads and the happy clappy water give her hope – yeah – they give her something to believe in. And you definitely can't argue with that, because *we* – she said it herself – we – me and Rox – we've given her nothing to believe in.

DAN: You'll make it up to her – I know you will.

PAULA: It got me thinkin' though – you know – what do I have to believe in. If I don't have things and I don't have what she has – blind belief and faith. What do I have?

DAN: Have me Paula. I'm here.

PAULA: That is what I said. In my head –

DAN: – Yes. Have faith in me.

PAULA: I thought – *That man. That good man. I can believe in him.* – We all need something –

DAN: – Yes.

PAULA: But it was one of those nights you know – in the hospital – with the Ma there and little Rox beside herself with the grief of the baby that she thinks she's lost – and we get to talking – three women – you can imagine it – and we all offered up our hurt and our hearts and many many tears and there was love and anger all swimmin' in the same broth – and it all came out that night – as the thunder hugged the windows – we three emptied our souls.

DAN knows what's coming.

DAN: Right.

PAULA: Yeah.

Pause.

You kissed my sister.

DAN: She – kissed me. I didn't kiss her back. I swear to god.

PAULA: Sixteen years old.

DAN: She kissed me Paula, and I stopped her. And I never said because I'm a fuckin' idiot – and of course I should have – I should have – I could kick myself – but she – ah fuck it – it's twisted – she made me believe that you'd choose her version of events over mine – ye know – choose her over me. But I stopped her – and it's been eating me alive ever since.

PAULA: I believe you.

DAN: Don't play with me Paula.

PAULA: She told me everything. The same story. Blow by blow. I made her. Once she'd started I wouldn't let up. Balling she was. Crying her heart out over what she'd done to me. Piece by piece.

DAN: Okay.

PAULA: Inconsolable. Couldn't believe that she could do that to me.

DAN: But me?

PAULA: I just can't have this in my house.

DAN: Paula, come on.

PAULA: I just don't need the distraction. Do you understand?

DAN: We're only starting. We can move on from this. A drunken episode – an overexcited teenager. We can move on.

PAULA: I can't have this in my house. It's too much.

Pause.

And I can't get rid of Roxanna – Me blood. I won't do that.

DAN makes to leave.

DAN: Would you even know how to be happy Paula? If it landed in your kitchen, would you know how to let your guard down? Would your heart recognise happiness? Or is it too far gone for that?

He exits.

SCENE FIFTEEN

PAULA's kitchen. STEPH and ROXANNA sit at the table – they should seem younger than ever. PAULA hovers around.

ROXANNA: Paula?

PAULA: What?

ROXANNA: Did you hate being pregnant?

PAULA: No, why?

STEPH: I would. I'd hate the gettin' fat.

PAULA: You wouldn't. Your mind does be elsewhere.

ROXANNA: Do you get used to it?

PAULA: No. But you move with it. You take it as it comes.

ROXANNA: And what else?

PAULA: You worry…

ROXANNA: Yeah?

STEPH: Do you be cryin' an' all?

PAULA: You'll worry about the baby.

STEPH: It's heart and it's health an' all?

PAULA: All of it. You'll stay awake at night wondering what's going on with your body and if you're doing all the things you should be doing, like not drinkin' or smokin' or eatin' greasy crap or anything like that. Its health yeah, you'll be thinking of its health a lot. But you'll have other worries as well.

ROXANNA: Yeah?

PAULA: Like you'll worry about Fitzy. You'll think everything through at the weirdest hours. The night time. The dead of night. The time when no one else is awake or thinking, you'll be thinking of Fitzy. Will he be there for me? Stick around like? Will he make a good father? Will we have enough? Will a baby turn him off me? Me body…and all of that. The crying. The sleepless nights. Shitty nappies. Some fellas are not able for that.

ROXANNA: Fitzy is. He will be.

STEPH: You won't know 'til you pop but.

PAULA: But you'll also be saying…in the back of your head… you'll be saying…and you won't let yourself think it out properly…you'll push this to the back, but you'll be thinkin': do I *want* to spend me life with this fella? Like, is this me now? Is this the lot?

ROXANNA: And do you be cryin' an' all?

STEPH: What about cravin's? D'you be eatin' coal an' all?

PAULA: Never had coal now…but I put tomato sauce all over ice-cream once.

ROXANNA: Fuckin' hell Paula!

STEPH: Would you do it again Paula?

PAULA: Don't know love. Never say never, you know that way?

ROXANNA: With the right fella you would.

PAULA: Would I?

ROXANNA: I think you would Paula. If you loved him, and he
loved you and it felt right…you would.

STEPH: Did it feel right the other times?

ROXANNA: It must have done.

PAULA: It did yeah.

ROXANNA: It must have.

PAULA: But feelin' that, that feelin'…it's not enough either…
you know? Later on…it's not enough…you…you never
stop worrying. You tie yourself in knots. Hate yourself
sometimes. Get all tangled up with the world askin' why
did I bring life into this? Why was I so selfish? How can I
look after these kids? And for yourself as well, ye know:
who is gonna look after me? Yeah…you have to ask
yourself…who is gonna look after me?

STEPH: I've to go home. Me Da has me on a curfew. Says in
all seriousness that he wants me tagged with one of those
electric bracelets.

PAULA: He knows you're not a bad young one.

STEPH: Thanks Paula.

STEPH makes to leave.

See you in school on Monday?

ROXANNA: Unfortunately.

STEPH: Breslin is gonna piss when he see's you. See yiz.

STEPH leaves. ROXANNA calls after her.

ROXANNA: Breslin wants puttin' on that sex offender's list.

PAULA: You all set?

ROXANNA: Me Ma said, *take a taxi*, and she'll pay for it.

PAULA: She's spoilin' ye.

ROXANNA: She's bein' all weird. All carin' an all.

PAULA: And Fitzy?

ROXANNA: Don't talk to me about that young fella. He's like a bleedin' lap dog. Between text messages and teddy bears. Like, give a girl some space to breathe.

PAULA: That's fellas for ye!

ROXANNA grabs her bag from the hallway.

ROXANNA: Fellas nothin' – Fitzy'll get a kick in the nuts if he keeps it up. I'm an independent woman me.

PAULA stands and stares at ROXANNA.

I'm scared Paula.

PAULA: I know. But you did the right thing you know?

ROXANNA: Yeah? Why's that?

PAULA: 'Cos you'd a mind of your own and that's a rare thing.

PAULA and ROXANNA embrace. A long loving hug. ROXANNA makes to leave.

Go easy on 'er yeah?

ROXANNA: I'll be like a sister of the immaculate conception. You wait and see Paula.

ROXANNA leaves.

See ya.

She's gone.

PAULA: Love you.

PAULA moves around her kitchen slowly. She touches surfaces, opens the fridge, closes it. She packs a load into the washing machine. She grabs a cloth and starts cleaning surfaces. JEAN's voice is heard offstage:

JEAN: *(Off-stage.)* Paula?

PAULA pauses for a long time, taking in her kitchen.

JEAN: Paula?

PAULA opens her window.

PAULA: What?

JEAN: That's me…

PAULA: What love?

JEAN: *(Barely audible.)* I said…that's me…

PAULA: Speak up – I can't hear ya.

JEAN: I said that's me love. I'm off… The last van load just left. I called down to ya earlier but you was out.

This is it.

This is the end.

PAULA takes a sharp intake of breath.

Whaaaat?

PAULA fights back tears maybe.

PAULA: Nothin' love. I'll miss yiz is all.

JEAN: Right back at you sister.

PAULA is left onstage alone. The lights fade.

Finish.

I ♥ ALICE ♥ I
BY
AMY CONROY

I ♥ Alice ♥ I

Written and directed by: Amy Conroy
Developed with: Clare Barrett

Cast:	ALICE KINSELLA	Amy Conroy
	ALICE SLATTERY	Clare Barrett

Additional credits listed below as applicable for each production.

2010 Dublin Fringe Festival
22–25 September 2010
Produced by: HotForTheatre
Venue: The New Theatre

RTÉ Radio 1
8pm on 22 May 2011
Presented by: Drama on One and HotForTheatre
Producer: Kevin Brew

Dublin Theatre Festival 2011 ReViewed
Autumn 2011
A showcase of successful Irish productions restaged in partnership with Culture Ireland and Irish Theatre Institute, touring venues around Dublin.
Designer: Ciarán O'Melia
Producer: Maria Fleming

Venues and Dates:
Civic Theatre 29 September–1 October
Project Arts Centre (Cube) 4–9 October
Draíocht Studio 10–12 October
Pavilion Theatre, Dún Laoghaire 14–15 October

Abbey Theatre
30 January–18 February 2012
Sound Designer: Jack Cawley
Set and Lighting Designer: Ciarán O'Melia
Producer: Maria Fleming

This show is fictional but presented as a documentary piece.

Both of the 'Alices' have been working with the director for nearly a year. They have been questioned and interviewed, directly and indirectly, alone and together. It has been a balancing act, keeping them happy and onboard.
They are not actors, so performing live is a huge challenge for them. They are nervous and, at times, vaguely reluctant.

The 'play' between the actors portraying the Alices is the unwritten script. The little prompts, encouraging glances, reluctance to speak on some subjects, light bolstering touches, stuttering, getting lost, forgetting words, the undeniable nerves.

The director and set designer will try to make the Alices comfortable on stage. They will have a table and chairs from the Alices' house centre stage, along with other bits and pieces (books, tea/coffee, cake, record player, postcards, photos, religious statue). There are obvious marks on the stage floor so the Alices know where their marks are.

The walls are covered with notes and transcripts from the interviews and the making of the show. There is a 'map' of the show, and a script, on the back wall… The Alices refer to it and can use it if they get lost or stuck.

Music plays: 'I Only Want to Be with You', Dusty Springfield.

ALICE SLATTERY and ALICE KINSELLA enter the stage. They are both nervous, this is obvious. They stand awkwardly on their downstage mark and look at the audience. Music fades.

A. SLATTERY: Walk on, and stand facing the audience.

A. KINSELLA: Look at the audience.

A. SLATTERY: Look left, look right. Take them all in.

A. KINSELLA: They are not your enemies, they are your friends.

A. SLATTERY: There is nothing to be nervous about.

A. KINSELLA: Breath. Smile. Relax. *(They attempt this, look uncomfortable, and fail.)*

A. SLATTERY: Just say the words as you said them to me. As we rehearsed them.

A. KINSELLA: If you get lost or stuck, stop, find your place on the map and carry on.

A. SLATTERY: Have fun.

A. KINSELLA: Enjoy yourself.

A. SLATTERY: Don't panic.

A. KINSELLA: Have fun.

They glance at each other; one subtly nods at the other to start.

A. KINSELLA: She tuts loudly when people drop litter. *(A. SLATTERY tuts.)*

A. SLATTERY: She expects people to move out of her way.

A. KINSELLA: I often say, 'ahh that's bass.'

A. SLATTERY: I watch *Nationwide*, and I think Michael Ryan is handsome.

A. KINSELLA: I like Turkish Delight…and rice pudding.

A. SLATTERY: I like a crease down the middle of my slacks.

A. KINSELLA: She eats marmalade on cheddar cheese.

A. SLATTERY: I wear 'stockings', and call a 'dint' a 'dint'… A 'dent' a 'dint' *(Confuses herself.)*…I say 'dint'.

A. KINSELLA: I always finish the first layer before moving down to the second.

A. SLATTERY: She has a post office account.

A. KINSELLA: I boil tea towels on the cooker.

A. SLATTERY: I consider chocolate biscuits a luxury.

A. SLATTERY: I have never, and will never have my hair set. We don't go for 'spins'; we count our own change and carry our own bags. We shop for groceries, not 'messages'.

A. KINSELLA: We normally go to Superquinn on Sundrive, better fresh fruit and veg. Failing that, Marks in Dundrum, but that's really an excuse for two packets of Percy Pigs and maybe the cinema, provided we bought nothing frozen. I made that mistake once and had Ben and Jerry's all over the boot. So I don't really know why we ended up in Crumlin Shopping Centre.

A. SLATTERY: The phone rang.

A. KINSELLA: Oh yes, Alice said she had a headache and then I got a phone call from my niece, which delayed us. At that stage traffic would have been a nightmare, so we figured Crumlin Shopping Centre was closer.
I was hungry and we had nothing nice.

A. SLATTERY: I had made spaghetti bolognese the night before, there was plenty left. It was raining and *Who Do You Think You Are?* was on at nine. I really didn't want to go shopping.

A. KINSELLA: I don't really like her spaghetti bolognese.

A. SLATTERY: I didn't really have a headache.

A. KINSELLA: We were cranky.

A. SLATTERY: *(Sharp look.)* I very seldom lose my temper with her, but when she speaks for me it makes me very cross.

A. KINSELLA: *(Sighs.)* Well, I was cranky. Alice is not normally moody, so I knew her headache must have been a bad one. I was trying to ease the tension and make her laugh by deliberately mispronouncing things: fajitas, 'Dolmyo' sauce, salmon darnes…

Making Alice laugh is one of my favourite things; her eyes close up and sort of change colour, they go from green to turquoise…from matt to gloss. I always say she has 'Dulux Weather Shield' eyes…beautiful, but tough.

The ice melted when I put the *(Mispronounce deliberately.)* Jalapeno relish in the trolley…

A. SLATTERY: *(Smirking/correcting.)* Jalapeno… *(Mispronounces it, both ALICEs laugh, she corrects herself.)*

A. KINSELLA: …And she smiled, a real smile, warm. I love that, when she smiles in spite of herself.

I winked at her just to be cheeky and she laughed. There it was. I couldn't help it, before I realized what I was doing… I kissed her, on the lips. By the marmalade.

A. SLATTERY: She kissed me! She kissed me in the soup and canned goods aisle in Tesco. Jesus Christ.

A. KINSELLA: I had a mild panic, I shocked myself. We've always been very discreet about things like that.

A. SLATTERY: Very, very discreet.

A. KINSELLA: It's easier I suppose, safer that way. No backlash. We were always aware of what could happen, we could lose our jobs.

A. SLATTERY: Public displays of affection. Our niece calls them PDAs.

A. KINSELLA: I kind of stunned myself; I didn't realize that I was doing it till I had done it. I scanned the aisle for stares or blushes, there were none. The place was fairly quiet and it looked like we got away with it. We skitted and laughed for ten minutes, with panic and relief. Alice was puce. We felt kind of liberated so I put a chocolate gateau into the trolley.

A. SLATTERY: I lost the car keys; I'm always losing things. There's a little tear in the lining of my handbag, and they had slipped inside. I found fifty euro in there once so I should have thought to look, but I wasn't thinking straight, I was flustered and a little all over the place. I was sure I left them on the deli counter. Alice said she'd wait for me by the door; I'm always amazed at her patience.

A. KINSELLA: I was still thinking about the kiss, so I told Alice I'd meet her at the exit.

A. SLATTERY: The two ladies that cut the ham looked for them, I searched the flat fridge with all the 'fancy' cheese, anything other than Kilmeadan is fancy these days apparently, and a manager humoured me and checked to see if I had dropped them by the tills.
I didn't recognize the woman Alice was talking to when I came back, but they seemed to be having a serious conversation, she wrote her number down, and was off before I reached them.

A. KINSELLA: 'Please don't panic,' she said, 'but I saw you two in Tesco. I saw your kiss and it was beautiful,' Oh dear God I thought! 'Bear with me, I'm not being weird, I'm an actor and a writer, I've wanted to make a show for a long time and you are exactly what I've been looking for. Can we sit and talk? I'd love to invite you to lunch or coffee? Here's my number, please think it over. I'm not mocking you, there's no ulterior motive, I promise.'
She saw us, I was mortified. Alice was going to kill me.

A. SLATTERY: Alice was flushed and her eyes were kind of electric, I can always tell when something has caught her attention. She was distracted, I told her that someone had handed the keys in to customer service; I don't know why I lied.

A. KINSELLA: I tried to explain the encounter, the conversation, to Alice in the car on the way home, I think I was rambling; I couldn't articulate what I was thinking… I didn't really know what I was thinking. At first I thought the girl was having me on. Obviously she wanted something, but I couldn't figure out what her angle was? Where was the catch, what was she up to? If I'm honest… something about her, something about what she said caught my attention. I believed her, I think?

Both ALICEs move back, ALICE SLATTERY prompts ALICE KINSELLA subtly; they check the 'map' on the wall. They give each other a reassuring glance.

A. KINSELLA: I'm Alice, and this is Alice.

A. SLATTERY: I'm Alice, and this is Alice.

A. KINSELLA: She's Alice Slattery.

A. SLATTERY: I'm Alice Slattery, and she's Alice Kinsella.

A. KINSELLA: I'm Alice Kinsella.

A. SLATTERY: I was born on the 27th of May 1948.

A. KINSELLA: I was born on the 20th of October 1946.

A. SLATTERY: She's two years older.

A. KINSELLA: I'm one year and seven months older. This doesn't really bother me.

A. SLATTERY: *(Pleased.)* It bothered her when she turned forty.

A. KINSELLA: It bothered me when I turned forty.

A. SLATTERY: And fifty.

A. KINSELLA: And fifty.

A. SLATTERY: And sixty.

A. KINSELLA: And sixty.

A. SLATTERY: And other times in between. It annoys her.

A. KINSELLA: It doesn't annoy me.

They both sit.

A. SLATTERY: *(Discreetly nods head, as if to say it does bother her.)* We threw her a surprise party for her sixtieth, I invited all our family, friends and extended family. They were all really excited about it and made a huge effort, decorating the restaurant, blowing up balloons, Mary even made the cake. I didn't have the heart to tell them that Alice already knew about it. I told her what we were planning. I knew she'd be irritated with the idea of it, but that she'd love it in the long run. And I wanted her to seem pleased after all the effort that was put in. So I gave her a month's notice, four weeks, to come around to the idea and work on her 'surprised' look. We had a great night, and Alice was spoiled rotten. She cried at the speeches, it was adorable.

A. KINSELLA: Alice doesn't seem to mind getting older, she's always been way more philosophical than me. Even when we were younger she had an old head on young shoulders, she was an old soul, sensible. Or so she'd have you believe. I think I'm a little rash, and can seem a little impetuous next to her. She can be very cautious and considered. We had to sit down for a week with pen and paper to weigh out the pros and cons of 'making the big switch'… From electricity to Airtricity. Lists, pros and cons…that's how all her decisions are made. It makes total sense, but… Lord almighty.

A. SLATTERY: Alice makes me move more than I would naturally, if that makes sense? She forces me to act fast and do things that, given the chance to think about, I probably wouldn't dare. Shouldn't dare. She is adventurous. She organises our holidays so they are jam-packed, fun from start to finish. Travelling is our luxury, our extravagance. I think my favourite trip was Greece, the scenery, the relaxed way of life, the food, the retsina, and the sandy beaches. No one bothering us, it was like pressing pause on the world. My least favourite trip was India, India, of all places. I really didn't like it. I don't understand why anyone would go on holidays to the third world. I needed a holiday to recover from my holiday.

A. KINSELLA: Alice fell off a camel years ago in Rajasthan, India. She wanted to go to Bali, but I wanted adventure. So it was kind of my fault. That day she wanted to see some palace but I wanted to do the camel ride across the sand dunes, I was having a Lawrence of Arabia moment.

I had bought a blue scarf and one of the guides had tied it for me... Alice tied her scarf herself and she looked like a pirate. It was one of the funniest things I have ever seen. Anyway, we were given brief camel riding instructions and then we were off. Something must have spooked Alice's camel because he took off like a shot, the saddle yoke came undone and she started to slide down the side of the camel, it looked like she was sitting horizontally. She landed with a thump and a billow of sand. The poor thing. There were about ten Americans sniggering into their sleeves... I'm embarrassed to admit that I laughed too. It was the look on her face that was funniest, total panic and absolute mortification. She laughed it off and got straight back on, I was so proud of her. She had to sit on a cushion for the next two weeks. We only went to palaces after that.

A. SLATTERY: I worked in the bank.

A. KINSELLA: I was a clerk in the National Gallery.

A. SLATTERY/ KINSELLA: Both retired.

A. SLATTERY: I could tell that Alice was quietly intrigued by the girl from the shopping centre. I was less convinced. She didn't say much about it but it was obviously on her mind. I can read her like a book. I kept catching her watching me doing mundane things. I finally cracked while doing dishes...
'Stop staring at me Alice.'

A. KINSELLA: One of us will die,

A. SLATTERY: she said.

A. KINSELLA: ...and then where will we be? When we're gone we're gone, that's it. What will we have actually achieved?

A. SLATTERY: I've never really wanted to bang drums, cause a scene or draw attention. I just wanted to live in peace, quietly. I thought that's what Al wanted too.
Fine, ring the girl; see what she has to say.

A. KINSELLA: She said.

A. KINSELLA: *(Stands.)* Pros
    Fun.
    Exciting.
    Challenging.
    Insightful.
    Triumphant.
    Beautiful.
    A testimonial, we will be seen. *(Sits.)*

A. SLATTERY: *(Stands.)* Cons
    Damaging.
    Boring.
    Indulgent.
    Frightening.
    Invasive.
    Insidious.
    Dangerous, we will be seen. *(Sits.)*

A. KINSELLA: I rang her and she invited us to lunch. Alice sulked.

A. SLATTERY: She went all out, very posh.

A. KINSELLA: She made antipasti of mozzarella, chilli and lemon crostini, aubergine and mint bruschette and a cous cous salad.

A. SLATTERY: I was impressed.

A. KINSELLA: We knew she meant business, we were expecting a ham sandwich.

A. SLATTERY: For afters we had lemon drizzle cake and espresso *(Mispronounced 'expresso')*. I love cake, any cake.

A. KINSELLA: She explained what she wanted to do; she wanted to make a show. She was a little unsure about the whole thing herself, she was only discovering it, but she wanted to make it with us.
    There was a lot of fun, flattery and attention. By the end of lunch I felt important, like our story mattered.
    We didn't commit to anything but discussing it and that we'd ring her in a day or two.

A. SLATTERY: She proposed that we should meet every week, sometimes together, sometimes separately, and she would ask us a series of questions. She was interested in memories, opinions and stories. A 'getting to know you' kind of a thing. She promised that there would be no judgement, and that if we didn't want to discuss something then we wouldn't have to.

A. KINSELLA: 'The more mundane the better'…

A. SLATTERY: …she said.
Well, why in God's name would we want to do that? I'd be mortified. Making myself vulnerable, ridiculous, God, the embarrassment? What would people say?
I've always cherished what Alice and I have, talking about it would feel cheap. Like we're belittling it or giving it away. Who in their right minds would want to know about this?
Anonymity. I used to crave it.

She stands and moves to her mark downstage right.

When Alice and I first started seeing each other, the anonymity and illicitness was delicious, it was our private world, our utopia. Unfortunately that can't be sustained, eventually you have to start letting people in, that's life. Then come the questions. Are you gay now? But you were married? Are you sure, maybe you're just lonely? Aren't you two just best friends?

A. KINSELLA: 'Isn't it nice for them to have each other,' 'You'd never think it by looking at them.'

A. SLATTERY: With every person I meet I have to decide, will I remain invisible or will I tell them? How do I tell them? Do I need to tell them? I'm embarrassed to admit that I've lied about us regularly over the years. It's a horrible guilt, denying the person you love, denying the life you've built together.
We don't fly the rainbow flag; we've never publicly danced or kissed…well, not until that day in Tesco's.
We seem to blend.

I decided not to be a part of the show, the interviews or the process. If Alice wanted to do it she had to do it without me.

A. KINSELLA: *(Stands.)* I was really disappointed in Alice when she said no, but it was her choice.

So I began without her. Coffees, meetings, tape recorders and cameras, 'what have I gotten myself into?'

I wanted to back out, but I didn't want to give Alice the soot of it.

She kept asking me what we were talking about, afraid we were talking about her. Well of course we were, we were talking about me, my life, my past and she's a big part of that.

I wouldn't give her any details. If you're in you're in, if you're not you're not, simple as that. I knew that would drive her mad. *(Sits.)*

A. SLATTERY: The secrecy of it, I think Alice thought she was changing the world. I was annoyed at her, for doing this, for wanting to do it. We didn't talk properly for about a week, it was the elephant in the room. I finally gave in about a month into it and got involved, primarily to keep an eye on what she was saying. I'm still not sure that it was the right choice.

A. KINSELLA: She left the process three times. Once over the title.

A. SLATTERY: It was almost called, *Old People Don't Smell.* That's just insulting.

A. KINSELLA: It was a joke, t'was never going to be called that. Being called 'old' didn't sit well with me though. I never really feel old. Sometimes I give myself a fright. When I see me accidentally, like in the window of a passing car, or in a mirror in a shop, one of those mirrors at a funny angle…where you look into one and look for yourself in another. And it takes my breath away. Is that me? Is that what people see? An old lady? An older lady?

A. SLATTERY: People don't see the life I've lived. They don't know that I've breathed in the misty air overlooking Niagara Falls. They don't know that I've been kissed in a hot air balloon, the type of kiss that made me blush. They don't see the 'me' that buried my husband. They just see an unassuming older lady. Well, I don't like scones, and I don't drink tea. I wonder would that shock them?

A. KINSELLA: *(Stands and moves to her mark downstage left.)* I am two years older than my sister, Mary, and we are polar opposites. I adore her and her family, we're very close. But when we were young it was a different story. She was always around, annoying me. I think that is a prerequisite for younger sisters.

A. SLATTERY un-pins an old photo from the set and passes it to the audience.

She and her little friend used to follow me everywhere. I remember making them laugh, especially Mary's friend, she was a quiet yet giddy girl...but once she started laughing that was the end if it, she was off, Mary was off and sure then I was off...
She was a small, skinny girl with big eyes. She was quick to flush, her hands were always pink and she was prone to cold sores.
She lived one street over, and was a constant in our house, part of the family. Her name was Alice Connolly, now Alice Slattery. I have known her all my life and, in some way, shape, or form I have loved her all my life.

A. SLATTERY: No. 44, The Kinsella's. A home away from home.

Music fades in, The Kinks, 'Sunny Afternoon'. A. KINSELLA acknowledges the music.

A. KINSELLA: I left Ireland for London when I was twenty. I was running away really.
Running away from myself. The funny thing about running away is that you bring yourself with you. I had done a secretarial course here and I had dreams of becoming a

journalist. I wanted to write, I wanted excitement, I wanted to live. I really believed that I was going to pen 'the great novel of our times'. Not really something I'd easily confess to.

A. SLATTERY: She was tall, cheeky and funny.

A. KINSELLA: I moved into horrible digs in Kilburn, into a house that smelled of boiled cabbage and damp sofa.

A. SLATTERY: Bossy, I remember her being very bossy.

A. KINSELLA: I always remember Dublin seeming black and white and London was in Technicolor. I started as a receptionist in a doctor's office and after a few months I saw an advertisement for a secretarial position in a prominent London newspaper.

A. SLATTERY: When Alice was in London she worked for *The Times*. She won't tell you that.

A. KINSELLA: It paid the bills, but really it could have been in any office, anywhere…

A. SLATTERY: The Times.

A. KINSELLA: …At the time I believed that it was my big break. I submitted an idea or two over my years there, but they really weren't having any of me. It makes me feel a bit foolish or naive now when I think about it.

A. SLATTERY: 'But I, being poor, have only my dreams;
            I have spread my dreams under your feet;
            Tread softly because you tread on my dreams.'

She had her spirit crushed a little, or bruised maybe. She still writes though.

A. KINSELLA: It was there that I met Louise. She was a secretary too. She was one of the funniest people I had ever encountered. For some bizarre reason she 'adopted' me, so to speak. Maybe she recognised herself in me, I can't see any other reason. If there was a party or a shindig happening anywhere in London, she and her pals knew about it, and we were there.

A. SLATTERY: *(Making herself busy. Self-conscious.)* Coffee?

A. KINSELLA: Please. Decaff. Thanks.

> They were kind of an arty, eccentric crowd, and I adored
> them. Mrs. Murphy, my landlady, detested them; she said
> they were 'dirty pagans' and that I should 'stay well clear of
> them.' Of course Louise was delighted when I told her this,
> and it was her idea for us to take a flat together. Louise,
> Jen, another friend of hers, and I shared a two-bedroom
> flat, a disgusting communal loo, and all our clothes.
> Louise was different, she wore her skirts too short, she
> smoked too much, she never really ate, she drank vodka
> neat…and she went to bed with women.
> I was shocked, amazed by this. I had never heard anybody
> say this; admit to it, like it was a real thing. No pretending
> or denying, she was a free spirit.
>
> You see, I was always on the outside, looking in at life,
> trying to figure out how to be a part of it. Frantically
> grabbing at every new thought or idea, thinking that it
> must hold the answer, but never really understanding the
> question. I think of it as a 'wanting', I wanted something
> but I had no idea what that 'something' was.
> One wet and thundery Friday night, Louise and I straggled
> home from the pub. We had drunk too much vodka on
> empty stomachs. We listened to 'Whiter Shade of Pale'
> over and over, and I finally figured it out. I figured out the
> question and the answer in one fell swoop.
> Louise and I went to bed together that night. It felt natural,
> it felt right.

A. SLATTERY: Cake?

A. KINSELLA: Thanks.

> It sounds idyllic, but believe me, it wasn't. It was a bloody
> soap opera.
>
> *Visibly gathering herself, drawing a big breath.*
>
> Louise and I were lovers, but Jen and Louise used to be
> lovers and were still occasional lovers. Jen had a boyfriend
> who loved her, she loved Louise, and she liked me. Louise
> had other lovers; I was unaware of this and believed we

were exclusive. Jen and I, in a bid to hurt Louise became lovers. Louise was hurt. Then Jen and I actually started to have feelings for each other, but she still had a boyfriend who loved her. He was hurt. Louise slept with him. Jen was hurt. Jen and Louise were sleeping together. I was hurt. This went on for the best part of two years, and in that time there were other lovers. Eventually Jen and I agreed to make a go of it, Jen broke up with the boy, I broke up with Louise, Jen broke up with Louise. Louise was…fine actually. She began seeing Fran. Fran used to go out with Jen's ex-boyfriend. It was all very incestuous really.

I only agreed to keep this section in the show if I could say it really fast and not have to elaborate on it.

A. SLATTERY: I only agreed to keep that section in the show if she said it really fast and did not elaborate on it. *(She passes cake to audience.)*

A. KINSELLA: I still hear from Louise occasionally, *(A. SLATTERY rolls her eyes.)* but I have no idea where Jen is. Last I remember hearing she had moved to the States. We lived together for two years, fought incessantly and never managed to trust each other. I think she was still sleeping with Louise. So was I.

(Sits relieved at table).

A. SLATTERY: *(Moves to her downstage right mark.)*

In 1974 Alice came home from London to nurse her mother, she was too thin *(A. KINSELLA, still eating her biscuit laughs an 'if you can believe it' laugh).* It looked like London had worn her down, but she swore that she was having a ball. She didn't look like she was having a ball, she looked sick. Liam and I were married for four years at that stage, we were happy but complacent. She regaled us with stories of her life, parties and people in England; we were avid letter writers so I felt I knew the people she was talking about from her letters over the years.

She moved in with her Mother and threw herself into caring for her. I think she felt guilty for not being there over the years, she also took a part-time job in a shop. I know now that she was punishing herself, making herself too tired to think.

The day we buried her Mam was awful, Alice took care of everyone, Mary, Declan and Jack, her brothers, and all their young families. Teas, coffees, sandwiches...porter and whiskeys later.

When everyone had left I looked for her to say goodbye, she was smoking down the garden, a habit she picked up in London. I walked down to her and found her sobbing. She looked like a child; she looked like the Alice I remembered from years ago. I threw my arms around her and held her, for ages. It felt like I was the only thing holding her up.

A. KINSELLA: Some time after my mother died, I told Alice about Louise and Jen...well about me really. I told her and didn't really give her an option to be shocked or appalled. I was in bad shape at the time, and it seemed trivial to me, incidental. Alice didn't bat an eyelid.

A. SLATTERY: I knew about Alice. I knew before she told me, Mary said it one night we were out. It wasn't something often spoken about in our circle, so Mary was kind of sheepish admitting it, worried more like. There was a fella' I'd see at mass said to be 'light on his feet'. People would snigger, roll their eyes behind his back, but they were nice to his face. It's easy to laugh when you don't really know the person, but I knew Alice, she was my friend, and there was nothing to laugh at.

(Sits down at the table).

A. KINSELLA: *(The Angelus bells ring softly, to prompt the women. Places a religious statue on the table)*

I refused to receive communion at a wedding, years ago. We didn't speak for about a week. I wasn't trying to upset her, I just... I just couldn't do it any more. I couldn't pretend to go along with something that offends me for posterity's sake. I had just had enough.

Alice prays. I don't understand why. Over the years I've seen enough to make me realize what a futile act it is. I'll do midnight mass at Christmas... I love the singing. People singing together moves me more than any 'miracle'. But that's it. I know it bothers her, deep down inside, I think she feels I need to come back to God so we can be together in heaven. I'm not so sure about that. Over recent years I've come to think that when you die you die. That's it. The end. This upsets Al, so we don't talk about it anymore; there are few things we don't talk about…

A. SLATTERY: 'There are no atheists in foxholes.'

A. KINSELLA: …But this is a big thing.
She calls me an 'atheist', joking…but only kind of.
I try to tell her it's not God, but the church that I have a problem with, but I think somewhere along the way they both got mixed up, intermingled in her eyes.
She goes to mass on Sunday mornings and always complains about getting up, especially when it's raining! Anyway, that's not the point.
While she's at mass I buy newspapers and breakfast bits. I always rush the shopping, I have about twenty minutes to get it done, so I can be back in bed when she gets in the door. She crawls back into bed and we have a 're-morning', that's what we like to call it; I ask her if she's been 'saved'. I suppose it sounds silly. We never discuss it…but this reclaims us, if you know what I mean, like the religion is a divide and this ritual brings us back together, you know? *(Sits.)*

A. SLATTERY: I came in one Sunday morning and she was still 'asleep'. I cajoled her like I always do, then I realised that she really was asleep, she hadn't been out to the shops, this was not part of the game. She was so tired; I had serious difficulty rousing her. She was cranky and off form, which was really not like her. After a week she suggested the doctor herself. She hates doctors and hospitals; the doctor said it was probably just a virus but while he had her there he'd give her the full overhaul, that's when she found the lump.

A. KINSELLA: My life did flash before my eyes. And it seemed very small. A small life, a small existence.

A. SLATTERY: Breast cancer. *(Moves to mark, downstage right.)*
I thought I had lost her when she was diagnosed. I had
never felt so low. When Liam died, I was devastated, I lost
my beautiful friend, my lovely husband. I had no idea how
to pick up the pieces, or where to even find the pieces. I
loved him dearly, I always will. But I was never in love
with him; I know it's a bit of a cliché but…what can you
do? Now here I was faced with it again, but this time…
I was furious with her for about a month, angrier than
I had ever been. I couldn't believe she would do this to
me, get sick, that she might leave me here alone. I started
playing this horrible, sick game in my head, I would
navigate the house and imagine she was gone; I'd see
the gaps in every room. I'd look around thinking…this is
where she used to sit, this is where she threw her car keys
every evening, this is where she scratched the paint on the
banister getting a new headboard up the stairs.
I would think of her in the past tense for an hour every
day, it sounds crazy I know, but I had to see what it would
feel like. I was pushing her away, and I did it at the worst
possible time. She ended up comforting me. I don't know
what I'd do without her. She…

A. KINSELLA: Had I done enough? Had I seen enough? Had
I sat on the sidelines, or played a full match? It made me
re-evaluate my life. The good, the bad, and the ugly.
(Stands and moves to mark downstage left.)

In the mid-Eighties 'Ann', not her real name, started
interning in the gallery. An American student living and
working in Ireland, she was ten years younger than me.
She was funny, smart, athletic, and very obviously gay. She
was like a breath of fresh air, full of American idealism. It
was the Eighties, when American idealism was popular.
I had sort of adopted an 'eyes down, hands in your
pockets' policy, and her openness was infectious. She made
me laugh, we'd have lunch together and on Wednesday
evenings I'd have a drink in Peter's with her and her
friends. I felt alive, more alive than I had in ages, almost

celebratory. Ann was flirtatious and charming, she knew I had a partner, and she didn't care, in fact I think that was what she found most attractive. She was bold and irreverent. I fooled myself into believing we were just friends but, truth be told, I knew what she was doing, and I knew what I was doing. We had an affair that lasted about six months. There are few things in my life that I regret, that I am ashamed of, this is one of them.

A. SLATTERY: I was collecting Alice from town one evening, it was pouring with rain and I wanted to surprise her with a lift. They walked out together, laughing, gesturing wildly, and then Ann brushed Alice's cheek with her hand. I knew then. My mouth went dry, and I sat there unable to move. Alice passed by, unaware, and got the bus home.

I was in shock, I was livid. How could she do this to me, to us? Ann was everything I wasn't; I wondered if that was why Alice liked her. I drove to Sandymount and walked for hours, thinking and thinking. I knew I had to talk to her, confront her.

'I saw you. How long? Do you love her?'

Alice cried. 'I'm so sorry,' she said, 'six months,' she said, and 'no, I don't love her.' 'But I love how she looks at me, I love that she likes who she is…that she likes who I am. You don't Alice, you're ashamed of yourself, and you're ashamed of me. I'm not asking you to live differently, just to think differently.' I was so hurt; she had never said this before.

I have always been uncomfortable with anything too 'overtly gay'. I used to deem it unnecessary; I thought that 'people like that' gave us all a bad name. I never stopped to think that we are all just responsible for ourselves, moreover that 'people like that' are a celebration. Kenneth Williams and Graham Norton used to make me cringe; now they annoy me simply because they're annoying. I'm not ashamed any more, but I was then. It took a long time to work things out, to trust her again, to fix things, but we did.

A. KINSELLA: We got through it, somehow. I was an absolute idiot.

An obvious shift here, both move to downstage centre. A little look and touch, as if to say, 'we got through that bit', a connection.

A. SLATTERY: Do we argue! That's gas. Yes, we argue. Not as much as we used to, but we pick at small silly things. I'm terrible at recycling, which really annoys her, when I hear her cry…

A. KINSELLA: How hard can it be…?

A. SLATTERY: I know I've put the plastic in the wrong place. And what's worse is it always makes me laugh…that she gets so upset.

A. KINSELLA: I'm not big on birthdays. I always say I don't want anything, just get me a card.
She says I'm impossible to buy for but I always know she'll get me something anyway. Five years ago she got me a lawn mower. A lawn mower…for my birthday. I think I sulked for a week. I would have preferred a watch.

A. SLATTERY: In my defence, she was looking at them in Woodies.

A. KINSELLA: She was looking at paintbrushes. I did not 'surprise you' with an extendable roller!

A. SLATTERY: *(Laughs.)* Menopause, that was intense.
Imagine two moody hairy women in one room, a recipe for disaster.

They move the two chairs from the table to downstage centre, like two car seats.

A. KINSELLA: I hate to be a passenger when Alice is driving.
(Swap sides so A. KINSELLA is driver side).
She makes me nauseous. Sorry Al, but you do.
She can't seem to maintain her speed; she's constantly accelerating and decelerating, faster, slower. It drives me crazy…literally.

She also drives way too close to the driver in front and it makes me really nervous. I keep saying *(Both together.),* 'If he brakes it's your fault.'
She fiddles with the radio, she's too hot, she's too cold, window down, window up, she talks, and talks, and talks and I'm sitting there thinking, 'we're going to die, we're going to die here on the Tallaght bypass!' By the time we get where we're going, I'm stressed and cross. I tend to do most of the driving.

A. SLATTERY: We argue about this a lot, it's not a real fight, it's kind of jokey…but serious at the same time. Passive aggressive is the term I'd use. *(Big inhale from A. KINSELLA.)* I think her real problem is lack of control; she hates not being in charge. I think it's being in the passenger seat that gets to her most, not my driving.

A. KINSELLA: You can't fake nausea Al.

A. SLATTERY: I think it's psychosomatic.

A. KINSELLA: Which is brought on by stress…

A. SLATTERY: The stress of not being in control…

A. KINSELLA: The stress of sudden braking at eighty miles an hour.

A. SLATTERY: Kilometres, see…you drive too fast.

A. KINSELLA: *(Both women pull the cushions from behind their backs.)* There are ten cushions on our couch. Ten. They range from oversized to small, like undersized…too small to have any purpose at all. In order to sit on the couch, you have to remove at least seven of them.
This drives me insane, totally insane.
I just don't see the point, don't get me wrong, I'm not aesthetically dim. I know what looks good and what does not. Ten cushions on a couch look daft, but apparently I have no taste, so the cushions stay. We cannot go to bed at night if they are left on the floor; I think she would have an anxiety attack.

A. SLATTERY: Alice has a painting of the 'mother and child'. It's a religious painting that she bought at a market in London years ago.

A. KINSELLA: Fifteen pounds, haggled down from twenty.

A. SLATTERY: It looks it. I had it reframed a few years ago; to try to make it less garish, but there is no saving it. It's appalling. It has pride of place in our sitting room, and clashes with our couch. When I walk into the room I feel it mocking me. Alice talks to it just to drive me mad.

A. KINSELLA: 'Hello Mary. Are you still holding the baby, you must be exhausted? Why don't you have a seat and put your feet up, but put the cushions back when you're finished, you know what she's like.'

A. SLATTERY: *(Trying not to smile.)*
Framing it cost me 180 euro, and I keep trying to move it to the upstairs landing.

A. KINSELLA: *(Discreetly shakes her head.)*

A. SLATTERY: She's not religious, and it's awfully ugly. I think she keeps it to annoy me.

A. KINSELLA: I know she thinks I keep that picture just to annoy her, but it's really not like that. I do love it, in all its tacky splendour, but I suppose I think of it as a totem, an anchor or link to another time and place.
Alice Slattery showed me what it felt like to breathe, to stop. That it's OK to stop and be still. She brings me a sense of calm and peace. I had never felt that before, I didn't know it was possible, or that I deserved it.
That picture brings me back, back to swinging London; back to the 'me' I was then, the girl who kissed Dusty Springfield at a party in an upstairs flat in Ealing.

A. SLATTERY: Allegedly.

A. KINSELLA: I did. It compounds all the choices I've made, because none of that compares to what I have now. None of it. I think Alice is gorgeous, I always have.

A. SLATTERY: I worried. At the beginning I worried. Am
I gay now, is that what I am? But I had been married,
was it even possible? Are there rules, was I allowed to
be gay? I didn't feel 'gay', but I loved Alice, so what,
did that make me? I prayed about it often. I prayed for
answers. I never told Alice this, but sometimes I prayed
for forgiveness. I thought I was weak, that I couldn't resist
this. Maybe feeling this kind of love, this kind of attraction
was common enough. Perhaps acting on these feelings was
the thing we needed to control? I was scared that we were
going to hell.
'Follow the way of love.' Corinthians chapter 14 verse 1.
I've made peace with myself. I know God loves me, as I
am.

A. KINSELLA: For me, the shift in our relationship happened
that year after my mother died. Alice was a true friend, so
supportive. We spent loads of time together and over the
year became closer and closer. Liam was supportive too,
in his own quiet way. I spent a lot of time in their house,
sitting at their table. He always welcomed me and never
made me feel like I was in the way.
Liam was such a lovely, lovely man. I couldn't figure out
why I disliked him so much.
One evening we were sitting up late listening to The
Temptations, she was singing along and looking at me,
everything in me wanted to kiss her, to hold her close
and dance with her. Liam had gone to bed earlier, as he
left he kissed her on the lips and I had to turn away I was
blushing so badly.

*'The Dutchman' by Makem and Clancy fades up slowly on onstage
speaker. This is obviously one of Liam's songs; both ALICEs
acknowledge it subtly.*

A. SLATTERY: My maiden name is Alice Connelly; I married
Liam Slattery in 1970.
I had wanted to stay in that night but Mary dragged me
along to a dance organizing committee meeting. I was
reading *Wuthering Heights*, and wanted to stay put, I was
quite shy back then, Mary was mad, sure where would she

be got! When we arrived in the hall we were swallowed up by a boisterous crowd, Mary got stuck straight in and was put on 'decorations'; I was put firmly in the background on 'sandwiches'.

Ham and cheese, and egg mayonnaise.

Liam was the other lost soul on sambos. He entered the kitchen looking shell-shocked and vaguely panicked; he blushed when I spoke to him.

I put him on egg mayonnaise as the smell was turning my tummy, and the onion was making me cry. We courted; I suppose that is the word you would use, for a few years after that. It's difficult to explain my relationship with Liam; I'm always terrified to sound dismissive of it, of him. I loved him. I didn't realise at the time that I was operating at half speed, that life is supposed to be faster and more passion filled. I thought that this is what love is supposed to be, sure how would I have known? He died of a massive heart attack, aged 31. That was fairly unheard of back then. I have a lot of guilt when I think about Liam, I feel I let him down, that I never loved him in the way that he loved me. He had a beautiful soul, and was a beautiful friend. That's all I have to say about that.

Shift, A. KINSELLA squeezes A. SLATTERY's hand and A. SLATTERY gets up to put on a record…and to move off the difficult topic.

A. KINSELLA: We always have music on in our house. Motown music is a favourite. I love it and so does Alice. I used to send records home from London to Mary and the boys, and Al used to write to me and tell me which was her favourite, she loved 'Forever Came Today' by Diana Ross and the Supremes. We saw Stevie Wonder last year, I was totally overwhelmed.

We listen to Stevie, The Temptations, The Supremes, Gladys Knight… Most meals are prepared on 'the midnight train to Georgia'.

Alice does most of the cooking and I love to watch her. There is something about how she moves in that space, her control and command that I find compelling and very attractive. She chops in time to the Pips!

She has great patience; I always rush and end up with lumps and under-cooked food. I'm more of a lunchtime cook, sandwiches, salads, soups…that kind of thing. She cooks; I do spiders, hoovering, and laundry. The laundry is a necessity as she refuses to separate colours and whites. I could wallpaper the house with pink and grey colour catchers.

Marvin Gaye, 'Sexual Healing', is faded in, and this next section is a pre-recorded audio. Presumably because neither ALICE would agree to do it live. Both ALICEs look terrified, nervous and giddy. They shoot glances at each other, and try to contain the nervous laugh that is close to the surface. They both pick up books/newspapers, sit at the table and hide behind them. It is clear that these props are only used to give both women something to do while this uncomfortable section is played. Their discomfort is still obvious from behind their papers; we hear them have a 'sneaky' whisper. There is a great sense of giddy fun, giddy nerves, and even a little flirting in the audio.

A. SLATTERY: *(Laughing and grimacing.)* I thought you said we wouldn't do this till next week?
Oh dear lord, right so, go on. You start Alice.

A. KINSELLA: *(Laughing incredulously.)* You start! I'll be in the kitchen. Opening more wine.

A. SLATTERY: You will in your eye. Sit down there.

A. KINSELLA: I'm just getting more wine.

A. SLATTERY: Are you now?

A. KINSELLA: Well…

A. SLATTERY: Well?

A. KINSELLA: Well, yes. Our first…time.

A. SLATTERY: It was arranged, like we had talked about it.

A. KINSELLA: No we didn't!

A. SLATTERY: Not talked about that, but we talked about the arrangements.

A. KINSELLA: Ahh, yes, Al is a planner.

A. SLATTERY: Well somebody had to take charge.

A. KINSELLA: I was invited to dinner.

A. SLATTERY: Dinner.

A. KINSELLA: 'Civilized'.

A. SLATTERY: I didn't call it civilized.

A. KINSELLA: Yes you did, you invited me over for a 'civilized dinner'…

A. SLATTERY: Oh God, did I say that?

A. KINSELLA: A civilized dinner, and I was to stay the night.

A. SLATTERY: I was petrified.

A. KINSELLA: You were drunk!

A. SLATTERY: I was not drunk!

A. KINSELLA: Well I was. Not 'drunk' drunk, but 'calm the nerves drunk'. I had somehow managed to get my hands on a bottle of…what was that horrible wine Al?

A. SLATTERY: God knows.

A. KINSELLA: Ahh, you know it… Blue Nun, that was it.

A. SLATTERY: Oh yes, that was it, in the dark bottle.

A. KINSELLA: We struggled through it over dinner. It was horrible, nobody drank wine at the time, but I was trying to impress. I was petrified too.

A. SLATTERY: I made quiche lorraine. I was also trying to impress, which was ridiculous, I had been cooking for Alice for years. I was flustered all day; I burned the first pastry base I made.

A. KINSELLA: She had made Victoria sponge-cake for dessert. My favourite.

A. SLATTERY: I know, it's hilarious now when I think about the whole thing.

A. KINSELLA: Ahh Alice, it's sweet.

A. SLATTERY: I kept telling myself to stop panicking, that nothing had to happen if we didn't want it to. It's difficult, if you have been friends before lovers.

A. KINSELLA: Yes, like, you already have an intimate relationship anyway…

A. SLATTERY: And you have to change those old dynamics.

A. KINSELLA: Well, you want to change those dynamics.

A. SLATTERY: I just keep thinking that you had done this before, I was so green. I hadn't a clue.

A. KINSELLA: But I had no experience with men, I didn't really know what I was up against.

A. SLATTERY: God bless poor Liam, but you really shouldn't have worried.

A. KINSELLA: Anyway…

A. SLATTERY: Anyway…

A. KINSELLA: The time came, for bed.

A. SLATTERY: We had been talking for hours…

A. KINSELLA: We had been kissing for hours…

A. SLATTERY: Alice!

A. KINSELLA: Well, we had.

A. SLATTERY: Don't be so graphic

A. KINSELLA: *(Laughing.)* I would hardly call that graphic. Considering the subject.

A. SLATTERY: I'm watching you.

A. KINSELLA: *(Laughing.)*

A. SLATTERY: We decided it was time for bed; Alice had brought over her toothbrush and a nighty.

A. KINSELLA: A nighty!

A. SLATTERY: I remember thinking how sweet that was. We both got into bed and…

A. KINSELLA: And we lay there in the dark, for what felt like an eternity.

A. SLATTERY: I was shivering.

A. KINSELLA: I thought she was freezing.

A. SLATTERY: Nerves.

A. KINSELLA: Alice got a fit of the giggles.

A. SLATTERY: I couldn't help it; I just kept thinking how funny it was, like in the greater scheme of things. Here I was 'in bed' with Alice Kinsella, and I loved her. Like 'loved' her loved her.

A. KINSELLA: That broke the ice, I kissed her and she stopped laughing. We stayed in bed for two days; we survived on cold quiche and coffee.

A. SLATTERY: It was fantastic…what were we so worried about?

A. KINSELLA: It was incredibly romantic.

Fade out chatter and laughter… 'That wasn't as bad as I had thought… Why did we put off that conversation for so long… Twice… Can I get the wine now boss…'

Marvin Gay fades back up and out.

The women put down their books/papers. Laughing at themselves, they share a glance. Look at the audience, they are both a little shy, but giddy.

A. SLATTERY: *(Blushing.)* Six months. It took us six months to work up to that conversation.

A. KINSELLA: It took a lot of convincing, and a lot of wine. We even had a toast around the table with a bottle of Blue Nun recording it. It's still terrible stuff.

ALICE SLATTERY takes out a laundry basket, sits at the table and begins to fold the clothes, she folds a bra and this is ALICE KINSELLA's cue.

A. KINSELLA: *(Move to mark downstage right)* Stage-two breast cancer. One modified radical mastectomy, one round of radiation therapy, three rounds of chemotherapy.
I don't think I have ever heard more terrifying words. I still wake panicked from nightmares…the cancer is back and spreading, I think the fear must have breathing-room in my dreams…because I don't feel it when I'm awake. I must suppress it.

I kept trying to figure out what I had done, what could I have done better, is there any way I could have avoided this? But in reality, this is what took my mother, so it was always a danger for me. I was totally numb, in shock I suppose, I felt nothing.

Alice felt it for both of us. I've never seen her so angry. She was mad at God, mad at the world, mad at me. She stopped going to mass and followed me from room to room, she watched me as if, at any moment, I would evaporate. I didn't have the energy to tell her it would be OK, I didn't have the energy for a brave face and hopeful lies.

One day I found her sitting on the bed, crying. She had just gotten off the phone with Mary and they were discussing my 'affairs'. I was outraged, I shouted at her…

A. SLATTERY: 'What are you doing that for? I'm not going anywhere.'

A. KINSELLA: At that very moment I knew I would be fine, I can't describe how or why, I just knew.

I think we both felt the shift. We both cried, then we went out and had a celebratory bag of chips. I figured if I were fighting cancer then a single of chips wouldn't kill me. Don't get me wrong, it wasn't easy, there were some awful days…

A. SLATTERY: Some awful days.

A. KINSELLA: …days when I could barely lift my head off the pillow, days when I just didn't want to talk to anyone, days filled with anger, with 'why mes'. Even now I find it hard to talk about, to think about. I was almost run over by a bus trying to make the lights on Parnell Street once, and I get the same feeling when I think about that.

A. SLATTERY: The 'what could have happened' panic.

I took Alice on a holiday when she was given the all clear, we went to Florida. Alice joked that that was where all the old people go, but I know she was excited.

We flew into Orlando International Airport and stayed in a posh hotel for three nights.

A. KINSELLA: We stayed in the Gaylord Palms Hotel! I laughed about that for the entire seven-hour flight. It was gorgeous and enormous. There was a massive indoor pond with alligators…real alligators. And a massive out-door pool…with no alligators obviously.

A. SLATTERY: Al wouldn't swim… She said she wasn't in the mood, that there was too much to see.

A. KINSELLA: We went to Sea World, I know it's for kids… but I loved it. Dolphins, penguins, sharks, sea lions, killer whales, and horses. I don't know why they have horses in Sea World. We reckon they're secretly feeding them to the orcas.

A. SLATTERY: She hadn't worn her swimming togs in public since her operation; I knew she was embarrassed and probably scared.

A. KINSELLA: We hired a car and headed for Boca Raton, we have friends who live there in a beautiful condominium. I'm still unclear as to the difference between an apartment and a condominium.
Anyway, theirs is a 'condo', apparently.

A. SLATTERY: We hired a car and headed for the Keys…

A. KINSELLA: I drove. We listened to Dusty Springfield on satellite radio.

A. SLATTERY: I don't care for Dusty Springfield.
The scenery was stunning, turquoise water, small squat palm trees, big old oak trees with hanging Spanish moss swaying in the occasional breeze. History seemed palpable the further south we went, we left plastic Florida behind and entered quaint, still and stifling Florida. Tennessee Williams Florida. We ate key lime pie in Key West. Alice swears she saw Kelly McGillis in a restaurant.

A. KINSELLA: We stayed in a stunning guesthouse with a wooden veranda and overhead fans. We drank gin and tonic in rocking chairs and we met Kelly McGillis, the girl from that film, *Top Gun*, in a restaurant.

A. SLATTERY: I did not see Kelly McGillis.

A. KINSELLA: You did Alice, she was lovely.

They both fold a sheet together.

A. SLATTERY: Alice finally swam in the Gulf of Mexico. She was beautiful. The trip was wonderful; it was exactly what we needed. I think it took about five years off us…

A. KINSELLA: And put about five pounds on us!

A. SLATTERY: *(Move to mark downstage left.)*
It really got me thinking, about my life, my future. Seeing Alice sick, really sick, scared me, it shook me to my core, the fragility of life. The emphasis we place on stupid silly things.
We met Frank and Jim on a cruise years ago, two beautiful men. Jim was a florist and Frank imported and sold antiques. I always considered them 'shiny', they sparkled. We struck up a genuine and easy friendship that deepened over twenty years. We visited them in Berlin once a year, and they stayed with us in Dublin. We used to meet for weekends in London, have dinner in Kettner's and see a show. They were full of fun, life, and extravagance, you were assured to drink too much and laugh too loud in their company. They died in an autobahn accident six years ago, wiped out in seconds. The paper reported…

A. KINSELLA has been putting the laundry basket away and moves back to her downstage right mark.

A. KINSELLA: 'Two men, in their fifties, were killed in a road accident.' That was it, no details.
They could have been strangers. When a husband and wife die you are immediately struck by the tragedy of the loss. A family lost. Their extended family and friends are interviewed in the paper, their funerals are covered on the news, their community grieves.
Frank and Jim were just 'two men in their fifties'.

A. SLATTERY: There are no words to express the sadness. I was devastated, I still am. We put a dozen white roses on their grave every summer, they were Jim's favourite.

What would happen if one of us died? We have no children, no legal binds between us, only a joint bank account and a co-owned house.

What would I do if I lost her? It took me so long to find her, it took me so long to realise I was looking for her. When she left for London all those years ago, I cried for days, I felt a sadness beyond the measure of the situation. The night before she left we all gathered for a drink in town, Bowes, I think it was. She was excited and nervous. Her friends from home and the girls from the secretarial college were all in flying form. Her mammy had given her twenty pounds for London; my mother gave her a fiver, which was a lot of money back then. I gave her a card and a hug on Fleet Street that lasted just a second too long. I promised I'd keep in touch. I lost her once. I couldn't lose her again.

We walked down Duval Street holding hands, that's the main drag in Key West. It's full of bars and restaurants that spill out onto the street, people eating al fresco and laughing over glasses of wine. Nobody gave us a second glance, except a young man with an arm full of tattoos who smiled at us. We walked away from the crowd and stood on this wooden walkway that overlooked the beach. We watched the sun set where the Atlantic Ocean meets the Gulf of Mexico. It was warm and still, almost dreamlike. I asked Alice to marry me. She said yes.

They move downstage centre, stand at the end of the table, and hold hands.

A. SLATTERY: We watched our first Gay Pride parade this year, under duress. I really didn't want to but it was for the good of the show apparently.

A. KINSELLA: All the colour, the costumes, the noise.

A. SLATTERY: A young man at the parade called us cute, we were holding hands. I swung around and was just about to tell him: 'I'm a grown woman, I'm not cute. Babies are cute, puppies are cute. I am not. Don't patronize me you arrogant idiot,' when I realised he was talking to his friend on the opposite footpath. I was mortified. He looked at me like I was mad. Alice thought it was hilarious. He wished me a happy pride. It was nice.

A. KINSELLA: There were all types of people there, young, old, gay, straight. With families and without. I realized that we all have a place, we all belong. We are all just people and we all just do our best. I'm sixty-four and I have a lot to learn.

A. SLATTERY: In making this show we have argued, cried, shouted, sulked, talked, remembered, smiled and laughed. We laughed a lot. Several times it begged the question, 'what in God's name are we doing this for?' It took me a long time but I finally figured it out, I don't want to hide anymore. I am proud of me, I am proud of us. We have been together for twenty-eight years. We plan to be married on our thirtieth anniversary, not a civil partnership, a marriage.

A. KINSELLA: We are here, we were here all along. Somebody has to do this, to stand up and be seen. We can't, in good conscience, always leave it to others. So here we are, warts and all. We have lived, lived well; we have loved, loved well. Alice, will you dance?

A. SLATTERY: I will.

The music fades up, 'Endless Love' by Lionel Ritchie and Diana Ross. The lights dim and flicker off a rotating mirror ball and the ALICEs dance… They kiss as 'my endless love' is sung.

Lights fade up.

A. SLATTERY: Fun.
Exciting.
Challenging.
Insightful.
Triumphant.
Beautiful. A testimonial.

TOGETHER: We will be seen.

Slowly the wigs come off and the actors reveal themselves.

They will be seen.

THE BIG DEAL
EDITED BY
UNA MCKEVITT

The Big Deal opened on the 10 August 2011 at Kilkenny Arts Festival, with a preview on 9 August. It was later performed at Project Arts Centre, Dublin, from 31 October–5 November 2011.

CATHY – Una Kavanagh
DEBORAH – Shania Williams

Directed by Una McKevitt
Lighting Design by Sinead Wallace
Production Manager: Conor Mullan

It received a work-in-progress performance on 8 and 9 December as part of Queer Notions, a festival of theatre and other performances, produced by thisispopbaby. On this occasion, the role of Deborah was performed by Niamh Shaw.

Scripted from original material provided by the contributors – including journals, poems, songs and interviews.

A long wide wooden bench is placed upstage centre right. At a short distance to the right of the bench is a mic stand. An actor on the bench can move to this mic easily in two short steps. Downstage left is another mic stand. Both mics frame the stage picture and the actors do not move beyond the circumference they mark. Above the bench is a vertical aluminium strip light and another perpendicular to this stage left. CATHY wears navy leggings, a long black lycra vest and over it a loose-fitting navy top with mid-length sleeves. DEBORAH wears khaki skinny jeans, a belt and a ladies vest top. Both are bare foot.

CATHY: I was at a wedding recently, and a woman asked me did I know where the happy couple were going on their honeymoon. I told her they were heading to the Caribbean and that the bride had a massage booked for every one of the ten days. This woman said, 'Ugh, that's horrible.' 'Horrible?' The woman said, 'Ugh, the thought of someone touching me like that every day. Horrible.' And I said, 'Like what? It's a massage.' And the woman said, 'It's unnatural. Ha! But look who I'm talking to.'

SCENE 1

The Runaways: 'Cherry Bomb'.

DEBORAH: 1994.

The Evening Herald.

'Men In Dresses'.

By Noreen Hegarty.

The atmosphere is a heady mix of subdued lighting, french perfume and cigarette smoke.

Deborah adjusts her short black lamé jacket and steps from one heeled foot to another. Her car, parked near the city centre club where she's socialising with her friends, has just been broken into and she's clearly upset.

It's only when Deborah turns and speaks that you would really know – the voice is unmistakably that of a man.

CATHY: It is the night before my operation.

I am remarkably calm.

Shouldn't I be doing something with my penis on his last night on earth?

He never did me any harm. In fact he worked rather well.

Shouldn't I be having second thoughts, doubts – I was born a boy after all.

Of course that's the whole point isn't it? Was I?

DEBORAH: Ever since I was twelve, my dad and I have discussed everything. He always said I was to come to him with any problems I had and if I was to smoke, drink, do drugs or 'go with girls', I was to do it at home – in front of him and my mum. At seventeen I decided to talk to him about something that was bothering me for quite some time. I believed I was a girl but none of this made sense. How could I believe this, I was born a boy after all, wasn't I?

So, I sat him down and told him, 'I think I am a girl, Dad.' He looked at me very calmly and said, 'It's just a phase you are going through, don't worry about it. Go get a new girlfriend and on Sunday go out and kick someone around the football field. You'll feel better and you'll be fine.' So on Sunday I did go out and kick some poor fool around the football field and a couple of weeks later got myself a new girlfriend. I tried to forget it, but it never went away.

Years later, when I told my Mum and Dad, my Dad was very quiet. He didn't say anything, he just agreed with my Mum: they would get me cured. I wondered if he remembered our conversation all those years previously. Who was I going to kick this time?

Dear Cathy,

These journals are yours; write whatever you are feeling, whatever you are thinking. They will have no effect on my own position, nor do I think you are rubbing my nose in it. Darling, I have tried to explain that I am OK with where I am in my life right now and I have struggled to get to this position. Like I said before, nothing is going to shake me off my path except me.

I suggested the journal, so later you can reflect on your experiences. These journals are not for criticism or explanation; they are how you are feeling right now. And that's what's important.

Love Deborah

CATHY: I was woken up at 6 a.m. for 'nurses check-up time'.

Blood pressure, pulse, temperature.

I had to finish eating by 7 a.m., fasting until surgery at 2.30 p.m., but the toast was cold and I got no enjoyment from my last meal on Earth as a Man. – God, doesn't that sound great. Now what else happened that day before they came for me. I did some Sudoku – watched some TV.

I played my iPod. Around 1 p.m. they gave me a sedative to make me drowsy. And then I was back in my bed – in pain –

very sleepy –

pain –

nurses check-up time –

pain –

and then it was Sunday Morning.

SCENE 2

The Runaways: 'Blackmail (Intro)'.

DEBORAH: Cathy has been there for me quite a lot.

She knows what I'm talking about and I won't go into that detail, it's personal between me and her.

She's helped me through a couple of rough patches with that.

CATHY: Dear Deborah,

– today is Day 2 after the operation and I'm a lot better but still very sore.

Being out here alone is not to be understated.

By and large I'm good. I walked around for the first time today and can now get out of bed. Everything I do is in slow motion. I can't use my Cathy voice because my chest

225

is so congested and this is really annoying me. I'm also wearing Patrick's face, as I haven't the energy yet for make-up.

Maybe tomorrow.

There is the problem of stitches where my adam's apple was shaved. Also very disappointed with my hair – see no difference to the way I was wearing it as Patrick last week – I did get the breasts done.

Now I'm a 38C.

I get a warm feeling at the thought that I now have a vagina – albeit a painful one for the time being. I am a bit petrified at its unveiling on Thursday. I don't have a good stomach for this sort of thing.

Six months of dilation to look forward to.

Still.

The pain will wear off.

Life is pretty good actually – Sore, but good! – And you helped get me here – Thanks.

DEBORAH: I only met Patrick once. I was passing by Cathy's office and she said call in. I said, 'okay, but I won't be me, I'll be Sean,' and she said, 'call in anyway, I'll be Patrick.' She thought it might be important for us to see that side of each other.

I felt weird in myself being there as Sean. I felt weird meeting Patrick. I would have preferred, if we were going to be friends, that we be friends the way we should always have been friends: just Cathy and Deborah.

At that time, I was trying to transition and I was doing it. OK, maybe in a haphazard way, but I was doing it. Cathy, on the other hand, was trying not to transition. She was trying to stay a happily married male, keep her family safe.

CATHY: Yes.

DEBORAH: At the time it meant a hell of a lot more to me to present myself as I saw myself. As Deborah.

CATHY: That's true.

DEBORAH: We are very different. Once Cathy decided to transition and live full-time as herself, she did it literally overnight; whereas, my transition from Sean to Deborah has been more like the tide coming in.

CATHY: I got my hair washed today and was able to put on my make-up, all of which made me feel more human again. Not just some banged up transsexual.

Your gift of an iPod Nano with 441 songs has proved invaluable. I carry it with me as I go. I also carry a white plastic bag which contains my urine bag and the bottle draining the blood from my vaginal area.

In the operation, Dr. Deeptha took my penis and literally sliced it down the shaft. He took away all the blood vessels inside that swell up and cause an erection. He also removed the testes.

My sons and I were joking, the day before I came here, that they should be mounted and perhaps be used as bookends or something. At least Shane was involved in that kind of slagging – as I remember, Peter thought it was gross and he's right.

The proudest moment of my life was handing my son to my father. I was totally chuffed. So was he. It was nice: to be a normal male at something. You know. I didn't know I'd feel the sense of pride I did, handing my son to my Dad. It was my Dad I was always trying to impress, not my Mum. I'm cut out of him, cut out of my father.

I haven't seen myself down there yet – I need to be sure I have, finally, been put right.

My days are filled with dozing.

Watching DVDs.

Listening to music.

Doing Sudoku –

thinking.

Missing my family.

The other thing is the rain. I haven't seen a blue sky yet. Bangkok is a lot bigger and more modern than I expected. The Skyscrapers are more impressive than New York. I can count ten of them from my 6th floor bedroom. I keep my curtains open all the time.

The view is great.

DEBORAH: 1993. It was a Thursday morning about 11am. Jean rang me on my mobile asking me to come home early to talk. When I arrived, the kids were gone, that's the first thing I noticed. We needed to talk, so that was OK. *'Who is Deborah?'* she asked. Fuck! Fuck, that came out of the blue. Minutes, Hours, Days, Seconds, A Lifetime seemed to pass. Do I tell the truth? Do I Lie? Do I say I am having an affair? How does she know? Be truthful, I thought. *'It's me.'*

SCENE 3

The Supremes: 'Come See About Me'.

CATHY: OK, I know this to be the worst day of my life so far. I think a good deal of the pain and horror occurred in my mind, rather than in the physical world, but, of course, the mind is where we actually live, isn't it?

The day starts off normally enough with a wake-up call at 6 a.m. and breakfast at 7 a.m., but all the time I am dreading getting the pack off, dreading the inevitable pain; dreading the cleaning of the vaginal area I know to be there but haven't seen yet, but which, as far as I am concerned, is nothing more than an open wound.

At lunchtime my sister visits me.

She is in Bangkok on her holidays. A total coincidence.

We talk about the traffic and the weather.

After lunch, Dr. Deeptha arrives to take the pack off. He and the nurse start. They remove the adhesive plaster that surrounds the groin.

They pull it from my skin – skin that had been operated on five days earlier and which was already sore.

Ouch! Oohhhhhhh! Painnnnnn! I don't know how to describe what I actually saw between my legs, but I'll try: I saw badly bruised, mounds of unrecognisable flesh. I felt pain and lots of it. I didn't want anyone touching me there – not from some sense of moral indignation, but rather, 'that's fucking sore – what do you think you are doing?'

They begin cleaning the area.

– that means touch me

there

– where I am so sore. I have waited my whole life to have my own vagina and knew that if I ever did get one, that this would be the type of introduction we would have. But OH GOD – what an introduction. I want to look down and see a healthy vagina where my healthy penis had been. That's all I want. Not this torn and battered flesh.

DEBORAH: Dear Cathy, first, let me say, **Congratulations**.

This is a major step in our lives to take.

You are so brave taking this step now.

Before taking this step, I want to be completely at one in who I am. I want to be happy within myself and like who I am.

I understand that you must be in so much pain and I can only hope and pray that you can cope. Remember that each day should bring you that much nearer to the day when there will be no pain.

Cathy, I know on the surface I may appear to be ready to go ahead with the operation now, but I feel I am not, not ready for both the mental and physical endurance test that you are going through. You Cathy, you are a lot stronger than me.

CATHY: After dinner I rang for the nurse. I still hadn't been shown how to clean my vagina and had to learn. So I rang for the nurse. She brought me into the bathroom and sat me on the toilet.

She filled the yellow pan with water and antiseptic solution and got some cotton wool.

She showed me what to do.

I remember using the cotton wool ball, soaked in the solution. The area was so sore and numb at the same time.

At first, I didn't realise what was happening,

but I was fainting –

my first time ever.

The nurse helped me from the toilet and somehow we made it to my bed.

That's where she left me –

naked –

dripping in antiseptic solution.

It was 4.45 p.m.

I was always like this, but the pain was in my heart.

The older I became, the more I thought of my mortality.

Not so much that I was afraid of death, but that the chance to have my life was slipping away.

So I was getting worse, the pain of the situation was getting worse.

I knew since I was about two or three, but I don't consider my life before as belonging to someone different.

I lived my life as a man because I had to.

When I was a man, I was called Patrick.

Now I live my life, thank god, as I was always meant to, as a woman and I'm called Cathy. But I'm the same person.

SCENE 4

The Velvet Underground and Nice: 'I'll Be Your Mirror. Final Chorus'.

DEBORAH: When I was in my late thirties, I was still playing football, not the perfect example of femininity I could have been. I had played football for over twenty years and had even played at League of Ireland level. I was quite good. I could play. I was fast and I was afraid of nothing. I think I was trying too hard, though, trying to be a man. But I did enjoy my football.

There came a time, though, when I needed to give it up. One Sunday I arrived, a little worse for wear, to play a match having been out the night before. The manager decided to play me as centre back. The team we were playing were not very good, so I wouldn't have much to do. Late in the game, we were winning 4-nil. The ball got kicked in my direction and a 6' 6", 20-stone farmer came rushing up the field at me with the ball. As he got closer, I started questioning what I was doing there. The night before, I had been wandering around Dublin in a short skirt and high heels, it just seemed mad to be involved in this macho pastime. So I stood to one side and let him through to score a goal. My team-mates were really pissed off. The next week, I played in the Cup Final, scored two goals and retired.

CATHY: It was 4.45 p.m. I remember that and I remember asking the nurse to come back in a few minutes.

I just needed a few minutes.

I managed to fit my sanitary towel by myself –

As Patrick I never felt vulnerable –

not really.

Now I just feel vulnerable.

I need Ellen.

I need my wife.

She wouldn't turn me away –

not tonight.

She's a saint –

a fucking saint –

we've agreed that so many times.

I love her. I love Ellen.

This is the single most important statement of my life.

I needed her that night.

I hope I will never need another human being as much again.

DEBORAH: Cathy, in your letter you say you don't feel any more of a woman now than before, why would you? You haven't changed your brain. You only had your penis removed. These changes over the next number of months will help you feel more like a woman. Firstly, you won't have to hide that penis and you will no longer be producing testosterone.

You are improving your lot, but, in doing so, you are losing someone important. Only you can decide if you can bring those around you with you and, more importantly, if you can live without them if they don't.

CATHY: Dr. Deeptha called in to see me. I am also due to get a full face lift, upper and lower eyelids done, and a nice set of feminine lips. I really want my lips. It is the one area of facial feminisation that I believe will be the most effective.

I haven't really had lips before –

none that you could see at any rate.

More pain. My head now ached also.

Pain. Pain. Pain.

– yea, yea, yea.

DEBORAH: Things I Hate

- People who don't return calls when they say they will
- My forehead
- Feeling lonely
- Cats
- People who constantly complain about money

- Pretending to be cool
- Birthday parties
- We'll get you sorted. We'll get you cured. We'll help you beat this thing.
- Psoriasis
- Broccoli
- Christmas
- Jack Daniels
- Never having enough money
- Conversations with strangers that end in a newspaper

I spent thirty-seven years apologising for my condition. Over those thirty-seven years, I always felt I was answering to someone else. I put other people's needs before my own. Now I'm shaking.

Moving out of my home, being told when and where I could see my children, accepting I will never have the same freedom with them as before. No one can ever understand what I experienced and, even if it is explained, no one can understand what it did to me. And maybe I don't want anyone to understand it; maybe I want to keep it with me.

That brings me to my children. I have caused them so much pain in their short lives; I would never wish to cause them any further pain than is necessary. Before I have the operation, I want those loved ones around me to accept me for who I am, and eventually they will.

CATHY: My head is completely bandaged all around my face. All that peaks out are my eyes, nose and mouth – even my chin is bandaged. Dr. Deeptha's assistant arrived to remove the bandages. Quick summary – pain. You see the bandages get glued to the head with dried blood.

After they left, I got up to get dressed and then I saw my face.

Really.

For the first time since surgery.

I look female.

It's still my face.

I really don't know what he did exactly.

I supposed he pulled the skin this way and that, but no bone restructuring work was done.

Still, I look more,

much more,

like a woman.

I hope it's not my imagination.

If I stand out, I will know.

I don't know why it matters to me that I pass in public –

it just does.

It always has.

It will make things easier on the kids when they are with me. Of course, if they are going to keep calling me Dad

(and I kinda hope they do),

people are going to look at us strangely anyway.

So here I am, staring at myself in the mirror and a woman looking back.

One that looks like she's gone a few rounds with Mike Tyson: but a woman nonetheless. So I smile at myself –

still my smile and really my face.

SCENE 5

Belfast FM: 'Killing in the Name Of'.

DEBORAH: 2004. It was a conversation that I knew I needed to have, but just never expected it to be now. I wasn't ready for it, but it had to be had. Michelle and I are eight years apart in age. I am the eldest. When I was eight, she was a baby, when she was eight, I was a teenager, when she was sixteen, I was getting married. We were close but not that close. I didn't really know her as a person; she was just my little sister. I sat on the bed and she sat across the room from me. I told her my big secret. I told her Mum and Dad had known for a few years now and that it had been the reason for the break-up of my marriage. I told her that I had to tell my kids. There was silence. Again, another point in my life when time stood still. I thought I had blown it. This was not going well. Eventually she spoke. She said: 'You mean after all these years, I have a big sister?'

SCENE 5.5

Belfast FM: 'Killing in the Name Of'.

CATHY: Today I was brought up to Dr. Deeptha's office so he could look me over and show me how to dilate before I was to be checked out.

By now, I just want to crawl inside myself and be left alone.

I sit up into these stirrups –

he begins checking out my face.

Then he moves down –

He produces some sort of metal instrument as he approaches my vagina and tells me he's going to insert it. But the odd thing is – that's okay with me.

If Dr. Deeptha says that's what he has to do, then that's what he has to do.

So he puts the metal device inside and pushes until he meets resistance – this feels like pressure inside me. Then he shows me how to cleanse myself and use the douche.

That's a red rubber ball with a point coming out one end. I have to fill the ball with antiseptic fluid mixed with water and squirt it up inside the vaginal cavity and repeat this four times immediately after I've spent fifteen minutes dilating.

I wasn't given the metal gadget, I was given two wax dilators, one slightly smaller than the other and both resembling a –

well –

I have to put a condom –

they gave me six free –

onto the dilator – cover it with KY Jelly and stick it up inside myself for fifteen minutes every morning.

Then I have to cleanse and douche, and after that I have to take a bath.

DEBORAH: My marriage was not happy. I submerged myself in work from at least one year after the marriage. I traveled extensively on business, not always coming home when I should have. I left Jean to bring up three young children. In 1989, with my condition getting stronger, I hid my self in alcohol and, for three years, I was a total alcoholic. Financially, I have never been dependable. After 1993 and my admittance to both Jean and my parents, I lost control and spent more and more time out as Deborah, despite having agreed to curtail it. No psychiatrist or psychologist. This is a very difficult life and I subjected both Jean and the children to it. This is how I caused my children so much pain.

This is the not the first time I have admitted any of this to myself, but it is the first time I have admitted it to someone else. As Sean, as a husband, and as a father, I was a total

Bastard…a failure. I was always hiding the real me. I hope in the last six years I have improved as a person. *(Beat.)*…

SCENE 6

50 things to do before I'm 50 (alternating Deborah – Cathy)

1. Gender reassignment surgery
1 Start Each Day by reviewing my 50 Targets and how I will get closer to achieving them today
2. Learn to play piano
2 Meditate for five minutes at the start of every day so that I can calm down
3. Buy a new acoustic guitar
3 Rejoin Weight Watchers
4. Inform my kids about the upcoming surgery
4 At work set particular times three days per week for careful managment of the Admistration of business.
5. The Frames tour of Ireland
5 Stand & Sit Straight
6. Open a record /coffee shop
6 Have a Health Check
7. Attempt to stop mum periodically calling me Sean
7 Weekend with J in her new House in Killarney
8. Talk to Jean and try to ease the tension
8 Organise Summer Holiday with the Kids
9. …
9 …
10. Meet JJ (my best friend from school)
10 …
11. Attempt to stop my Mum watching Sex Change Hospital
11 Fix Leak and Paint Hall
12. Submit poetry for publishing

12   Hang Photos

13.   Record some of my songs professionally

13   Develop Cooking Recipes

14.   …

14   Play Tennis at least twice a week to develop my game

15.   Read Ulysses again

15   Organise Tennis Coaching

16.   Visit the Aran islands

16   Help Develop *The Big Deal* story for Play

17.   Visit Skibbereen

17   Spanish Trip with the Kids at Easter

18.   Trip to Paris (on my own)

18   Reconcile my relationship with Ellen

19.   Weekend away with T

19   Reconcile my relationship with Mammy

20.   …

20   Reconcile my relationship with Sister 1

21.   Start cycling

21   Reconcile my relationship with Sister 2

22.   Lose a stone in weight

22   Reconcile my relationship with Brother 1

23.   Get my ears pierced

23   Reconcile my relationship with the Catholic Church and separately with God

24.   Stabilise financial situation

24   See Counsellor again to check if she thinks I'm still sane

25.   …

25   Have Father-and-Son day with my eldest son Shane

26.   …

26   Have Father-and-Daughter day with my eldest daughter Louise

27.   …

27 Have Father-and-Daughter day with my youngest daughter Charlotte

28. …

28 Have Father-and-Son day with my youngest son Peter

29. …

29 Stop watching so much TV with the Kids. Learn to relax in their company and enjoy the time with them. Stop trying to organise something to do all the time

30. …

30 Develop more Adult relationship with Shane take an interest in his friends, school and sports

31. Fiftieth Birthday dinner with family

31 Keep Income Levels sufficiently high to meet all the bills

32. 50th Birthday dinner with closest friends

32 Go on the Tennis Weekend & join in the Club's social activities to develop friendships there

33. Party at home August weekend

33 Write a decent short story

34. Night out with ML & SH

34 Write a decent poem

35. €1000 shopping spree

35 Develop a plan for my novel

36. Boxing Match (to see Katie Taylor)

36 Push Ellen to have her house renovated

37. Laser Eye Surgery

37 …

38. Start a club

38 Have friends to Dinner once every 6 weeks

39. …

39 Buy a New Tennis Racquet

40. Buy a copy of The Frames' 1st album on Vinyl

40 Go on a Solo Weekend Trip abroad

41.   Bands To See: The Frames

41   Go for a Solo Weekend Trip in Ireland

42.   The Swell Season

42   Go to London with Deborah

43.   James

43   Acquire nice Jewellery piece – an opal perhaps

44.   Gemma Hayes

44   Complete the Pandora Bracelet

45.   Duke Special

45   Purchase a nice Gold Fountain Pen or Biro

46.   Vyvienne Long

46   Consider 3D TV and DVD Acquisition

47.   Paul Tiernan

47   Consider benefits of acquiring a Laptop or iPad

48.   Wallis Bird

48   Acquire a Silk Nightie

49.   Lisa Hannigan

49   Acquire Silk Sheets

50.   Christy Moore

50   Minimise working weekends to once a month

   Song: 'Lisdoonvarna'.

CATHY: I first tried to transition in 1984 when I was twenty-three years old. I told my mother in the kitchen and she said, 'Oh, Jesus!' or something like that. Then she went into my Dad in the living room and turned off the TV. Now I broke it to them gently. I gave them a physical reason; I think I told them I had a womb. That was the cowardly thing to do, not to stand up and say, 'These are my feelings. I've no evidence of it.' I pretended there was a physical manifestation. Of course there was a physical manifestation as far as I was concerned. I had the wrong fucking body. It was 1984. My parents were very supportive, although it was covered up. I went and lived as Cathy for four months in London and I tried to be what was in my mind the ideal woman, what a woman should be. That involved not talking too much. That wasn't me. Now, you cannot be someone you're not, and so I wasn't any happier. I knew my family would be happy if I went back to being Patrick and as I wasn't happy anyway… Very simple. I went back. I fell in love. I got married.

DEBORAH: Cathy,

It's 10.30 p.m. on Tuesday night. I have just finished your recent e-mail. All nineteen pages.

You are now on the way to recovery.

You are here now as you should have been and will be from now until the day you die.

So whilst I struggle slowly onward and upward, you are already there,

Love Deborah.

CATHY: I woke up this morning with a very determined view that this was the first day of the rest of my life. I got up and had my weekly shave – the first since I arrived – I do hate that.

I shaved very gingerly as my face is sore from the face lift.

I went down for breakfast which was the best meal I've had since I got here.

Coffee, Cornflakes, orange juice, toast, rashers cooked in the crispy way I love them.

I returned upstairs ready to dilate the first time myself.

I find it very difficult to come to terms with touching my vagina and surrounding areas.

After my bath I open my card and presents from the kids.

The card read 'To the best Dad: in the world.'

And I'm crying again.

Each child had signed their own name.

Nothing from Ellen. No present. No card.

This is the scariest, loneliest, most rotten time of my life.

While I was waiting for the plane to Thailand, Deborah
gave me an iPod Nano – not just an iPod Nano because
that's just buying someone a present – she did something
I wouldn't be able to do, she uploaded 441 songs and,
I have to say, about 80% of them I liked, which is an
amazing achievement. When she puts her mind to helping
someone, she really knows how to do it.

I had a very bad brush with myself one time. I went to
Deborah's house the next day. She got me through one
of the darkest periods of my life, and then she helped me
produce a CD of about eighteen/nineteen songs that were
basically appealing to Ellen – don't leave me. She has an
amazing music library and an amazing music mind and she
helped produce for me an album that I love and still listen
to and call *Without You.* One of the songs in particular has a
lot of meaning for me.

I will learn to live before I die

Will learn to love and learn to try

Not to give it all away

She may be the one that's meant for me

Or for the man that I used to be

Till I gave it all away

Today was probably one of the most boring days so far –
thank God.

I finished the Alias series –

It was OK.

I then opened my DVD box set of *The West Wing* –

I did get out of the hospital for a short time today – I got
lunch at McDonald's. I also purchased my first pack of
sanitary towels. That is probably the weirdest part of all

of this. Having to get used to needing those things and wearing them.

Later on, I settled down for probably the best film since I got here.

Enemy of the State.

I finally got my journal off to Deborah.

It was eighteen pages long – poor Deborah.

Dr Deeptha told me I could now wear make-up. I can't tell you how much this cheered me up. It allows me cover up all the bruising on my face and look normal. I couldn't believe the results.

It gave me some pep in my step and I decided to go shopping.

I took the sky train.

And there I was,

moving around the shopping centre,

nothing special about me anymore,

just another woman.

Every time I passed a man,

especially one in a tie,

I smiled to myself.

I will never again have to pretend to be something I'm not.

The horror is over.

DEBORAH: Dear Cathy, can you let me know if I am collecting you on Monday from the airport and if so what time…? Just so you know, I would be honoured to… Lots of love, Deborah.

CATHY: I always feel better about myself when my hair is washed and I have my make-up on. So I made a huge effort this morning to do just that. I had my breakfast and then went up to my room and forced myself to sort things out and tidy. For the past half-hour, I have been working on legal contracts. They are complex, but if they are drawn up correctly, I can save my client a few tens of thousands of euro. Even though I am thousands of miles away, having surgery – surgery that many people think is weird

– the client (God bless him!) doesn't trust anyone else to get the job done right. So he's paying me, to make sure everything is done properly.

Life can be sweet.

Today seems very like yesterday.

Breakfast, clean-up, writing, skipped lunch altogether, clean-up, didn't feel like dinner.

After clean-up, I started writing – to Ellen. I never stopped. Except to cry.

I don't think I will ever recover from losing Ellen.

I am mortified at the thought of meeting her tomorrow.

Mortified that my wife is going to see me as I am now.

How I have let her down.
My feelings of disgust are almost drowning me.
I am in love with a woman who is not gay and must hate me for killing her husband.

I don't expect to find anyone else.

For God's sake, I'm not even looking.

And if I were, who or what would have me.

DEBORAH: 2011. The Westbury Hotel, Dublin.

I ask Jean to meet me so I can tell her of my impending surgery. When she sits down, she asks what this meeting is all about. I thought maybe one of the kids might have mentioned it to her. Obviously not.

I tell her that I am going for surgery. I tell her that I've asked for this meeting out of respect for her, that I didn't want her hearing about it from someone else.

'You should have shown me some respect by not marrying me or having children. Then you wouldn't have the need to tell me anything.'

Janis and I arrived in London, early Sunday, at 9.30 a.m. After having a late breakfast and a leisurely glass of wine in Covent Garden, we went for lunch. This was my last meal before I checked in to Charing Cross Hospital at 4 p.m. It felt like a last meal. 4 p.m. came around quickly and we headed for the hospital. A girl I knew from Dublin, Edel, was also in the ward, she was due to have surgery the same day as me.

I was awoken at 6 a.m. by a Philippino nurse called Amour Resurrection. She gave me an enema and told me to put lovely white surgical stockings on, which I was to wear the entire time I was in hospital. Amour came and Edel left for her surgery. I wished her good luck.

At 12 a.m., the doctor arrived. Dr Bellringer. I'm not making these names up. He was dressed in a football shirt, shorts and sneakers. He looked like he was going for a kick around in the park. He asked if I would donate my scrotal skin for research. Sure. I don't need it anymore, knock yourself out. He told me he would see me later. He did but I didn't see him.

At 1.30 p.m., Amour came to bring me to theatre, a long walk to the fourteenth floor. We caught the lift to the fifteenth floor. Amour told me that Edel, on her way to surgery that morning, had admired the view of London.

I came to in the recovery room. Holding my hand was a nice man. I asked his name. He said it was Raj. I told him he had a really nice face. I looked at the clock, it said

4 o'clock. This was all very real. I was awake, I wasn't dreaming, I was ALIVE. Raj informed me that he was bringing me back to the ward…

SCENE 7

Fade up so DEBORAH can be heard talking over the song.
David Bowie: 'Space Oddity'.

I started singing. I don't know why, but I did. I didn't stop, couldn't remember any more lyrics, so I kept repeating that bit. I kept on smiling at that beautiful face looking down on me. I sang out loud. They could hear me coming…

SCENE 7.5

Fade up much louder. Fade out fast after 'the stars look very different today'.

I texted a few friends to let them know it was over. The nurse told me how to manage the pain. There was no pain, some discomfort, but no pain. I was sitting up enjoying my fish pie and, more importantly, my orange marmalade pudding with custard. I had a morphine drip with a little button attached, should I need it. I didn't need it. I felt great. *'Just like riding a bike around Ireland for five hundred miles,'* I told Janis, *'a sore ass, wobbly legs and a little bit woozy.'* Cathy had five surgical procedures in one day and was alone in Bangkok. I had one and was with my friends and family. Amour arrived and removed my bandages. I got to see down there. I got a warm feeling.

My mum rang me at 10 p.m.. Dad had gone to bed. We talked about the op, how I was in myself, coming home, dad, and how great it was for me to have Janis here. She asked would I like to go down to her house for a couple of weeks after I got home so she could look after me. She had stressed herself out watching *Sex Change Hospital* on the telly.

Later that day I got my energy back and did 10 laps of the corridor. 3200 steps of about 2ft each. So I walked 6400 ft. I was tired so I went back to bed.

I didn't sleep too well that night. I started to feel a little down. I was missing the kids. I don't know why. I had seen them last Saturday night, and normally go for weeks without seeing them. It was just tiredness. My daughter sent me a text to tell me she got herself a job for the summer. It lifted my spirits.

The next day we had a party in the ward. I played DJ and had all the nurses dancing. Even the nurses not on our bay came to join in, smiling and dancing – 'You Sexy Thing'. It was fun. Everybody was singing.

At 8 a.m., I peed. I didn't think I could be so overjoyed about peeing. This meant I could go home. I walked outside the hospital and thought:

Freedom, and fresh air. I've escaped.' I was glad to be out. It had been a short week, but I was glad it was over.

I was always Deborah. This operation did not make me a woman; all it did was make me physically female.

But I will never be completely female.

I will never have a menstrual cycle.

I will never experience the joy of being able to bear children.

And I will never experience growing up as a girl.

On the Saturday before I went to England, my mum insisted that I take her rosary beads. I don't subscribe to the church anymore and I certainly don't pray. I tried to explain this, but she insisted I do it for her. On the morning after the surgery, I found myself saying a decade of the rosary. I didn't use the beads, I counted with my toes. Why, I don't even know now, I don't believe in that sort of thing, but it continued all week. Every morning I would wake up and say one. I stopped as soon as I got out.

CATHY: I packed,

    had dinner,

    did my clean-up,

    finished packing.

    I had no time for a last cup of coffee when my driver arrived at 8:30 p.m. to bring me to the airport. The flight got in in good time and I arrived at the connecting gate an hour early.

    I think I will always be annoyed with the man who didn't help me as I struggled with my case on the carousel.

    Patrick would have rushed to help.

    Interestingly, I'm not prepared to ask a 'gentleman' for help.

    Not yet anyway.

    Deborah met me in the arrival's lounge.

    I got the thumbs up from her.

    I can't wait to see the kids.

    I can't wait to see the kids.

    I just finish dilating and have my make-up in place when everyone arrives.

    Charlotte, my youngest, hugs me first.

    Then Ellen appears at the door.

    We give each other a polite hug and a kiss on the cheek.

    We both hold it together and everything is fine.

    One time not too long after the operation, about three or four months in, I woke up with an erection and my hand around my penis and I thought, 'oh my god, it grew back during the night.'

I was still dreaming, only I didn't know I was dreaming. This felt so real and I could feel my penis throbbing and I was horrified thinking, 'oh my god, I have to go through all that again,' because there was no way I wanted it.

I was already trying to work out how would I hide it, who would I tell, and then I realized, 'this is silly, penises don't grow back, I must be dreaming,' and as I began to wake up, I could literally feel the penis dissolve into thin air and my hand was where the penis might have been but wasn't.

What word do you put on people like us? I prefer to solve the problem and ignore the working. Call me what you like. I'm a woman.

DEBORAH: Don't call me what you like. I'm Deborah. That's it…

SCENE 8

(Loud.)

Transvision Vamp: 'Baby I Don't Care'.

OEDIPUS LOVES YOU
BY
SIMON DOYLE AND GAVIN QUINN

TIRESIAS – Ned Dennehy
JOCASTA – Gina Moxley
OEDIPUS – Karl Shiels
ANTIGONE – Ruth Negga
CREON – Dylan Tighe

Text: Simon Doyle and Gavin Quinn
Direction: Gavin Quinn
Set Design: Andrew Clancy
Lighting Design: Aedín Cosgrove
Music: Gordon Is A Mime

Performances:

Smock Alley, Dublin; 9–24 October, 2006

High Performance Rodeo, Calgary, Canada; 11–13 January, 2007

University of Lethbridge, Canada; 17–18 January, 2007

The Banff Centre for the Arts, Banff, Canada; 20 January, 2007

Timms Centre for the Arts, Edmonton, Canada; 24–26 January, 2007

Recto–Verso Festival, Quebec City, Canada; 9–10 February, 2007

FFT, Dusseldorf, Germany; 15–17 March, 2007

The Arches, Glasgow, Scotland; 16–17 April, 2007

Auawirleben Berne, Switzerland; 26–27 April, 2007

Kilkenny Arts Festival. Kilkenny, Ireland; 16 & 19 August, 2007

Carnuntum Festival. Austria; 26 August, 2007

Das Schauspielhaus, Hamburg, Germany; 2–3 September, 2007

Espoo City Theatre, Espoo, Finland; 30 October–2 November, 2007

Euro–Scene Leipzig. Germany; 9–10 November, 2007

Hebbel am Ufer (Hau Zwei), Berlin, Germany; 14–15 December, 2007

Riverside Studios, London, UK; 8–24 February, 2008

The Oriental Pioneer Theatre, Beijing, China; 3–6 April 2008

Shanghai Grand Theatre, Shanghai, China; 10–13 April, 2008

Wexner Center for the Arts, Columbus, Ohio, USA; 15–18 May, 2008

PS 122, New York, , USA; 21–25 May & 28 May–1 June, 2008

Project Arts Centre, Dublin; 26 November–6 December, 2008

Everest Theatre, Seymour Centre, Sydney, Australia; 21–25 January, 2010

Powerhouse, Brisbane, Australia; 3–7 February, 2010

Granary Theatre, Cork; 4–6 November, 2010

Town Hall Theatre, Galway; 15–16 November, 2010

ACT I

SCENE 1

Curtain opens. THE SPHINX is revealed.

SPHINX: *(Sings 'Crackerass'.)*
Second
Fill any second,
Take off take too much and the room
Silly now, Exhausted
Oh oh, it's so open
Oh god, So hot, Sticky
Oh I'm gonna puke
So sick
Oh take too many
So warm
Slowing down and sicken
I love you baby and if it's quite all right
I need you baby, if it's really right
I really love you baby
Really love you, Really Love you
Really Love you, Really Love you
Really Love you, Really Love you
Really Love you, Really Love you
Don't dance in front of me, come here and make me
Agree with the song, the loneliest drug
Back to your bed, holding yourself
There's no one to hold you
Bring you back down
Wake up on bad days, desert and lies
Nothing too sick
Drown in your own eyes
Wanted to throw your arms around something
Anything that's warm or possibly breathing
Don't dance in front of me, come here and fuck me
Don't dance in front of me, come here and make me
The loneliest drug here

The loneliest drug here
The loneliest drug here
All the little faces
Pretty and gorgeous
Still all women with sweat so obvious
No one to hold you
There's no love here, There's no love here
There's no love here, There's no love here
There's no love here
Don't dance in front of me, come here and fuck me
Don't dance in front of me, come here and fuck me
Don't dance in front of me, come here and fuck me
Darling, darling, darling
Da da ba ba ba ba ba ba ba
Ba ba ba ba ba ba ba ba ba
Da ba ba ba ba
I love you baby and if it's quite alright I need you baby
I love you baby and if it's quite alright I need you baby
I love you baby
Ha bee ba, ha bee ba, ha bee ba, ha
Ha ha ha ha ha ha ha ha ha ha

The SPHINX finishes singing, OEDIPUS enters.

SPHINX: I have a riddle for you. What has four legs in spring, two legs in summer and three legs in winter?

OEDIPUS: Man.

SPHINX: Yes. You're right.

(Pause.) Oedipus, you mother fucker.

SCENE 2

OEDIPUS and JOCASTA are in bed together.

OEDIPUS: Touch me.

JOCASTA: I don't want to.

OEDIPUS: Why?

JOCASTA: I'm not into it.

OEDIPUS: What's wrong with you? Lately you're so dulled.

JOCASTA: There's a plague.

OEDIPUS: What kind of a plague?

JOCASTA: A plague. I don't know what kind of a plague. I have no expertise in plagues. Ask Tiresias. It was his diagnosis.

OEDIPUS: Why haven't you told me about this before?

JOCASTA: It's not really of much consequence.

OEDIPUS: What do you mean it's not really of much consequence? It's a plague. We need to find a cure.

JOCASTA: I don't know that we do. I kind of like it. It suits me. It suits my lifestyle. It makes sense of my inertia.

OEDIPUS: How long has this been going on?

JOCASTA: For a while. Since my first husband Laius died.

OEDIPUS: And what have you done about it?

JOCASTA: Nothing.

OEDIPUS: But you have to do something.

JOCASTA: I'm not sure. It's kind of reassuring. Like being half asleep and knowing that you don't have to wake up. I think it suits us here this plague.

OEDIPUS: Who do you mean by 'us'?

JOCASTA: Everyone's got it here. Everyone except Tiresias. And you. So maybe it's you who have the plague? Maybe we're the un-afflicted ones. Anyway, I don't see what business it is of yours how we live our lives. You barged in here like you owned the place. You thrust your dirty feet into my husband's shoes. You took his place in my bed without a passing thought for the consequences.

OEDIPUS: It was my right.

JOCASTA: Who gave you the right?

OEDIPUS: I vanquished the Sphinx.

JOCASTA: You vanquished the Sphinx. Did she need vanquishing? She had some good songs, that Sphinx.

Maybe we enjoyed her routine. What made you think we needed rescuing?

OEDIPUS: But she was a Sphinx. She had to be vanquished.

JOCASTA: Who told you that? Tiresias? He's living in his own fantasy world. We stopped listening to him ages ago. He's insane.

OEDIPUS: He's a psychoanalyst.

JOCASTA: What's the difference?

OEDIPUS: I think we need to call a family meeting.

JOCASTA: I think you should take your medicine. You're demented.

OEDIPUS: This isn't right. We need to address this problem.

JOCASTA: You're worse than Tiresias.

OEDIPUS: What about Tiresias? Antigone is making such progress with him. Maybe he can take us through some family therapy?

JOCASTA: He's gotten to you, hasn't he? That crazy blind old bat. He used to be in a band, you know. You can tell. You can always tell. He always needs to be the front man. He was the bass player. Till he deadened all the nerves in his fingers. He never changed the strings. He'd heard somewhere that it would give him a proper dub reggae sound. Eventually they fired him. They replaced him with a special amp that put the bass in the mix automatically.

OEDIPUS: I think he might be able to help. I think you just don't want to get better. It's a plague. It can't be good for you. Why don't you want to be cured of it? You're addicted to sickness.

JOCASTA: Just let me put it to you this way. I used to have to take pills every day, and now I don't. That's something, isn't it? I mean, that's something, at least.

SCENE 3

In the garden, ANTIGONE is in therapy with TIRESIAS.

TIRESIAS: Your father's very stubborn.

ANTIGONE: Yeah. He's very proud, I guess.

TIRESIAS: He always has to have his own way.

ANTIGONE: Big deal. Lots of people are like that.

TIRESIAS: Are you like that?

ANTIGONE: I don't care. I take what comes my way.

TIRESIAS: Amazing, just like Jocasta.

ANTIGONE: Whatever. If that's what you believe?

TIRESIAS: Yes. I think so.

(Pause.) How are you feeling these days? Anything on your mind, you'd like to talk to me about?

ANTIGONE: No, not really.

(Pause.) I feel normal.

TIRESIAS: What are you interested in?

ANTIGONE: Everything.

TIRESIAS: Everything.

ANTIGONE: I'm interested in everything. Everything that's going on around me.

TIRESIAS: I suppose that's an okay way to be.

(Pause.) Are you listening?

ANTIGONE: I am listening avidly.

TIRESIAS: Your life is like a scene in a film except it really could happen. Think about that.

ANTIGONE: Yes.

TIRESIAS: Do you have many pals? Your own age, I mean?

ANTIGONE: No.

TIRESIAS: I suppose it can be difficult to meet people with like interests. I mean you're quite unique. You're not the same as everyone else. You're very different. You come from a very special family.

ANTIGONE: If you say so.

TIRESIAS: Your mother asked me to talk to you about your recent behavior with your father.

ANTIGONE: What do you mean?

TIRESIAS: She thinks you're being a bit too friendly, you know, you're a grown woman now. It's just a little unnatural, she thinks, the way you sit in his lap and kiss him on the lips good night.

ANTIGONE: What the fuck are you talking about, you slimy creep?

ANTIGONE storms out, goes to her bedroom and throws pillows about her room. And sheets…

SCENE 4

OEDIPUS and ANTIGONE are in the kitchen.

OEDIPUS: Do you think I look sexy?

ANTIGONE: I don't know, you're my dad.

OEDIPUS: It's only a bit of fun, relax. It makes me feel better.

How come you don't have a boyfriend?

ANTIGONE: I don't want one.

OEDIPUS: You're not gay are you?

ANTIGONE: No! Dad!

OEDIPUS: Sorry. I didn't mean to.

ANTIGONE: It's okay.

OEDIPUS: You seem to hang around with your uncle Creon a lot. It's just I don't think it's healthy. You should hang around boys your own age – ones that aren't related to you would be even better.

ANTIGONE: I do hang out with other boys, I just never bring them home, that's all. What does it matter to you anyway? Why the sudden interest?

OEDIPUS: Just making conversation, that's all. I'll drop the subject if you like. Are you still a virgin?

ANTIGONE: I'm leaving.

OEDIPUS: Please don't. I'm sorry. I promise I'll stop.

SCENE 5

CREON tries to drown himself in the pool. ANTIGONE tries to save him.

CREON: Don't worry. I'm just trying to find out who I am.

ANTIGONE: Very funny. Asshole.

CREON takes his clothes off.

CREON: I have a hopeless tenderness for you. I understand the anxiety, the fear, the disgust.

CREON dances to Turkish folk music and changes into his Speedos. He looks at ANTIGONE first to silently ask for permission. She nods approval. When he is finished he gestures to her to do the same.

ANTIGONE: No way.

She rubs lotion into his body at his request. Especially around his breasts.

CREON: Ooh. That's nice.

They look at each other in the eyes. They practice kissing for a while. They then go swimming in the pool. He plays music on his ghetto blaster and jumps on top of her.

ANTIGONE: Why are you behaving like this?

CREON: I'm sorry.

ANTIGONE: Maybe you should go.

CREON: Why don't we rehearse for a while?

ANTIGONE: Did you know Tiresias used to be in a band?

CREON: He said something about that all right.

ANTIGONE: He was talking to me. He wants to join the band.

CREON: Join the band?

ANTIGONE: Join our band, yeah.

CREON: But he's fucking ancient.

ANTIGONE: You're no spring chicken yourself.

CREON: What does he play?

ANTIGONE: He used to play bass.

CREON: Bass.

ANTIGONE: But he says he doesn't play bass any more. Something wrong with his fingers. He wants to play drums.

CREON: But we don't need drums. Oedipus plays a bit. And besides, we've got a machine.

ANTIGONE: Yeah, I know. I told him.

CREON: What did he say?

ANTIGONE: He said that humans sounded better.

CREON: But they don't keep time as well as a machine.

ANTIGONE: No. No they don't.

CREON: So he's not much use to us, then.

ANTIGONE: No. No he's not.

CREON: So what did you tell him?

ANTIGONE: I told him he could join.

CREON: You're crap. You get embarrassed too easily. You need to learn how to turn people down. Just tell him to fuck off.

ANTIGONE: I can't.

CREON: Why not?

ANTIGONE: Cause he's old. I feel guilty. Old people make me feel guilty somehow.

CREON: You're a fucking spa.

ANTIGONE: Shut up and play.

CREON: I'm bored of your songs.

ANTIGONE: Then write some of your own.

CREON: I couldn't be bothered. What's the point? They all sound the same in the end.

ANTIGONE: Maybe Tiresias can write us some new songs.

CREON: Is he your 'special friend' now?

ANTIGONE: No he's not. Shut up ye tit. It's just about the band. It's all about the band. He just wants to join the band. He's really enthusiastic.

CREON: I'll bet he is.

ANTIGONE: We've been practising secretly.

CREON: I'll bet you have.

ANTIGONE: I'll play you one of our songs.

CREON: Go on then.

ANTIGONE: *(Sings.)*

> Sex, Sex with real women
> I can tell you it's over-rated
> I tried it myself and I can tell you I hate it
> Oh but I love them all when they're sedated

TIRESIAS enters.

TIRESIAS: So. What's all this about a band then?

CREON: It's just me and Antigone. It's experimental. We jam. I process her. She processes me. We listen back to the tapes and splice together the songs in real time. We write each other's lyrics and sing on the spot. One take. Purity. Never rehearse. Never play a song twice. Never think. Just act out the moment.

TIRESIAS: That sounds… Interesting.

CREON: And what do you have to offer us?

TIRESIAS: I'm a seasoned musician. I used to be in a glam rock band. I had very intricate make-up. Hair right down to my ass. These days I'm a percussionist. I bang stuff. It's quite a unique form. Very ancient. Full of possibilities. You are, of course, aware that I study the ancient Greeks. Well,

I try to reconstruct their epic poetry in percussion and
song. With a contemporary angle.

CREON: You're completely outmoded.

TIRESIAS: You haven't heard my songs.

TIRESIAS: *(Sings 'I'm A Ladies Man'.)*
Sex, Sex with real women
I can tell you it's over-rated
I tried it myself and I can tell you I hate it
Oh but I love them all when they're sedated

I'm a ladies man
I'm a ladies man
I'm a ladies man
And there's nothing queer about that
And there's nothing queer about that
I'm a ladies man
I'm a ladies man
I'm a ladies man
And there's nothing queer about that
And there's nothing queer about that
La La La La La

You were so soft so uncomplicated
I loosened your clothing
My heart palpitated
I felt so alive
I felt so elated
I'm a ladies man
I'm a ladies man
I'm a ladies man
And there's nothing queer about that
And there's nothing queer about that
I'm a ladies man
I'm a ladies man
I'm a ladies man
And there's nothing queer about that
And there's nothing queer about that

SCENE 6

OEDIPUS is barbecuing in the back garden.

ANTIGONE: Where's Creon?

OEDIPUS: I sent him away. To the oracle.

JOCASTA: Why did you do that?

OEDIPUS: To find out what's wrong.

JOCASTA: But nothing's wrong.

ANTIGONE: What do you mean? Everything is wrong.

OEDIPUS: She's right. Everything is wrong.

JOCASTA: Why do you always have to side with your father in these things? There's nothing wrong. Tell me what's wrong.

OEDIPUS: There are problems in this house. That's why I sent Creon to the oracle.

JOCASTA: Did you give him money?

OEDIPUS: Yes. I gave him a few quid. For the bus.

JOCASTA: Oh no. He'll be gone for days. You know you really shouldn't give him any money.

ANTIGONE: That's not the answer, you know. Going to the oracle. The solution is only to be found in a just morality.

OEDIPUS: You're so full of crap, Antigone. You're young. You think that you can control the world. Wait till you get to my age. Then you'll find out that the world controls you. That's why I sent Creon to the oracle. To find out what it is that's controlling us.

JOCASTA: Nothing is controlling us. Nothing is wrong. Except for your own fuck-ups. And you can take responsibility for those without infecting us all with the blame. You're a fool.

OEDIPUS: Are you finished?

OEDIPUS busies himself with the barbecue. JOCASTA takes ANTIGONE to one side.

JOCASTA: Antigone. Come here. I have to tell you something.

ANTIGONE: Yes? What is it?

JOCASTA: It's about your father.

ANTIGONE: Yes?

JOCASTA: It's about the barbecue. He's burning the meat. Watch him. He throws on a few sausages. He turns his back and they're frazzled.

ANTIGONE: But that's not such a terrible thing, is it?

JOCASTA: You don't seem to understand. I don't think he can be trusted with meat.

ANTIGONE: Then you can do the barbecue.

JOCASTA: The man of the house must be the one to do the barbecue. But your father cannot be trusted to cook the meat properly. This is a dreadful omen.

ANTIGONE: We could just order pizza.

JOCASTA: You can't have pizza at a barbecue. There must be burgers and ribs and sausages and chicken legs. There must be sauces. There must be salads, which nobody remembers bringing, and nobody bothers to eat. There must be ice cold beers in rubbish bins full of ice. There must be paper plates incapable of holding anything. There must be plastic cutlery which shatters very easily. Because all that matters is meat, barely cooked, taken in the hands and ripped from the bone. Now that's what a barbecue is all about.

SCENE 7

CREON returns. He begins to tell OEDIPUS what he learned in Delphi. He is prompted through headphones.

CREON: What I learned was, 'Drive the corruption from the land, don't nurse it in the soil, root it out.' We all, especially you, have to be honest with ourselves and go into therapy, and get our problems out in the open.

OEDIPUS thinks for a moment. They look at each other.

OEDIPUS: Okay. Fuck it. Why not?

CREON gives him a hug. CREON receives another prompt.

CREON: There's one more thing. The oracle thinks we should try to solve the murder of Jocasta's first husband, Laius. She thinks that would help.

OEDIPUS: Okay. No problem. Maybe we'll finally catch the bastard.

(To himself.) But if he hadn't been killed, I wouldn't be here right now sharing his wife's bed.

(To CREON.) And besides it's a good idea to try and find the murderer because whoever killed Jo's first husband might try and kill me.

CREON: Absolutely. You're so right. Finally we can begin a year of living honestly.

OEDIPUS: That would be great, brother.

CREON: Yes, brother.

(They hug.) I think you should know. The people hate you.

OEDIPUS: What people?

CREON: All the people. Out there. You know the ones. Hate you. Can't stand you.

OEDIPUS: And how do you know?

CREON: I stayed out there. To see. To check them out. I wanted to see if there was anything out there. For me. I mean, it's nice here and everything. And I really love you all. Love my family. I mean I really love my family. In a very special way. Even though you've totally ruined my life. But I just wanted to get out and see how I would get on with other people. See if I could make some friends. Tiresias thinks I spend too much time with my family. Even though I really love them. Even though they fuck me over constantly.

OEDIPUS: And how did you get on?

CREON: Terrible, mostly. People are so awful. I mean, not like here. My family is so wonderful. But out there… Wankers. They hate you, you know.

OEDIPUS: How can they hate me? They don't even know me.

CREON: That's exactly what I said to them. And you know what they said? They said that that was besides the point. That it wasn't so much you personally that they hated, but what you stood for.

OEDIPUS: Really. That's just – That's just too much.

CREON: I really admire you. You've got guts. I don't know how you do it. But I'll tell you this much, I won't be going out there again. I don't need them. I've got everyone I need right here.

CREON kisses OEDIPUS.

TIRESIAS: He's mixed up.

JOCASTA: I know.

ANTIGONE: What's going on?

JOCASTA: Apparently we are all going to enter therapy.

ANTIGONE: Spare me.

(Pause.) The dead are spreading death and therapy is going to rescue us. Come with your face aflame with drink and your raving women's cries and we'll get to the bottom of this mess.

ACT II

SCENE 1

Everyone is sitting around in a therapy session.

VOICEOVER: Act Two. Therapy.

TIRESIAS: Let's start.

OEDIPUS: I wasn't here when all this happened. But I will try and help.

JOCASTA: We don't have to tell everyone our shortcomings do we?

TIRESIAS: Not exactly, just what's on your mind, really. To get the thing rolling.

JOCASTA: Oh. I feel embarrassed.

TIRESIAS: Okay. Why do you think you feel embarrassed?

JOCASTA: Isn't it obvious? Being here like this, in front of you all.

TIRESIAS: Go further. That is not the full reason.

JOCASTA: I feel embarrassed for myself, I feel a general embarrassment for the whole family, as I am the mother, you see.

TIRESIAS: Okay. Thank you. Anyone else embarrassed?

They all put their hand up.

V.O.: I know. Why don't you turn the lights off? That might help. Or put on those masks. Then maybe you'll feel more comfortable when you have to speak about yourselves.

TIRESIAS: Well if you really want to. I think you are missing the point, though. Isn't that just further secrecy, murkiness?

ANTIGONE: Oh. Come on. Let's try.

CREON: Yeah. It's a good idea.

TIRESIAS: Okay.

OEDIPUS: Okay.

JOCASTA: *(Nods.)*

Blackout. They put the masks on.

CREON: I used to masturbate a lot as a teenager, mostly thinking of Jocasta's breasts.

ANTIGONE: Creon!

JOCASTA: Creon!

CREON: Sorry. Only joking. Sorry.

TIRESIAS: So let's try again. Who feels awkward, let's say, when we are all having dinner together?

OEDIPUS: I do. I feel awkward.

Laughs.

TIRESIAS: Antigone, can you remember a happy moment? From your childhood?

ANTIGONE: Let me think.

(Pause.) No, I can't. I'd need more time to think.

TIRESIAS: Are you sure? Nothing at all?

ANTIGONE: I just can't think of anything in particular. None of it really stands out. I mean, I'm not saying that it was an unhappy childhood. No. But I can't think of anything to single out. I'm sorry. I'm bad at this, aren't I?

TIRESIAS: That's fine. We'll do an exercise. A role play. Creon, you be me. Jocasta, you be Antigone. The rest of us will observe, as if from outside a goldfish bowl. You will ask her to recall a happy memory from her childhood. All right. Are you ready? Go.

CREON: Antigone.

JOCASTA: Yes?

CREON: Tell me something. When and where were you happiest?

Pause.

JOCASTA: In my mother's womb.

CREON: Thank you.

Pause.

TIRESIAS: What did you think of that?

OEDIPUS: It didn't hang together for me.

ANTIGONE: Yes. No. The body language was all wrong. And she spoke too quickly.

TIRESIAS: It was an interesting answer, though. Wasn't it?

ANTIGONE: It was the sort of answer I'd expect from her. Self-serving. Flippant. Pat.

TIRESIAS: Do you think she tried to understand you?

ANTIGONE: No more or less than usual.

TIRESIAS: What did you think of him?

OEDIPUS: He was good. I liked the eyes especially.

CREON: Are we finished? Can we speak?

TIRESIAS: Yes. How did you find it?

CREON: It was very intense, being you.

TIRESIAS: Yes. I know. I'm a very intense person.

JOCASTA: I really feel that I got something out of that.

TIRESIAS: Good. That's great.

ANTIGONE: Why can't I think of a happy memory? I'm useless.

TIRESIAS: Antigone. Relax. Don't forget. The person is not the problem. The problem is the problem.

ANTIGONE: I suppose.

TIRESIAS: Now. Let's go again. This time, Oedipus, I want you to be Antigone. And Antigone, I want you to be me. The rest of us will observe. All right. Are you ready? Go.

ANTIGONE: Antigone?

OEDIPUS: Yes, Tiresias?

ANTIGONE: What is the happiest that you have been?

OEDIPUS: When I was a child.

ANTIGONE: Tell me about it.

OEDIPUS: I can't remember much about it. There was just the sense of profound happiness. It's slippery. The more I try to remember it, the more it recedes.

TIRESIAS: Can we have the lights back on now, please?

The lights go on.

CREON: I think this is stupid.

TIRESIAS: Thank you for that, Creon. Your opinion is valued.

CREON: This is really fucking stupid.

TIRESIAS: Thanks for that, Creon. We already had that point. Let someone else speak.

CREON: You are not playing drums in our band.

TIRESIAS: Percussion. I play percussion. There is a difference.

OEDIPUS: Can I just say how happy I am that everyone came along today?

CREON: So fucking stupid.

OEDIPUS: I thought that we needed to get together to talk about the plague.

CREON: There is no plague.

TIRESIAS: It might be helpful if we go around the room and everyone explains what it is that they mean by the plague. Let's start with you, Jocasta.

JOCASTA: I don't know. I suppose that yes, it's there. But it's nothing major. It's just like you're feeling a little tired all the time. A little resigned. Like an interesting prescription medicine. I don't have a problem with the plague. I think he's the one with the problem.

TIRESIAS: Let's not get into value judgments just yet. Creon?

CREON: This is stupid. I'm fine. There's no problem. So what if I get a little upset from time to time. It's no one else's business. Are you saying that I have a problem? Stop looking at me. Leave me alone. I didn't do anything. So what if everything is fucked up. Everything always fucks up, eventually. That's just the way things go. So what if I get a little hurt from time to time. Wouldn't you? Wouldn't you if it was fucken you?

TIRESIAS: Thank you, Creon. Antigone?

ANTIGONE: It's a moral illness. It's symptomatic of a failure in morality. Like a life support machine in a power cut. The emergency generator is running down. The first organ to go is morality. What will be next? Sanity? The plague is a symptom of a greater disease. None of you care any more, do you? About what's going on beyond? About what's happening outside your airless cocoon? All the oxygen of decency has been sucked out, and you just keep on going. Bacteria. That's all you are. Bacteria.

TIRESIAS: And you, Oedipus, what does the plague mean to you?

OEDIPUS: I don't know. I don't really have a clue. It doesn't really affect me. But it saddens me to think of you suffering under it. I'm the head of the household. I can't be running a plague-ridden household now, can I? So we need to sort it out. Don't you agree? That it's a bad thing?

TIRESIAS: It's really for you to decide. What does the plague mean to you?

OEDIPUS: It's – It's a sort of a sadness, I suppose.

TIRESIAS: Thank you. Thank you for that.

V.O.: Why don't you take a short break.

(Beat.) And play a game to help you relax.

TIRESIAS: We're going to play a game of wink murder. Everyone sit in a circle and close your eyes. I'm going to choose the killer by touching one of you on the shoulder. Then when I tell you to, open your eyes. If the killer winks at you, then you're dead. If you guess who the killer is, put up your hand and say their name but if you're wrong, you die. Okay. Everyone open their eyes.

OEDIPUS is the chosen killer, and proceeds to dispose of everyone, except TIRESIAS, who can't see him wink.

TIRESIAS: Oedipus is the killer.

End of game.

OEDIPUS: You seem to have all the answers. What's going on?

TIRESIAS: I think you already know the answer to that question.

OEDIPUS: What are you talking about?

TIRESIAS: Don't play dumb. You're such a bad actor.

(Beat.) Any bad memories? Anyone? Anyone?

JOCASTA: Not really.

ANTIGONE: I have to go.

JOCASTA: Please stay, we're only just getting started.

ANTIGONE: Don't fucking touch me.

(ANTIGONE storms out. She returns.) I just want to be left alone. Get off my back. I just want to be left alone like any normal teenager.

CREON: If you mention the plague again, I'm going to be sick.

OEDIPUS: I think that's the point right there.

CREON: I'm too lazy to talk. What does that make me, then?

TIRESIAS: Tiresome.

OEDIPUS: You're spoilt.

CREON: What do you care? Are you an oracle?

JOCASTA: Sometimes there are no words…

TIRESIAS: Anyway, there are some interesting points there for us all to consider.

JOCASTA: I'm talking. I'm talking. It might be nice to finish a sentence from time to time.

TIRESIAS: Of course. Sorry. Please continue.

JOCASTA: I can't. The moment is gone…

OEDIPUS: Well, I'm quite outgoing.

JOCASTA: He butts in, so sneaky, as if his sentence is better than mine. He thinks he rules this house and he doesn't. Every time I breathe he's next to me, it's suffocating, very, very draining.

OEDIPUS: I don't really understand women, that's my problem. I don't know how to look after them.

TIRESIAS: But you got on very well with your mother, you told me.

OEDIPUS: I know. But that's different. I mean, stranger women. Women that I bump into.

TIRESIAS: Oh.

Pause.

OEDIPUS: Why can't you tell me what happened twenty years ago when I first came here?

ANTIGONE throws a full milk carton to the floor making a beautiful 'don't-cry-over-spilt-milk' painting.

JOCASTA: What's going on?

ANTIGONE: Sorry.

JOCASTA: It's okay. I'll clean it up.

TIRESIAS: I think it would be better to concentrate on now.

OEDIPUS: You're all driving me crazy. What's wrong with me?

TIRESIAS: Can I suggest some visualisation techniques. Sometimes it helps to write yourself a letter.

OEDIPUS: I'm sorry. I can't…

(Writes something, privately.) 'Dear Oedipus…'

(Stands up, reads what he has written.) 'I am going to track down Laius's murderer. I'll fight for him as if he was my own father.'

TIRESIAS: Really. That's magnificent.

OEDIPUS: How could you leave the crime unsolved so long? What's wrong with you all?

CREON: We tried to find out but all we got were useless rumours.

OEDIPUS: What were the rumours?

CREON: That Laius was killed by strangers, traveling on the same road as him. Somewhere near a crossroads.

OEDIPUS: Brilliant work, Creon. But no one can find the murderer...

CREON: If anyone can, Tiresias can. They say, 'The truth lives inside him.'

OEDIPUS: Is that what they say? Okay, tell me. We are in your hands. Save us. Rescue us from everything being infected by the dead.

TIRESIAS: How terrible it is to see the truth. It's so painful.

OEDIPUS: Why are you so morbid?

TIRESIAS: I want to go home.

OEDIPUS: Why do you want to hide the truth?

TIRESIAS: Why dig up all this now?

TIRESIAS gets up to leave.

OEDIPUS: Please, if you know something. Tell us.

TIRESIAS: None of you know anything. And I will never tell you.

OEDIPUS: You know but won't tell us.

TIRESIAS: Trust me, you don't want to know.

OEDIPUS: You killed him. Or you arranged it. If you weren't such a coward you would have done it yourself.

TIRESIAS: Is that so? Actually, you are the murderer you hunt.

OEDIPUS: Are you mad? Who put you up to this?

TIRESIAS: You did. You had to go and force it out of me, didn't you?

OEDIPUS: Creon. Is this your idea or his?

TIRESIAS: Creon is not your problem. You are.

OEDIPUS: I didn't ask to be King. You asked me. Is this the reason you made me King so you could steal it from me later?

ANTIGONE: Please Dad, he didn't mean it. He just gets angry sometimes and says the wrong thing. It's not what we need right now. We need to concentrate and find the best solution to our problems.

OEDIPUS: Get out. Go back to where you came from. Fuck off. Vanish.

TIRESIAS: I would never have come here if you hadn't invited me.

OEDIPUS: If I'd known you were completely insane and were going to talk to me like this...

TIRESIAS: Insane, am I? Maybe to you but not to your parents. They found me sane enough.

OEDIPUS: Parents? What about my parents?

TIRESIAS: This day will bring your birth and your destruction, Oedipus.

ANTIGONE: The horror too dark to tell. I am terrified. I can't accept it. I don't know what to say. I'm lost and the wings of dark foreboding are beating. I cannot see what's happened and what's still to happen. Never will I convict my dad, never in my heart.

ACT III

SCENE 1

ANTIGONE and CREON are talking in the kitchen. CREON is sitting sideways to the audience, we see his profile in an exaggerated way. ANTIGONE is facing the audience.

ANTIGONE: This place is a nut house.

CREON: Yes.

ANTIGONE: Do you have any cigarettes?

CREON: Sure. What are you doing?

ANTIGONE: I'm practising my killer stare.

CREON: Let's see?

ANTIGONE: There. What do you think?

CREON: How is it a killer stare?

ANTIGONE: It goes on for miles and can last forever.

CREON: It's okay, I suppose. I'm still alive, though.

ANTIGONE: No, no, no, no, no. It's not supposed to be a deadly stare. It's a killer stare. It's a stare which says, 'I could kill you if I wanted to, but I choose not to.' It's a cool stare.

CREON: Aloof.

ANTIGONE: Exactly. It's for the band. When we perform.

SCENE 2

OEDIPUS is with CREON in the kitchen.

OEDIPUS: Creon. You're the source of this plague. Get out of here.

CREON: You've got me all wrong. What's this really about? If I knew something, I would tell you. I swear…

OEDIPUS: We would never have even heard about the killing of Laius if you and Tiresias hadn't got together. But you will never convict me of the murder.

CREON: Why would I want to get rid of you? I don't want to be King. Go to Delphi yourself and talk to the oracle personally. I've reported the message word for word. If I'm lying, kill me.

OEDIPUS: What? Do you want me to relax and sit back while everyone shits on me from above?

CREON: What do you want? Do you want me to go away?

OEDIPUS: No, I want you dead.

CREON: Calm down. Try and relax.

OEDIPUS: You don't think I'm serious. I am going to kill you.

CREON: You're insane. I haven't done anything.

OEDIPUS: It doesn't matter. I don't believe you.

JOCASTA comes out from the house.

JOCASTA: Can you keep it down? You're going to wake everybody. Oedipus, go to bed. And Creon, get lost, leave us alone. Why are you making such a racket? Are you drunk?

CREON: Your husband is threatening to kill me.

OEDIPUS: Yes, because I caught your brother about to stab me in the back.

CREON: No way. I swear. You've got it all wrong.

JOCASTA: Oh god, just believe him. Do it for me.

OEDIPUS: What do you want from me?

JOCASTA: He's your friend.

OEDIPUS: Do you know what you're asking? If that's what you want, then you want me dead, or out of this family.

JOCASTA: I feel sick.

OEDIPUS: I'm sorry. I'll leave him alone. But don't ask me to stop hating him.

SCENE 3

ANTIGONE and CREON are alone together.

ANTIGONE: I've lost my earring. I need to find my fucking earring. Right now.

(Pause.) There it is.

CREON: *(Eating an apple.)* Do you know what your problem is? You're always fishing for compliments.

ANTIGONE: Piss off. No I'm not. I'm genuinely quite quiet, some people accept that.

CREON: Everyone does. But that doesn't mean you're not always fishing for compliments.

ANTIGONE: You're saying just fucking nothing. Everything's a joke to you.

CREON: Just having a laugh. Relax, will you. That's how I get by.

ANTIGONE: Fucking hell. You annoy me.

ANTIGONE introduces her band. The gig begins.

(Sings 'Miss Dún Laoghaire'.)
I don't know what happened to me
I used to be such a nice girl
I used to be Miss Dún Laoghaire
I used to be Miss Dún Laoghaire
Now look at me Antigonised
Like a clown in my underwear
Playing darts through the night
Don't be too nice to me
It only makes me nervous
It only makes me nervous
It only makes me nervous
They've all had me
Yet they talk to me
As if I'm still a virgin
Still a virgin, still a virgin
Still a virgin, still a virgin
La la la la la la la la

La la la la la la la la
La la la la la la la la
La la la la la la la la

CREON introduces the song 'Limp'.

CREON: *(Sings 'Limp'.)*
Sometimes I feel like setting my clothes on fire
So I can be naked with you
I would burn all my skin just be in sin with you
You are my small personal alarm grenade
I fell in love with a girl with a limp
But she never fell in love with me
She only liked me as a friend she said
So one day I stole her walking stick
I'm really down like being in a tunnel
Don't see any light
I have a few questions
I have to write them down
What is the benefit of the medication I take?
I am on now
Play pool, play pool, play table tennis
Pool, pool, table tennis
Pool, pool, table tennis
And she never left her house again
No, she never left the house again
No, she never left the house again

ACT IV

SCENE 1

Stravinsky's 'Oedipus Rex' plays. The characters sing along to it through headphones. It fades out. Everyone is prompted through headphones throughout this scene and the following scene.

JOCASTA: Oh god, I need your help. My husband is paralysed by fear.

MESSENGER: I'm looking for someone called Oedipus. I have some good news for him.

JOCASTA: What news?

MESSENGER: I'm from Corinth. And the good news is that we want to make Oedipus our King.

JOCASTA: Isn't there a King already? Polybus?

MESSENGER: He died last week.

OEDIPUS: What's going on? Who's he?

JOCASTA: He's come from Corinth and he's here to tell you the good news that your father is dead.

MESSENGER: It's true. Polybus is dead.

OEDIPUS: How did he die?

MESSENGER: He died in his sleep.

OEDIPUS: He died and it had nothing to do with me. So much for oracles.

JOCASTA: That's what I have been trying to tell you all along.

OEDIPUS: Sorry. I was afraid.

JOCASTA: This fear you have of marrying your mother, lots of men dream about that, it doesn't mean it will ever happen.

OEDIPUS: I know that you're trying to help, but as long as my mother is still alive, I'm afraid of her.

JOCASTA: But surely your father's death is a good omen.

MESSENGER: What's the problem with your mother that makes you so scared of her?

OEDIPUS: Not her personally, but the oracle which foretold that I would kill my father and marry my mother – that is what scares me.

(Beat.) And that's why I never really visited them much.

MESSENGER: *(Shakes his head.)* That's unbelievable. All this time you thought that Polybus and Merope were your real parents? That's so incredible.

OEDIPUS: Of course they're my real parents.

MESSENGER: They loved you as a son but they were not your real parents. You were a gift from me.

OEDIPUS: What do you mean, a 'gift'?

MESSENGER: I found you abandoned on the side of a mountain with your ankles and feet shackled together, helpless. I took you back to Corinth and gave you to Polybus and Merope who brought you up as their own.

OEDIPUS: *(Removes his shoe.)* My limp and these awful scars, I've had them for as long as I can remember.

MESSENGER: And your name comes from them too. Oedipus, meaning pussy foot.

OEDIPUS: Who did this to me?

MESSENGER: I don't know. Actually, it wasn't exactly me who found you. It was another man who passed you on to me.

OEDIPUS: Who was he?

MESSENGER: I didn't know him but I remember he said he worked for someone called Laius.

OEDIPUS: Jocasta, do you know the man we are talking about?

JOCASTA: Jesus. Let it go, will you? Don't listen to this fool. He's talking rubbish.

OEDIPUS: I have to know. Don't you understand?

JOCASTA: Please stop. Please. Please Oedipus, let it go.

OEDIPUS: I can't. I want to know the truth.

JOCASTA: For your own sake. Stop right now.

OEDIPUS: You know I can't stop.

JOCASTA: Oh no.

> *JOCASTA goes into the house. OEDIPUS and the MESSENGER turn to watch her go. TIRESIAS enters, reluctantly.*

OEDIPUS: Is he the one you mean?

MESSENGER: That's him, definitely.

> *The MESSENGER leaves.*

OEDIPUS: Tiresias?

TIRESIAS: Yes. I tried to warn you, but you never listen.

OEDIPUS: Will you answer all my questions now?

TIRESIAS: If that's what you want.

OEDIPUS: Did you give him a child as he says you did?

TIRESIAS: Why are you doing this?

OEDIPUS: DID YOU GIVE HIM THE BABY?

TIRESIAS: Yes. Yes. Now, are you satisfied?

OEDIPUS: Where did the baby come from?

TIRESIAS: No more questions, please. Leave it.

OEDIPUS: Who did the baby belong to? Tell me. Or I'm going to kill you with my bare hands.

TIRESIAS: Your wife, Jocasta, she gave me the child, it was her child, Laius and hers.

OEDIPUS: Why?

TIRESIAS: To kill it.

OEDIPUS: Murder her own baby?

TIRESIAS: She was afraid of the prophecies.

OEDIPUS: What prophecies?

TIRESIAS: That the boy would end up killing his father.

OEDIPUS: So why wasn't the boy killed?

TIRESIAS: I couldn't go through with it. I hoped that the boy would grow up somewhere far from here and never meet his real parents.

(Pause.) But the boy is you.

OEDIPUS goes into the house. CREON comes out from the house. They remove their headphones.

CREON: The Queen is dead.

TIRESIAS: How?

CREON: She ran into her bedroom pulling at her hair. We all heard her screaming out Laius, her dead husband's name. Then Oedipus knocked down the door, to find her hanging by the neck. He cut her down and laid her on the floor. Then he took a knife and scissors in either hand and held the points of both above his eyes. And plunged them deep into his eyeballs, screaming. He kept screaming as he kept stabbing his eyeballs, until the river of blood stopped flowing and gushing, and it was only clots and sinewy nerves peeking out of his decimated skull.

TIRESIAS: The poor bastard.

SCENE 2

Later, CREON and ANTIGONE are on the lawn.

ANTIGONE: How are things?

CREON: I finally unblocked the toilet.

ANTIGONE: Great.

CREON: Do you think I'm a little autistic?

ANTIGONE: Yes, a little.

CREON: Really, this is serious. Do other people know? Do strangers know when they meet me? Should I get tests done?

ANTIGONE: Oh don't be silly, there's something wrong with everyone, just chill out.

CREON: That's like telling someone to relax who's stressed. That's bad.

ANTIGONE: Or 'snap out of it' to someone depressed. Bad too. You're not autistic enough for tests. The doctor would think you're mad. You just have to live with it.

CREON: I'm not sure how I feel about that. I know. I feel scared.

ANTIGONE: But you've been the same all your life. Nothing has changed.

CREON: Are you 100% sure? I want to know. You see, I feel different.

ANTIGONE: Yes, Creon, you are the same as always.

CREON: Is that good or bad?

ANTIGONE: It's good, of course. We all have stuff we need to work on. I have to fight my deep-seated melancholia.

CREON: How do you do that?

ANTIGONE: Struggle, struggle.

CREON: Struggle is a beautiful drug.

ACT V

SCENE 1

An instrumental song, 'Every Hard-on Needs Love'. Everyone dances. When the song ends, they are all sitting around in the kitchen. OEDIPUS goes to the front of the stage.

OEDIPUS: Hello, my name is Oedipus, Oedipus Rex. And I think I have been unhappy for a very long time.

(Pause.) Let me be happy.

TIRESIAS: Sorry. Not on the cards. You'll just have to face it.

OEDIPUS: I have limited imagination. Tell me something straight.

TIRESIAS: You were fucking your mother and you murdered your father. Is that straight enough for you?

Pause.

ANTIGONE: What was your favourite song when you were growing up?

OEDIPUS: 'Freebird' by Lynyrd Skynyrd.

Pause.

If I leave here tomorrow
Would you still remember me?
For I'm free traveling on now
Because there's too many places I've got to see

OEDIPUS cries inconsolably.

SCENE 2

A barbecue. Everyone is sitting around in the back garden. OEDIPUS' eyes are bandaged.

TIRESIAS: Where did you get the sausages?

OEDIPUS: At that butcher down the road. The one that's always smiling.

TIRESIAS: They're… Interesting.

CREON: Moist.

OEDIPUS: What?

CREON: I said, they're moist. The sausages.

ANTIGONE: I should have bought a new dress. For the summer.

JOCASTA: That's all right. It's raining.

ANTIGONE: It might stop.

JOCASTA: It never stops.

OEDIPUS: Does anyone else's eyes hurt? I think it might just be the smoke.

JOCASTA: Who made the potato salad? Has anyone tried it?

CREON: Hard.

JOCASTA: What?

CREON: It's hard.

JOCASTA: You always have to find fault in everything, don't you?

TIRESIAS: Life is hard. The potato salad is just a little chewy.

ANTIGONE: You're so deep, Tiresias.

TIRESIAS: You should hear my poetry.

CREON: Why aren't there any ribs?

JOCASTA: Oh, come on. It doesn't matter.

TIRESIAS: Yeah. Where are the ribs?

OEDIPUS: I fucked-up the marinade. I mistook tablespoons for teaspoons. They were inedible.

CREON: And what about the steaks?

OEDIPUS: They went off. I forgot to put them in the fridge. There were little worms crawling out of them. Sorry.

TIRESIAS: And where are the burgers?

OEDIPUS: They were in the freezer. I thought they'd be okay. But they came out all grey and mushy. There wasn't time to get any more. Sorry. But the sausages are good, aren't they?

CREON: Moist.

OEDIPUS: See? We have moist sausages. Grand.

CREON: Moist is not a good thing.

TIRESIAS: Tender. Tender is a good thing.

ANTIGONE: They're disgusting.

JOCASTA: At least it's not raining.

ANTIGONE: It is raining.

OEDIPUS: Have some potato salad. I made it.

TIRESIAS: It's chewy.

JOCASTA: You ruined the barbecue.

OEDIPUS: I always ruin the barbecue.

JOCASTA: I live in hope that some day you'll get it right.

OEDIPUS: At least the weather held.

JOCASTA: It's pissing rain.

OEDIPUS: Not as much as it might be.

JOCASTA: You're blind.

OEDIPUS: You're dead.

JOCASTA: Have you got a problem with that?

OEDIPUS: I'm going to go away.

JOCASTA: I thought you might.

OEDIPUS: There's nothing left for me here.

JOCASTA: No. Nothing.

OEDIPUS: And what about you?

JOCASTA: I'm dead. I'll be fine. It's the children I worry about.

SCENE 3

ANTIGONE speaks into a mic.

ANTIGONE: I'd like to say something.

TIRESIAS: Go ahead.

OEDIPUS: Go ahead.

ANTIGONE: I think it's all been a big misunderstanding.

JOCASTA: It usually is.

ANTIGONE: I mean, we get on okay. We just need to be kinder to each other. And forgive more…

TIRESIAS: Yes, but it's getting too hard for some of us to truly accept that. To truly forgive. That's why we need to go through this process. To discover how upset, angry and hurt we really are with each other so we can work it out. Work out how much we are really being asked to forgive.

OEDIPUS: Wouldn't it be easier if I just left?

TIRESIAS: Maybe. But that's kind of giving up isn't it?

ANTIGONE: I'd like you to stay. I want us to be a family, no matter what.

JOCASTA: Antigone, darling, it's just too fucked-up, I can't bear it.

OEDIPUS: You know what the biggest regret of my life is right now? That I was born. That's pathetic, isn't it? As miserable as it gets. What did I do to deserve this? I love you all.

(He takes out a piece of paper and reads.) 'I'm a bad person. I want to apologise for all the terrible things that I've done. I'm not doing this to make myself feel better, it's so you all know the truth and are not sitting there thinking that I'm something great, something special, to be looked up to, to be admired.'

TIRESIAS: Come here, come here.

TIRESIAS gives OEDIPUS a hug. OEDIPUS' face is covered by TIRESIAS', then we see TIRESIAS' eyes open.

OEDIPUS: *(Sings 'I Think We Are Just Waving Ourselves Goodbye'.)*

Everything is different now
But I still can't give you up
I won't believe the dreams till they are gone again
I can't hide my face till I'm awake
I hope one day to find a way
To learn how to give you up
Even though you are just scraping by
We are all just waving ourselves goodbye
In hotel rooms
And airport bars
And quiet streets
And public parks
Even though you are just scraping by
We are all just waving ourselves goodbye
In hotel rooms
And airport bars
And quiet streets
And public parks

THE YEAR OF MAGICAL WANKING
BY
NEIL WATKINS

Written and Performed by Neil Watkins
Directed by Phillip McMahon
Designed by Ciarán O'Melia

Produced by thisispopbaby
Producers Jenny Jennings and Lara Hickey

Performances:
Queer Notions Festival 2010, 10–11 November 2011, Project Upstairs
Cork Midsummer Festival 2011, 23–25 June 2011, Half Moon Theatre
Outburst Belfast 2011, 20 November 2011, Lyric Theatre, Naughton Studio
Dublin Fringe Festival 2011, 9–17 September 2011, Project Upstairs
Melbourne Midsumma Festival, 17–29 January 2012, Theatre Works
Fringe World Festival Perth, 31 January–11 February, Metcalf Theatre
Sydney Mardi Gras Festival, 14–18 February, Sydney Theatre
Adelaide Fringe Festival, 22 February–18 March, AC Arts

Great Spirit and Great Mystery hear my prayer.
Bless all the beings gathered in this room.
I bid your tastebuds welcome to my womb.
This is my truth. I bare my fruit. Let's share.

Tonight, Great Spirit. Shine. Infuse my heart
With courage so sublime that I may say
The details of my story and my way.
I am a wanker. Know this from the start.

I am Neil Martin Watkins and I am
A sex and love addicted innocent.
There's patterns I've adopted that would taint the
Love of Saints. I wank, therefore I slam.

It's normal to love sex; to love to love.
But it's not healthy when you're feeling shame;
When sex becomes a drug to kill the pain.
When pain is all your sex life's smacking of.

I'm into every act the mind can dream.
But intimacy isn't on the list.
For me to cum, I'm either stoned or pissed.
So I'm not really there to hear my screams.

This intimacy thing flies over my head.
I'm startled by the sight of same-sex bliss.
Why haven't I been healed by true love's kiss?
And so I wank because I haven't wed.

Sure everybody wanks their willy. Right?
And everybody hurts and needs to heal.
But I find healing hurtful. Hurts to feel.
I deal with stuff by wanking day and night.

I've got this little ritual. I score
Weed from a dealer, poppers, then begin.
I dress in leather. Get out of my bin.
So, safe in my cocoon, I go to war.

My right hand pulls the trigger. Consummate.
No other hand could possibly compete.
My left hand is in permanent retreat.
Except to feed me weed. I get my hit.

Me laptop's primary use is finding porn.
The weirder and the sicker does the trick.
You know, like sharp things shoved up through the dick.
Four Windows of Insanity are born.

The icing on the cake for perfect wanks
Is Poppers for that Crystal paradise.
I yield to feel oblivion's high price.
It's kind of you to hear me out. My thanks.

I cum and sure it's brilliant. Love being high.
I love forgetting that my life is shite.
Forget about the money owed, take flight.
And stuff those comedown feelings. I won't cry.

I'm 33. The age when Jesus died,
Rose from the Dead, ascended out of Hell.
If she can resurrect, I can as well.
Me bell end's battered and my hands are tied.

NOVEMBER

There's nothing like ten years of migraine pain
To needle you and tease a leap of faith.
A White Witch Doctor set with me a date
In Ireland's garden Wicklow. I'll explain.

Sweet Medicine Horse Nation is her name.
This woman changed my life forever. Fact.
She held a workshop, this was not an act.
And like the moth I am, I fed her flame.

Inside an earthen teepee twenty prayed
And listened to her ancient wisdom sing.
She'd flown from Oregon, on metal wing
To Ireland for my spiritual upgrade.

My pessimistic pout for the occult
Or anything religious was my shield
To any of the bullshit she might deal.
But I'd an inkling she would bring results.

She looks at me with genuine goodwill.
'I so desire to say, "look who's here,"'
Sweet Medicine addresses me. I fear
That she will say a queer gives her a chill.

Instead she glows. 'I thought that you'd be shy.
My people hold your kind in high regard.
We call you Winkta, Twin Spirited. Scarred
Though you are, you're angelic. You're God's child.'

Moth to the flame I fly now. My sad heart
Begins to heal as I unfeel the mean
And nasty lessons of the Pope's regime.
Sweet Medicine continues in her art.

'You are evolved. It is your last time here.
You are a woman's spirit, and a man's.
You are Winkta, God's servant, and you can
Be who you are, be kinky or be queer.'

Now obviously she doesn't speak in rhyme.
But what's a little poetry 'tween friends.
Sure Sweetie wouldn't mind these odds and ends.
She'd say no finer way to paint that time.

Take stock, give thanks and dream your precious dreams.
For who's to say your dream life isn't real.
And that this is the dream. It's time to deal
And to let go of past complaints. So scream.

I smoke some dream tobacco. And I dream
My mother sits beside me watching porn.
We're smoking joints. Somehow I've got a horn.
'So this is what you're into, son. Extreme.'

Me mammy's right. This nightmare of her sees
Some fetish porn. It even bothers me.
It's one giant slug all dressed up rubbery,
Alright enough, Wake up, ASAP.

A fetish slug, alright, you know…it's fine.
And perched above the slug there sits my debt.
In garish digital my debt is set.
My mother's off her box and I am dying.

A magpie taps the roof. Then I'm awake.
The countryside is silent. It is dawn.
I make my way into the kitchen's warmth.
Sweet Medicine is there. She sees me shake.

Just us alone. The morning bares my soul.
I sense that she has seen the dream I've held.
I tell her every detail. I'm compelled.
Her tone is tender. And her words are gold.

I want to extricate my clustered thoughts.
There's nobody around, It's not yet 8.
'Sweet Medicine I would like to be raped.
Does that mean that I'm bad? 'Coz I'm distraught.'

She doesn't flinch. I've taken quite the chance.
'Raped as a child you were, my husband too,
He prayed for violation, just like me.
Explore that, you are free to be, so dance.'

Permission from the light to be so dark.
God's servant, Sweetie lets me make the choice
To live inside the consequence. Rejoice.
I'm free to be a dirty little… 'Hark,

'Not dirty,' suggests Sweet Medicine, 'explore.'
I don't recall that I was raped I say.
'You were,' she gently tells me. 'There's no way
That I was raped. Molested. Yes.' No more

Is said about this and I have to wait.
Until some memory invades my day.
I thought he just molested me but hey.
Why would you want to know when you were eight?

DECEMBER

It is a council flat where I reside.
Since I confessed to having HIV
My family all agree it should be me
Who holds the fort for Grandad who's just died.

Somehow the Council buy he's still alive.
No legal right have I to warm his bed.
But I sure need a place to rest my head.
I couldn't just inherit it. I lie.

The rent's still paid by 'Grandad'…hardly costs.
This flat; two bedrooms, on two floors. It's bang
Right in the heart of Dublin town. I hang
Out on the balcony and smoke. I'm lost.

I cannot go on living in this town.
Why did they have to give the flat to me?
It's very rough. No place for me to be.
This posh puff is so easily put down.

Grandparents dead. Me in their bed…a queer.
My granny died when I was diagnosed.
So I could cry and nobody would know
That my tears were for her and my new fear.

It's magic 'coz the flat is right beside
The centre for those who have HIV.
I go there for my meals. I get them free.
You could say that I'm lucky. God provides.

The Council after two years have copped this
And wish for me to leave. It's time to go.
I'm shocked. This is so sudden. I don't know
Where I'll end up. I fear the street's abyss.

I have until February to leave.
And with this news my disposition lifts.
I get a job as Santa giving gifts.
December and I'm broke.

I'm Santy in the Wax Museum. It's true.
My friend Patricia says she has a gig.
This isn't anything too strange. A wig.
Another frock. This is the job I do.

We strike a pose with Bono and The Edge.
Madonna would collapse. The state of her.
It's nothing strange. Another frock and wig.
Just like that drag act that I used to do.

We come to life and put the fear of God
Into the old and young. It matters none
'Coz it's escape and this is giddy fun.
It's like we're cumming up, the laughs. I plod

Along till Christmas comes then I succumb.
I'm trying not to notice but it's cold.
Another year without someone to hold.
You'd think by now the drugs would leave me numb.

I make a stab at rescuing my health.
My HIV's under control with pills
But it's my attitude to it that's ill.
I'm tired of studying its stain in stealth.

Do yoga for an hour every day.
One week I live like this. I feel divine.
I wonder will I keep up this routine?
The weekend comes. The addict has her way.

A party in a fancy part of town.
A penthouse, it is homo wall to wall.
And yeah the yoga gives me pick of all.
I choose the one who's dark. When I sit down,

He smoothly takes position straight ahead.
I rise to meet him. Want to give my all.
He offers me cocaine but I'm appalled.
That turns me to a cunt. I'll drink instead.

But go ahead. I say. Just not my drug.
I'll have some of that joint that he's got there.
Within a very short time I'm aware
I've one thing on my mind. And it's bear hugs.

He offers coke again, so I say yes.
Then ketamine, more grass. Wired. I confide
To him, my handsome black-haired bear and ride
'I knew you in a past life.' I'm a mess.

He says he'd really love to play with me.
But since his boyfriend's here. It can't be done.
This always happens. They ruin all the fun.
Fuck boyfriends. Ah but magic number three.

Your boyfriend is my type as well. Ah tits.
My bear is now unconscious on the couch.
And I am on my chair. I'm in a slouched
Presentiment. Then home alone in bits.

On alcohol, on ketamine, on coke.
On poppers, on my own, on with the porn.
On headshop herbal smoke, I am reborn.
On x-tube I'm abused and used by ghosts.

Projectile vomit onto my laptop.
I puke some more into a plastic bag.
The porn still plays. I mop up with a rag.
I take more poppers. Really I can't stop.

I drain my Santy's sack in Satan's gaze.
I guess this is taboo for Christian boys.
Who wouldn't love intense transgressive toys?
I clench my jaw, and roar. My lamp's ablaze.

JANUARY

Look I'm no muscle Mary. God I wish.
But I love big and scary. You're a lash.
I'd love to lick your boots, sir, nice moustache.
You look like Freddy Krueger. He's a dish.

I've got some coke. Let's play like blokes. You're hot.
You've HIV? Yea, me as well. It's cool.
You know they only changed that awful rule.
The Visa ban is lifted.

Yer man, Obama, restored hope in me.
Now I can see the States despite my blood.
I can live in America. It's good.
The world got bigger this January.

You're hotter than a double whopper meal.
It's nice to meet you, Rick. You kiss so well.
I'm Neil. Ich bin lihr houndin. Ring my bell.
I love the way your leather looks and feels.

Destiny has joined us don't you think?
I live in Dublin. But I'm moving here.
New York is so much better if you're queer.
To moving here. Cheers, Rick. You're slick. Cheers. Clink.

I'm here on tour. I'm in a show. Ten days.
We tour the world. Well, let's just say, my dream
Came true this week. It really makes me beam.
Do you believe in magic, Rick? Yea, same.

I'm grateful everyday for stuff I've got.
Just like the flat that keeps me safe 'n warm.
I give thanks for ten things. Yeah ten's the norm.
I then give thanks for ten things I have not.

A decent home, a boyfriend, holidays.
These last few days I prayed that my mentor
Would come. And lead me through the magic door.
I prayed that he would be a genius gay.

John Cam'ren Mitchell came to see the show.
You know him. Good. He's great. You know his stuff?
I feel like he's instilled in me self-worth.
He took me out to dinner. I'm like Whoa.

His *Hedwig*, and, well *Shortbus* I just love.
I said, I love your work. And he said, you're
Performance was like poetry…yes sir.
John Cam'ren Mitchell came from up above.

It's not like this stuff happens all the time.
We go to the Cornelia St Cafe.
It's where he first performed back in the day.
We sit right down the back. The food and wine

Is lovely. So is he. I don't feel he is
Playing or objectifying me.
Well, says he.
The movie is called *Rabbit Hole*. So see,

This was a play on Broadway with your one,
Cynthia Nixon. Rick, sir, I am mix-
Ing with the leader of my A-Gay List.
I ask who's in the flick? Nicole Kidman.

My heart just does a high jump to my throat.
And Aaron Eckhart's in it. Diane Wiest.
First John. Now you. I'm floored, to say the least.
Sex and the City. Rick, you got a note?

I will do anything you want, so here.
Put on your monster mask. Come home to bed.
You're Freddy. Rape my soul. And fuck my head.
I've always wanted to get fucked by fear.

I love you, Freddy Krueger. Thank you, Fred.
Oh thank you, Freddy Teddy. Make me die.
Your fingernails are kissing me goodbye.
Oh thank you, Freddy. Fuck me till I'm dead.

I'm such a lucky fucking little bitch.
Oh Freddy, I'm your faggot. Fist my soul.
I'm worthless and I'm nothing. Make me whole.
I'm cumming, Freddy Daddy, scratch my itch.

Oh Daddy Freddy, Baby loves to pop.
My little dicky wicky sicky oh.
I'm sorry. I'm a faggot. Fuck me… No.
Oh God. Sweet Jesus. Rick. This has to stop.

FEBRUARY

HEIDI: Oh Neil, you're such a wanker.

NEIL: Shut up Konnt.

HEIDI: Just call me Heidi. Neil you never call.

NEIL: Because you're not my friend.

HEIDI: Ah Neil. Zat all?
    Zat all the thanks you give me?

NEIL: I'll be blunt.
    Miss Konnt, you're my addiction. You're insane.

HEIDI: The friction Neil, my God, what brought this on?

NEIL: Get off the stage.

HEIDI: You need my rage. Come on.

NEIL: I'd like to try to have sex without pain.
    Alternative Miss Ireland was a scream.
    This pageant raised some funds for HIV.
    I won as Heidi Konnt. So I could be somebody when I
    went out on the scene.

HEIDI: I see.

NEIL: Now, Heidi, look we've had our fun.

HEIDI: I gave you the best handjobs, Neil. Fuck you.
    You faggot little wanker. 'I'm so true.'
    You tell the people all the things you've done?

NEIL: I have.

HEIDI: Oh no you haven't.

NEIL: Yes I have.

HEIDI: Oh no you haven't.

NEIL: Yes I have.

HEIDI: You have?

NEIL: Oh yes I have.

HEIDI: Oh no you've not.

NEIL: I have.

HEIDI: Have you a smoke?

NEIL: I haven't.

HEIDI: Well I have.

NEIL: Where did you get that?

HEIDI: Fuck sake, Neil, let go.
You know you love your joints. He does.

NEIL: I did.
I've knocked that on the head.

HEIDI: Please, Neil, don't kid
A kidder. Kiddy Fiddler Heidi knows.

NEIL: I'm not a kiddy fiddler, Heidi Konnt.

HEIDI: Alas, when you've been fiddled, you will too.

NEIL: I've worked this with my therapist. Not true.
Fuck you, there'll be no smoking.

HEIDI: But I want to.

NEIL: I won't let you do another show.

HEIDI: It's 'coz I am a woman. You're ashamed
Of femininity. How could you blame
Me for my need for love, my need to grow.
I only want to give you sex, Neil.

NEIL: Stress.

HEIDI: Remember how it feels tied up by thugs.
Or Daddy types, or half-retarded mugs?
You loved that cop from Kerry.

NEIL: Heidi?

HEIDI: Yes?

NEIL: I'll tell the story.

HEIDI: Tell it gay face then.

NEIL: The cop was a distraction from my shit.

HEIDI: The cop was fucking cute. Mad out of it.
He rode you up the gick.

NEIL: Heidi… Ahem.
    The only reason that I gave a shit
    About that guy was –

HEIDI: you thought he was straight? –

NEIL: No mate. I fancied we might have a date.
    He was a guard. That got me hard. Now split!

HEIDI: Okay relax. It's just a fucking play.

NEIL: You aren't in this play.

HEIDI: I make more cash
    Than all your faggy acting gigs.

NEIL: I'll bash
    Your fucking head in Konnt. Now take
    A Heidi hike. I made you.

HEIDI: So you'd think?
    I'm what you think of girls. Your mother here
    Tonight to see your wank? You mincing queer.

NEIL: She's not invited.

HEIDI: Not without a drink.
    Is this not what it's all about? Your shame
    Is with your mother. Don't you miss her love?
    Before you got your kicks from rubber gloves.

NEIL: It's your hand that I wank with. You're to blame.

HEIDI: Neil fantasises that he is a child.
    Who's getting baby-sat by skinheads.

NEIL: Stop.

HEIDI: That time Neil spent the night with that cute cop,
    Neil's fantasy, even for me, too wild.

NEIL: Konnt leave me be.

HEIDI: Sweet Neil, I keep you safe.
    Without me, Neil, your mother would be dead.
    I save her from you when I'm in your head.

NEIL: That isn't true, Konnt. You begin to chafe.

HEIDI: The night that Neil spent with the cop. The cop's

Asleep. So Neil wanks on the sleeping guard.
Imagines he's got down's syndrome, he's mad,
Our Neil, a pervert through and through, can't stop.
Neil, tell me how you're feeling.
Ah, Neil, please don't ignore me.

NEIL: Miss Konnt, if you don't go, I'll kill us both.

HEIDI: Sweet Medicine says suicide is wrong.
It's fine. I'm off. Go have your wank-a-thon.
You'll never get your intimacy, Neil.
A head like yours can't deal with stuff that's real.
But, by all means, I dare you, prove me wrong.

MARCH

Shit. Sorry I'm late. Twenty past twelve.
I smoked some blow this morning but I'm grand.
Had coffee. Sue, I do not understand
Why I'm still here. This has been, fucking hell,

Three, four, five, years confessing all my fears,
My shame, my secrets. And what must you think?
I watched *The Hours* twice this week. I'm sink-
Ing slowly into my worst rut in years.

Mark doesn't want to go out anymore.
Not that we really dated. Just two nights.
His core belief is no gay person's right.
He wouldn't let me sleep with him. I roared

And shouted while I walked home drunk. The flat.
They've still not let it out. Nobody there.
At least I didn't have to pay cab fare.
That's where I crashed 'coz I was mashed. That's that.

I smashed a cup. I just want to have sex.
I just want to wake up in someone's arms.
I always pick the thicks. Mark meant no harm.
He sort of has a boyfriend. I'm perplexed.

They always have a boyfriend. Or they're weird.
Or unavailable emotion'lly.
Am I emotionally present, free?
I guess I'm not. That's why I grow my beard.

To hide. Where I have moved isn't as rough.
But still not great. Got called a faggot when
I left the house today. No, they weren't men.
They were just kids, at play. Hi, Faggot, Puff.

I daren't interfere. They've got tough clans.
I cannot even go out my front door.
That is fucking disgraceful. Sue. I swore,
Fuck them and fuck this world. I wash my hands.

Mark's lovely but I guess he's not my style.
The fantasy of someone who's got class.
But can't imagine him raping my ass.
Essentially, my taste in sex is vile.

Sure I've been on a wank binge since last week.
Like, Mark was not that frightening. But stoned
I fantasised he was a thug. I moaned
And shot my load. My headache eased. Eurek…

Perhaps there's something in this. Like, perhaps
My higher self loves S & M. Combine
Some whipping with vanilla love. Divine.
Perhaps I won't need drugs to wear my chaps.

I keep recalling when I was abused.
His name was also Mark. Do I attract
And recreate him? Because their names match.
Okay that part is normal. So I choose

To recreate the sense of shame. That's great.
I'm fine. No, something has come up. I see
Him jump out from behind a door. Marky
Has heard me telling all my friends. He'll bait

Me if I say another word. I got
A fright. How could a person be so mean?
It's like being chased by Freddy in a dream.
How can a person interfere like that?

What? What? What you just said. Say it again.
That Freddy Krueger cannot penetrate
Your dreams. That's lovely. Look, it's getting late.
Just need to get my self in shape. And then

I will be off. He cannot penetrate
My dreams. It's so poetic. So this means
That my abuser cannot have my dreams.
I want to thank you for these words. They're great.

NEIL WATKINS

But I can't go just yet. What's with this flood?
It's been locked up inside of me so long.
It isn't right to interfere. It's wrong.
I don't know why I'm crying. For my blood.

You're not supposed to touch a kid down there.
I trusted him and I looked up to him.
I liked him touching me. Now that's the sin.
I liked it. And I wanted more. So there.

APRIL

Come 'ere you. You're my best and oldest friend.
You know I love you, don't you. But I can't
Go on your stag night. See this sycophant's
An elephant. It's time to make amends.

There's too much going on inside my head.
I'm trying not to drink or smoke the blow.
So if it's cool with you. I cannot go.
And to be honest I'd rather be dead

Than be stuck on a stag night with the lads.
Such male machismo bullshit. Titty bars.
And shots and driving round in racing cars.
It's not my thing. Big toys for boys. It's sad.

I can't afford it anyway. No way
I'm just about surviving in this kip.
How can I justify a little trip?
I won't regret it on my deathbed. Hey.

You're not losing your friends. It's just too much.
So have your stag in Ireland. Just one night.
Then everyone could make it. Now, I'm right.
This fashion for big stags is out of touch

With the recession. One would think that you
And other grooms and brides would play it down.
You've got a text. No, check it. I won't frown.
Who is it? Oh Bom Bum. He's overdue.

He's not been round in ages, then he swans
Into your life just for your stag. That's bull.
Now he can't go because his workload's full.
I do not want his ticket. Please come on.

So even if it's free. I hate stag nights.
They're shite. You've been through therapy. These days
Are tough and I've enough of holding face.
Old memories are surfacing. Alright.

Je hear that young McGinley broke his back?
Your Ma was telling my Ma there at mass.
Remember how we bet McGinley's ass?
Sure we were only messing, having craic.

But, sorry, we were cunts to deaf John Dunne.
Je'member I sprayed fart gas on his coat?
Knocked in for him, 'Is Bom Bum coming out?'
Sure everybody bullied poor Bom Bum.

Don't make me go. I'll be there the big day.
I'll dance and sing, I'll mind the ring. Please don't.
Bom Bum can get a refund if he wants.
I'd have to pay him back. Stop trying to sway

Me. Please don't make me go. Okay, then. Fine.
But know I'm only doing this for you.
I can't believe I'm doing this. So who
Exactly will be going? There'll be Brian…

Do any of them smoke the whacky? Well,
Here, find out how we'll get some or I'm fucked.
I need to have the option so just look
Into it, will you, and I'll go. With bells.

Is the accommodation paid in Spain?
What airline? Ryanair. Oh nice. Fuck no.
The colour scheme is Fisher Price. I'll go.
I'll just get drunk before I board the plane.

Now listen to me, pal, this breaks my heart.
It seems that I've a problem with…well…cock.
The truth is…I'm sure it comes as no shock…
My therapist has said that I should start

To work the steps, that I've become, well…hooked
To porn and dirty weekends and to reef.
I'm stony broke. I'm wallowing in grief.
Addicted to my dick. You see I'm fucked.

I have a lot of stuff to process. So.
I'm striving to acknowledge my gay shame.
I'll be there on your stag. Right. But don't blame
Me if I take an early night. I'll go.

MAY

HEIDI: My dear beloved gathered here today.
What can I say? Neil Watkins loved a wank.
The church is black. So I'll crack off. I thank
You all for coming. All; straight, bi and gay.

Your Holiness, Pope Ratzinger, the Cunt.
You're very welcome. Watkins loved your work.
From Sesame Street, Bigbird, Ernie, Bert.
And all the Muppets sitting in the front.

Please put your hands together. Elton John,
Tom Selleck, Mickey Mouse and Bernie Dunne.
She isn't famous. Listen. She's just from
Neil's estate. State. I can't get through so long

A list of Nobel-winning scientists.
And politicians, porn stars, paedophiles.
If Neil were here, I know he'd wear a smile.
I knew him well. It's hard to swallow this.

The death of Watkins is a blow to all.
Nelson Mandela says he can't go on.
The Dalai Lama's gone and bought a gun.
And Nickie Kidman won't return my calls.

Oh what a lovely wanker. Blond and Kind.
He grappled with his gearstick. But, alas.
Neil Watkins wanked with a degree of class.
He gave himself to wanking. Wanked his mind.

His very name revealed an anagram.
'Silent I wank'. The letters jumbled round
Disclosed Neil's special role. So he did pound
His pound of flesh, his little leg of lamb.

That lanky laddy wanked his wand and waved
Like Voldemort himself casting a spell.
With Michael Jackson, Neil resides in hell.
He was found on a cross, he died a slave.

The wanking couldn't get Neil's fire lit.
In his last days he searched for something more.
So on the internet he found amore.
A man who promised crucifixion's hit.

He looked just like a paedophile might look.
Old, bald and fat, with glasses and red nose.
He stood and watched while Neil removed his clothes.
His dog barked out the back. Neil Watkins took

Out from his pocket pre-rolled joints. And smoked.
The crucifier once had been a priest.
And nailing Jesus to the cross released
For him a sense of love. Neil tried to cope

As finger nails clawed deep into his chest.
His arms tied to the cross, he was the Lord.
And Satan was the paedophile who gnawed
Into the face of rape, and hate. Impressed?

Neil didn't fight the pain that swarmed his thoughts.
He felt just like a virgin. Felt so pure.
Like he had been enlightened. He'd been cured.
He'd finally found the love oft he had sought.

He died there on the cross, and flew to rest
And finally knew that he was Christ indeed.
I took him down. And watched Sweet Jesus bleed.
At thirty-three, molested, freed and blessed.

Some call it S & M. I call it love.
Neil Watkins didn't fight our Father's call.
And he embraced the light. And rose to fall.
He'll come again of course. As God above.

JUNE

I don't know many people who were not
Abused. That's just being Irish. Forty shades
Of shame. We all submit when men invade.
Rape is the culture that we know. So blot

Out all that pain with all your might and drown
In drink. Our water's blessed with alcohol.
Don't think. Just stay asleep. Do not recall
The way you felt when you were small. Play down.

Sure is it any wonder it's called locked?
The Irish have so many words for drunk.
So many words for cum and jip and spunk.
The drugs make porn seem real. No websites blocked.

I spunk another chunk. I beat the meat.
Ten times repeat. The sheet has not been changed
In bleeding weeks. Me Ma would freak. Deranged,
I piss into a bottle. I'm not neat.

It's just a thing I do from time to time.
It's my idiosyncrasy. Sure who
Does not enjoy a little crutch. Eschew
This practice? This keeps me alive.

I used to be good looking. But who cares.
I'll die soon with some luck. Won't have to face
Up to the years I've put on weight. My waist
Is fine. It keeps the predators in their

Apartments. Out of mine. Can't give them AIDS.
I call it AIDS sometimes. I know I'm fine.
I shouldn't have told anyone. To thine
Own self be false and to them all. Display

A milky mask of cow manure and moo.
Why can't I just get on with life? There's queers
Are riddled years and they seem grand. It's fear
That keeps me locked inside my rut. I know.

I watch the real boys pick each other up.
I am the last of the great gay ashamed.
I do not understand the dating game.
I've only ever known the sick pick-up.

Was phone lines first, my first fuck an old man.
I hated him. But thought I better, well,
Who knew when I would get another yell?
On toilet doors were numbers scribbled and

I followed the instructions. Then the parks.
All my seductions, shadows in the shade.
And degradation paid for my free trade.
And then just boozy, druggy, sleazy lark.

I always had a good time. In my head.
I liked to feel afraid. Adventure play.
I did eventually date this guy.
He never kissed. I stayed three years. Then fled

Because I fancied someone straight. They say
That's symptomatic of self-hate. Do they?
I'm not a sex- and love-addicted freak.
I'll have a healthy love life by next week.

JULY

She doesn't say I love you more than God.
Her word is 'Fuck'. I'm seventeen. I cry.
My father has a breakdown. I decide,
'Return to Narnia.' May my façade

Remain a closet where I weep and sleep.
I am too much for Mam and Dad to take.
The atmosphere at home is of a wake.
I've really let them down. Their hurt is deep.

They seek a local doctor's sound advice.
I see a psychotherapist for help.
And we agree the ice had best not melt.
I date a few more girls for Jesus Christ.

My coming out had not been a success.
'My God is telling me that you're not gay.
I know it in my heart that you're okay.'
My mother's tears have power to suppress.

Who can I sue or blame for this abuse?
Just like the time when I thought I should broach
The subject of being fondled by the coach.
She ran out of the house. So I produced

A fabrication. My 'magination
Let run loose. I make her estimation
Not so devastating. She comes back home.
She grabs the phone. She calls his Mom. Psycho.

Some poor old woman and my poor young Mam
Are losing all the love they'd won in prayer.
This isn't news of any gay affair.
You're son's a paedophile. An evil man.

Mam's threatening to kill both her and him.
'I'll tear your son asunder limb from limb.'
It isn't any wonder she's dismayed.
Nevertheless, I feel like I've betrayed.

The same thing when I said I'd HIV.
I'm not as angry with my Dad. 'Coz he
Stays calm these days when I'm in need. Oh sure.
I'm hypersensitive. I'm insecure.

Embrace whatever lonely fat old man
Will take control of me. I understand.
I'm acting out my nightmare. This is how
I cope. Don't feel. 'Coz feeling's not allowed.

Sometimes my parents cross my mind in sex.
What can I do? Each morning with my ex
Was like I woke up with my Dad. Could be
That's normal, possibly, conceivably?

So silent I wank floor-bound in Paris.
Some French leather Daddy is slaughtering me.
I capitalise on the pain I feel.
A nameless exchange with a stranger. Big deal.

Sweet Medicine said accept my desire.
I crawled on the floor, then he killed his fire
Four times on my arm. Which scars. But no harm.
There's cigarette burns on my forearm. Yes, charmed?

Monsieur is asleep with his husband all warm.
Silent I wank on the floor. It's like porn.
Sun's coming up, so I get dressed and split.
The addict's been fed. Her fire is lit.

A weekend in Paris binge-fucking is slick.
Where nobody knows me, or knows that I'm sick.
Not that you would ever catch me taking a chance.
But we all take a risk when we dance in our pants.

Last tango in Paris for me and for me…
I grab a cab in search of chi.
I, like,…meditate in Père Lachaise.
I listen to Jim Morrison, he says,

'Heal, Heal, Heal, Neil, if Christ could be
A Jew born to a Virgin, and be me.
He sure as hell can be a riddled gay.
They only washed your brain so they could stay

'In power. They're devouring themselves.
The ones who criticise are stuck in hell.'
I'm suddenly officially the Christ.
I sense a bit of pressure. But it's nice.

AUGUST

Here yous, I've got the need for weed.
My head is pounding off of me.
Roll up, roll up, roll up the green.
The universe is loving me.

It's August. I'm in Finland. Drunk.
Got thrashed with twigs by naked men.
And jumped into a lake. I froze.
But it feels good to live again.

It's 3 a.m. No orgy in my room.
The hotel carpark down below…shows
Three skateboarders smoke. They're chilled.
From three flights up I smell the blow.

Forget about my fear. I want
To get out of my head. Hi there.
You guys from Finland? Have some sweets.
Would you be so kind as to share?

The marijuana kills my pain.
These headaches are a fucking curse.
These lads seem nice. There'll be no fight.
I say I'm gay. They're all adverse.

But they're too stoned to raise a hand.
We don't like gays. We think it's wrong.
And monged I say. I understand.
There's people I hate too. It's grand.

I tell them that I do gay plays.
All their faces are dead. They look like this.
I look dead too. So we liaise.
One takes his cock out, has a piss.

They're fifteen, sixteen, thereabouts.
No sexy feelings for these teens.
I like my men post-puberty.
When they're older, they can treat me mean.

They're just three stoners. I'm some fag.
I ask them what their passions are.
One loves his skateboard. One can't speak.
And the other says that drugs by far

Are all he does day in day out.
That drugs are totally what life is.
His pal butts in and says he's hooked.
The silent skater shows unease.

I'm totally stoned. Now I'm on fire.
We hang by trashcans, carpark's dark.
A bit of light…the hotel sign.
This lad's too young. I must remark.

'You think that you love drugs. You don't.
You're on the run from painful shit.'
His pal chimes in. 'He's got a problem.'
'Me as well,' I say, 'Let's quit.' He's got a problem, man.

Don't be like me. My life's a mess.
Because I ran away from pain.
Don't you see that I was sent to warn you?
This is huge. It's massive. 'Don't you see, we're the same?'

The one who can't speak faints at my feet.
My words are blowing his mind. 'I'm Christ.'
I say. 'My words have just blown his mind. He's just getting
a healing. Let me deal with him. Back off. He's like ice.'

I say that my power has even scared me.
One translates what I say. When the other's, like, what?
Now he's conscious again, Mr. Silent is like,
Get your hands off my chest. Whoops, I forgot.

I'm stoned. I'm Christ. Ascend to bed.
I long for porn to soothe my shame
The shame that I must come again.
Again. Again. Again. Again.

In bed I wank and act out hurt.
Need better props to get me there.
Next week, I'll get some crystal meth.
Some problems are beyond repair.

SEPTEMBER

Because I could not stop Miss Konnt
I had to stop us both.
I tied a rope around our throat
And eased the pain with dope.

My dearest darling Mother,
How I wished I had been good.
I cannot go on troubling you.
Your lot's more than enough.

You're from the time when little girls
Were not allowed to smile.
You're not to blame, Mam, for my pain.
I'm sorry. I've been vile.

Now I'm released. So you'll have peace.
It's better where I am.
No need to honour monsters now.
Sweet Jesus understands.

My obsession with *The Hours*,
It's that film that I love,
Has finally come to this, my death.
What was I thinking of?

I've watched it every week for years.
Since headaches first appeared.
Virginia Woolf knew pain like mine.
And voices 'tween her ears.

You've given tears straight from your heart.
God drove us round the bend
And built a wall between our hearts.
In heaven we'll be friends.

Watch *Rabbit Hole.* It stars Nicole.
It will help with your grief.
It's all about bereavement.
It will change your core beliefs.

This pain has driven me insane.
I tried to find a cure.
I couldn't give up wanking, Mam.
It's just how I've matured.

I couldn't help my isolation.
And I hate that you could see
The way your little flower waned
To mediocrity.

I hope my suicide works out.
I'll be scarlet if it doesn't.
Just one more act of shame to share
With aunties and with cousins.

God says that I am not the Christ.
It's just me being mad.
So now I take my punishment
In purgatory's hands.

OCTOBER

Last October my friend knew that I was depressed.
So she invited me to join her on a trip out to Swords, Co.
Dublin to a warehouse normally reserved for dog-shows.
In order to get a hug from an Indian lady called Amma.
The usual Friday night out, you know.

Turns out Amma is known as 'The Hugging Saint'. It's
said that her hugs are healing. That night, thousands had
shown up for a spiritual squeeze. And Jacinta and I waited
in line until four in the morning along with all these people
dressed in cloaks and sandals, with little dots on their
forehead. We basically took the piss out of all of them.

When Amma hugged me, I felt this huge sense of…relief. I
felt a very deep feeling of…unconditional love.

The following night at home, I was having a dream about
Jacinta. I dreamt she was putting giant multi-colored
curtain tassels around her neck. And I don't know why but,
I thought that this was the funniest thing ever. I laughed so
much in my dream that I woke myself up.

I sat up in my bed, laughing to myself in the dark.
My heart was heaving with happiness.

At the foot of my bed, I saw an orange glow. And in the
glow I saw the face of Amma. This wasn't a dream.

And Amma's face turned into the face of Jesus and back
again. And they said to me, 'Neil, do you still want to
die?…because you can come with us now…' And I'm
genuinely afraid that my time is up. And I push myself to
speak. 'No,' I say, 'I want to stay.' And Jesus and Amma
reply as one, 'Then tell your story.'

Contributor Biographies

THOMAS CONWAY

Thomas works as a director, dramaturg, lecturer and journalist. He teaches contemporary theatre practices at National University of Ireland, Galway, and The Lir Academy for Performing Arts, Dublin. He is Literary Manager with Druid.

GRACE DYAS

Grace is currently researching and developing HISTORY (the third part of THEATREclub's social history trilogy) as part of her Public Art Commission Residency in St. Michael's Estate.

She is also working with The Abbey Theatre on *The Young Covey's* project about young people and politics to coincide with *The Plough And The Stars.*

Grace is one third of THEATREclub. She is a theatre director, writer and producer. Recent work for THEATREclub includes *TWENTY TEN, THE FAMILY, HEROIN* (Spirit of the Fringe Award), *THEATREclub stole your CLOCK RADIO what the FUCK you gonna do about it?, GROUP THERAPY FOR ONE* and *ROUGH* (Fishamble New Writing Award). Other theatre includes *I am A Home Bird (It's very hard)* which she produced for Talking Shop Ensemble.

Grace has also worked as an assistant to directors Jason Byrne, Annie Ryan and Wayne Jordan.

Grace is a proud board member of Dublin Youth Theatre.

MARK O'HALLORAN

Mark is a writer/actor from Ennis Co. Clare, Ireland. His screenplays include *Adam & Paul* and *Garage.* He has also written a television series, *Prosperity.* Plays include *The Head of Red O'Brien* and *Mary Motorhead. Trade,* which premiered at the 2011 Dublin International Theatre Festival, won the Irish Times Irish Theatre Award for Best Play of 2011 as well as the Irish Playwrights and Screenwriters Guild Zebbie award for best new play. Mark has been nominated for numerous other awards, including a European Film Award for the screenplay of *Adam & Paul,* Irish Film and Television Awards where he won for both 'best screenplay' and 'best TV writer' 2007. He also won the London Evening Standard award for Best Screenplay in 2005.

LYNDA RADLEY

Lynda Radley hails from Cork and lives in Glasgow. In 2011 Lynda won a Scotsman Fringe First for her play *Futureproof*, a co-production between Dundee Rep Ensemble and the Traverse Theatre. She recently took part in the Dream Plays programme for Edinburgh Fringe 2012, also for the Traverse, and shared in a Herald Angel Award. Other recent work includes *Berlin Love Tour* – a walking tour of Berlin that can take place in any city – which sold out at the Fierce Festival in Birmingham, Cork Midsummer Festival and Dublin Fringe (Playgroup). In February 2012 Lynda travelled to the National Play Festival in Australia, with a delegation from the National Theatre of Scotland, where her play *DORM* received a rehearsed reading. With visual artist, Jenny Soep, she is currently developing a graphic novel. Her solo show *The Art of Swimming* was short-listed for Meyer Whitworth and Total Theatre awards and toured internationally. Other works include *Birds and Other Things I am Afraid Of* (in association with The Arches and Poorboy), *Integrity, Dark Week, The Heights* and *Soap!:* a ten episode live soap opera co-written with Ciaran Fitzpatrick (Playgroup).

PHILLIP MCMAHON

Phillip is one half of pop culture outfit THISISPOPBABY. As a theatremaker he has worked as actor, director, producer and playwright. His plays include *Danny and Chantelle (still here), All Over Town, Investment Potential, Pineapple, Elevator* and the musical *Alice In Funderland* at the Abbey Theatre. Directing credits include *In These Shoes?, All Dolled Up* and *A Woman In Progress* all written and performed by drag superstar Panti, *The Year of Magical Wanking* and a live arena show for the Rubberbandits at Electric Picnic Music and Arts Festival. Phillip is co-creator and co-curator of the 'POP' performance venue at Electric Picnic Music and Arts Festival, 'Queer Notions' cross-arts festival at Project Arts Centre and 'WERK' Performance/Art/Club at the Abbey Theatre.

As a teenager Phillip was a member of Dublin Youth Theatre, National Youth Theatre and Australian Theatre for Young People. He was 'Writer-in-Association' at the Abbey Theatre 2009/10.

AMY CONROY

Amy Conroy has been a professional actor for over ten years and founded HotForTheatre 2010.

She wrote their debut show *I* ♥ *Alice* ♥ *I*, which premiered in ABSOLUT Fringe 2010, winning her the Fishamble New Writing Award, nominations for the Stewart Parker Trust Award and a Zebbie Award. *I* ♥ *Alice* ♥ *I* was programmed in the Ulster Bank Dublin Theatre Festival, the Peacock stage of Abbey Theatre in Dublin, the Irish Arts Centre In New York, LÓKAL Festival in Iceland, and was recorded and broadcast on RTÉ Radio One. Her second show, *Eternal Rising of the Sun*, for which she won the Best Female Performer Award, premiered in ABSOLUT Fringe 2011 and transferred to the Dublin Theatre Festival 2012. Both shows will tour nationally and internationally in 2013. Amy has begun working on HotForTheatre's next show which will premier in late 2013. Amy wrote and recorded *Hold This*, a radio play for RTÉ Radio One, and was a participant on the New Playwrights Programme 2011 in the Abbey Theatre.

HotForTheatre believes theatre should provoke, move and delight in equal measures.

UNA MCKEVITT

Una McKevitt is a Dublin-based theatre practitioner interested in making theatre from everyday life. The ambition and focus of Una's work is to derive a dramatic text from a documentary practice and abstract personal histories and social realities through performance and design to create theatre that is both artful and innovative. Inspired by Quarantine's Production of *Susan and Darren*, Una developed her first documentary work *Victor and Gord* in 2009 based on the dysfunctional friendship of her sister Gord (Aine McKevitt) and Gord's friend Victor (Vickey Curtis). *Victor and Gord* was published by Cork University Press in *Queer Notions 2010*, edited by Fintan Walsh. In 2010, Una premiered her second work, *565 + 'My name is Marie O'Rourke'* at the Ulster Bank Dublin Theatre Festival 2010. In *565 +* Marie discusses her compulsive attendance of the theatre and her ongoing battle with depression. In 2011 Una, in collaboration with two contributors, edited and directed *The Big Deal*, based on the contributors' real-life experiences of gender re-assignment and performed by actors. Una is currently developing a new show *Singlehood* with a cast of ten and based on over fifty interviews with single men and women. *Singlehood* will premiere at the 2012 Absolut Dublin Fringe Festival.

SIMON DOYLE

Simon Doyle is a writer based in Dublin. Texts for stage include: *Thwaite* (2003), a libretto for an opera by Jürgen Simpson, directed by Dan Jemmett for Almeida Aldeborough Opera and Opera Theatre Company and staged in London, Dublin and Aldeborough; *Oedipus Loves You* (2006), co-written and directed by Gavin Quinn for Pan Pan Theatre, which premiered in Dublin and toured internationally; *Off Plan* (2010), an adaptation of *The Oresteia* by Aeschylus, directed by Rachel West for RAW productions, premiered at Project Arts Centre, Dublin; *The Truth of the Moon* (2010), a monologue written for Sonya Kelly and directed by Sophie Motley for ANU Productions, premiered at The New Theatre, Dublin.

GAVIN QUINN

Gavin was born in Dublin in 1969. He is joint artistic director of Pan Pan Theatre, which he founded with Aedín Cosgrove in 1991. Selected productions include, *A Bronze Twist of Your Serpent Muscles* by Gavin Quinn (winner of Best Overall Production, Dublin Fringe Festival, 1995), *Cartoon* (1997), *Standoffish* by Gavin Quinn (Best Production, Advertiser, Adelaide, 2000), *Deflowerfucked* by Gavin Quinn (2001), *Mac-Beth 7* (2004), *One: Healing with Theatre* (2005), *The Playboy of the Western World* by John Millington Synge (in both Beijing and Dublin, in Mandarin and with a Chinese cast, 2006), *Oedipus Loves You* by Gavin Quinn and Simon Doyle (2006), *The Crumb Trail* by Gina Moxley (2009), *The Rehearsal, Playing the Dane* (Winner of best production, best design, Irish Times Theatre Awards, 2010), *All That Fall* by Samuel Beckett (2011), *A Doll House* (2012).

Opera directing credits include, *The 4 Note Opera* (Tom Johnson, 2000), *The Magic Flute* for OTC, *Hamelin* for OTC (Ian Wilson, 2003), *The Abduction from the Seraglio* for ETO (Hackney Empire, London 2007), and *Così Fan Tutti* for Opera Ireland (2007).

NEIL WATKINS

Neil Watkins lives in Dublin City. A former member of Dublin Youth Theatre, he went on to study acting at Drama Centre London. He has written and directed *The Ugly Penguin Scenarios* and *Covers* for Dublin Youth Theatre. Neil founded Gentle Giant Theatre Company to produce his own writing and to create opportunites to perform and direct. For Gentle Giant he has produced; *The Ugly Penguin Scenarios, Love In A Time Of Affluence*, (nominated for the Stuart Parker Award for Best New Writing), *A Cure For Homosexuality* (published by Cork Press in *Queer Notions*), *The Heidi Konnt XXXmas Story, Dublin City Counselling* (Spirit of the Fringe nominee) and *The Dark Room* (Spirit of the Fringe nominee). Neil has worked as an actor in theatre, TV and film in Ireland, appearing in the national soap opera *Fair City* as a Norwegian child minder called Karl Hansen and the nation's favorite satire *The Savage Eye* as various characters with Dave McSavage. Neil recently appeared opposite one of his acting heroes Martin Sheen in the film *Stella Days*.

He emceed the performance art night club Werk at Ireland's National Theatre with thisispopbaby. He has toured internationally with Sean Millar's Brokentalkers' *Silver Stars*. And with support from the British Council in Ireland he was mentored by renowned Manchester/London-based performance artist David Hoyle. He has guest appeared at The Royal Vauxhall Tavern with David in London. Neil has also proudly performed alongside Gavin Friday and Sinead O' Connor for Gavins' "Catholic" concert at the Olypmia Theatre.

He scored the first international try for the Irish Gay Rugby Team at the Bingham Cup in London 2004 and won the title of Alternative Miss Ireland 2005 as Heidi Konnt.

As singer-songwriter Neil has recently formed the band Buffalo Woman with criticically acclaimed musician and theatre-maker Sean Millar.

At the time of print Neil is under commision to Calippo Theatre Company to rewrite his 2007 Fringe Show, critically acclaimed smash (***** *Irish Times*), *Dublin City Counselling*.

Neil enjoys New Writing, Cinema, Art, Music Festivals, Bikram Yoga, DaftPunk's soundtrack to *Tron* and having the craic with buzzers. Neil is delighted and proud for *The Year of Magical Wanking* to be included in this anthology.

Namaste to one and all.

WWW.OBERONBOOKS.COM

Follow us on www.twitter.com/@oberonbooks
& www.facebook.com/OberonBooksLondon